*Primary Readings in Philosophy
for Understanding Theology*

BOOKS BY DIOGENES ALLEN
PUBLISHED BY WESTMINSTER/JOHN KNOX PRESS

✦ ✦ ✦

Christian Belief in a Postmodern World:
The Full Wealth of Conviction

Philosophy for Understanding Theology

Primary Readings in Philosophy for Understanding Theology

Edited by
Diogenes Allen
and
Eric O. Springsted

Gracewing
Leominster, England

Westminster/John Knox Press
Louisville, Kentucky

First published in the British Commonwealth in 1992 by Gracewing, Southern Avenue, Leominster HR6 0QF, England

First published in the United States in 1992 by Westminster/John Knox Press, 100 Witherspoon Street, Louisville, Kentucky 40202-1396

Book design by The HK Scriptorium, Inc.

This book is printed on acid-free paper that meets the American National Standards Institute Z39.48 standard. ∞

PRINTED IN THE UNITED STATES OF AMERICA
9 8 7 6 5 4 3 2 1

British Cataloging-in-Publication Data

A catalogue record for this book is available from the British Library.

ISBN 0-852-44229-7

Library of Congress Cataloging-in-Publication Data

Primary readings in philosophy for understanding theology / Diogenes Allen & Eric O. Springsted, editors.
p.   cm.
Includes bibliographical references and index.
ISBN 0-664-25208-7 (pbk. : alk. paper)

1. Philosophy.   2. Religion—Philosophy.   3. Christianity—Philosophy.   I. Allen, Diogenes.   II. Springsted, Eric O.
B73.P75   1992
102'.42—dc20   92-6139

CONTENTS

CONTENTS

PREFACE

When *Philosophy for Understanding Theology* was published in 1985, its stated goal was "to give a person the philosophy needed to understand Christian theology better because often the lack of knowledge of some key philosophic term or concept impedes significant understanding of a vital issue." In this respect it was meant to give not a history of philosophy for the needs of philosophers but a book fitted to the needs of theological students.

These are the goals also for now publishing an accompanying selection of primary sources. The present volume, however, meets an additional need that *Philosophy for Understanding Theology* by its very nature could not: to engage the reader in the texts themselves and to appropriate them personally.

The introductions to each selection are precisely that: introductions to help situate the author and the passage. They are not full-fledged explanations; for that the reader should consult *Philosophy for Understanding Theology.*

While this is an anthology designed to help one understand philosophic concepts in order to better understand Christian theology, it is also a highly selective history of some very important questions and answers that have entered the human mind from Plato to the present. It can be used and read in that light too. Such a history is a feature frequently missing in most collections designed for courses in the philosophy of religion, and therefore this volume can easily be used to supplement such courses as well as some courses in the history of philosophy.

We would like to acknowledge the generous assistance of Princeton Theological Seminary and Illinois College in the preparation of this book.

DIOGENES ALLEN
ERIC O. SPRINGSTED

✦ ✦

PLATO

Alfred North Whitehead once suggested that the history of philosophy is
nothing but a series of footnotes to Plato (428–348 B.C.). Although the same
suggestion would be an overstatement in the history of theology, nevertheless
probably no single philosopher has contributed as much to Christian theology
as Plato has. Indeed, for many early Christian thinkers it was a perceived affinity
between Platonism and Christianity that allowed Christian thought to accom-
modate Greek philosophy. In turn, it was Plato who gave Christianity crucial
conceptual tools needed to articulate its doctrines. The following texts are two
of the most important ones used by Christian thinkers. In the first, taken from
the *Republic,* Plato first offers the simile of the sun to help understand the nature
of transcendent Good (which Christianity took to be God) and then proceeds
through two successive images, the Divided Line and the Cave, to discuss how
human beings can be related to that ultimate reality. In the second text, taken
from the *Timaeus,* Plato discusses divine creation. While his view is not the
Christian doctrine of creation *ex nihilo,* it became an important way of discussing how a good and perfect being could create and impart goodness within
a world that is not simply an extension of God.

The Sun, the Line, and the Cave
(*Republic,* 505–518)

A right noble thought; but do you suppose that we shall refrain from
asking you what is this highest knowledge?

Nay, I said, ask if you will; but I am certain that you have heard
the answer many times, and now you either do not understand me or,

as I rather think, you are disposed to be troublesome; for you have often been told that the idea of good is the highest knowledge, and that all other things become useful and advantageous only by their use of this. You can hardly be ignorant that of this I was about to speak, concerning which, as you have often heard me say, we know so little; and, without which, any other knowledge or possession of any kind will profit us nothing. Do you think that the possession of all other things is of any value if we do not possess the good? or the knowledge of all other things if we have no knowledge of beauty and goodness?

Assuredly not.

You are further aware that most people affirm pleasure to be the good, but the finer sort of wits say it is knowledge?

Yes.

And you are aware too that the latter cannot explain what they mean by knowledge, but are obliged after all to say knowledge of the good?

How ridiculous!

Yes, I said, that they should begin by reproaching us with our ignorance of the good, and then presume our knowledge of it—for the good they define to be knowledge of the good, just as if we understood them when they use the term 'good'—this is of course ridiculous.

Most true, he said.

And those who make pleasure their good are in equal perplexity; for they are compelled to admit that there are bad pleasures as well as good.

Certainly.

And therefore to acknowledge that bad and good are the same?

True.

There can be no doubt about the numerous difficulties in which this question is involved.

There can be none.

Further, do we not see that many are willing to do or to have or to seem to be what is just and honourable without the reality; but no one is satisfied with the appearance of good—the reality is what they seek; in the case of the good, appearance is despised by every one.

Very true, he said.

Of this then, which every soul of man pursues and makes the end of all his actions, having a presentiment that there is such an end, and yet hesitating because neither knowing the nature nor having the same assurance of this as of other things, and therefore losing whatever good there is in other things,—of a principle such and so great as this ought the best men in our State, to whom everything is entrusted, to be in the darkness of ignorance?

Certainly not, he said.

I am sure, I said, that he who does not know how the beautiful and the just are likewise good will be but a sorry guardian of them; and I suspect that no one who is ignorant of the good will have a true knowledge of them.

That, he said, is a shrewd suspicion of yours.

And if we only have a guardian who has this knowledge our State will be perfectly ordered?

Of course, he replied; but I wish that you would tell me whether you conceive this supreme principle of the good to be knowledge or pleasure, or different from either?

Aye, I said, I knew all along that a fastidious gentleman like you would not be contented with the thoughts of other people about these matters.

True, Socrates; but I must say that one who like you has passed a lifetime in the study of philosophy should not be always repeating the opinions of others, and never telling his own.

Well, but has any one a right to say positively what he does not know?

Not, he said, with the assurance of positive certainty; he has no right to do that: but he may say what he thinks, as a matter of opinion.

And do you not know, I said, that all mere opinions are bad, and the best of them blind? You would not deny that those who have any true notion without intelligence are only like blind men who feel their way along the road?

Very true.

And do you wish to behold what is blind and crooked and base, when others will tell you of brightness and beauty?

Still, I must implore you, Socrates, said Glaucon, not to turn away just as you are reaching the goal; if you will only give such an explanation of the good as you have already given of justice and temperance and the other virtues, we shall be satisfied.

Yes, my friend, and I shall be at least equally satisfied, but I cannot help fearing that I shall fail, and that my indiscreet zeal will bring ridicule upon me. No, sweet sirs, let us not at present ask what is the actual nature of the good, for to reach what is now in my thoughts would be an effort too great for me. But of the child of the good who is likest him, I would fain speak, if I could be sure that you wished to hear—otherwise, not.

By all means, he said, tell us about the child, and you shall remain in our debt for the account of the parent.

I do indeed wish, I replied, that I could pay, and you receive, the account of the parent, and not, as now, of the offspring only; take, however, this latter by way of interest, and at the same time have a care that I do not render a false account, although I have no intention of deceiving you.

Yes, we will take all the care that we can: proceed.

Yes, I said, but I must first come to an understanding with you, and remind you of what I have mentioned in the course of this discussion, and at many other times.

What?

The old story, that there is a many beautiful and a many good, and so of other things which we describe and define; to all of them 'many' is applied.

True, he said.

And there is an absolute beauty and an absolute good, and of other things to which the term 'many' is applied there is an absolute; for they may be brought under a single idea, which is called the essence of each.

Very true.

The many, as we say, are seen but not known, and the ideas are known but not seen.

Exactly.

And what is the organ with which we see the visible things?

The sight, he said.

And with the hearing, I said, we hear, and with the other senses perceive the other objects of sense?

True.

But have you remarked that sight is by far the most costly and complex piece of workmanship which the artificer of the senses ever contrived?

No, I never have, he said.

Then reflect: has the ear or voice need of any third or additional nature in order that the one may be able to hear and the other to be heard?

Nothing of the sort.

No, indeed, I replied; and the same is true of most, if not all, the other senses—you would not say that any of them requires such an addition?

Certainly not.

But you see that without the addition of some other nature there is no seeing or being seen?

How do you mean?

Sight being, as I conceive, in the eyes, and he who has eyes wanting to see; colour being also present in them, still unless there be a third nature specially adapted to the purpose, the owner of the eyes will see nothing and the colours will be invisible.

Of what nature are you speaking?

Of that which you term light, I replied.

True, he said.

Noble, then, is the bond which links together sight and visibility, and great beyond other bonds by no small difference of nature; for light is their bond, and light is no ignoble thing?

Nay, he said, the reverse of ignoble.

And which, I said, of the gods in heaven would you say was the lord of this element? Whose is that light which makes the eye to see perfectly and the visible to appear?

You mean the sun, as you and all mankind say.

May not the relation of sight to this deity be described as follows?
How?

Neither sight nor the eye in which sight resides is the sun?

No.

Yet of all the organs of sense the eye is the most like the sun?

By far the most like.

And the power which the eye possesses is a sort of effluence which is dispensed from the sun?

Exactly.

Then the sun is not sight, but the author of sight who is recognised by sight.

True, he said.

And this is he whom I call the child of the good, whom the good begat in his own likeness, to be in the visible world, in relation to sight and the things of sight, what the good is in the intellectual world in relation to mind and the things of mind.

Will you be a little more explicit? he said.

Why, you know, I said, that the eyes, when a person directs them towards objects on which the light of day is no longer shining, but the moon and stars only, see dimly, and are nearly blind; they seem to have no clearness of vision in them?

Very true.

But when they are directed towards objects on which the sun shines, they see clearly and there is sight in them?

Certainly.

And the soul is like the eye: when resting upon that on which truth and being shine, the soul perceives and understands and is radiant with intelligence; but when turned towards the twilight of becoming and perishing, then she has opinion only, and goes blinking about, and is first of one opinion and then of another, and seems to have no intelligence?

Just so.

Now, that which imparts truth to the known and the power of knowing to the knower is what I would have you term the idea of good, and this you will deem to be the cause of science, and of truth in so far as the latter becomes the subject of knowledge; beautiful too, as are both truth and knowledge, you will be right in esteeming this other nature as more beautiful than either; and, as in the previous instance, light and sight may be truly said to be like the sun, and yet not to be the sun, so in this other sphere, science and truth may be deemed to be like the good, but not the good; the good has a place of honour yet higher.

What a wonder of beauty that must be, he said, which is the author of science and truth, and yet surpasses them in beauty; for you surely cannot mean to say that pleasure is the good?

God forbid, I replied; but may I ask you to consider the image in another point of view?

In what point of view?

You would say, would you not, that the sun is not only the author of visibility in all visible things, but of generation and nourishment and growth, though he himself is not generation?

Certainly.

In like manner the good may be said to be not only the author of knowledge to all things known, but of their being and essence, and yet the good is not essence, but far exceeds essence in dignity and power.

Glaucon said, with a ludicrous earnestness: By the light of heaven, how amazing!

Yes, I said, and the exaggeration may be set down to you; for you made me utter my fancies.

And pray continue to utter them; at any rate let us hear if there is anything more to be said about the similitude of the sun.

Yes, I said, there is a great deal more.

Then omit nothing, however slight.

I will do my best, I said; but I should think that a great deal will have to be omitted.

You have to imagine, then, that there are two ruling powers, and that one of them is set over the intellectual world, the other over the visible. I do not say heaven, lest you should fancy that I am playing upon the name (οὐρανός, ὁρατός). May I suppose that you have this distinction of the visible and intelligible fixed in your mind?

I have.

Now take a line which has been cut into two unequal parts, and divide each of them again in the same proportion, and suppose the two main divisions to answer, one to the visible and the other to the intelligible, and then compare the subdivisions in respect of their clearness and want of clearness, and you will find that the first section in the sphere of the visible consists of images. And by images I mean, in the first place, shadows, and in the second place, reflections in water and in solid, smooth and polished bodies and the like: Do you understand?

Yes, I understand.

Imagine, now, the other section, of which this is only the resemblance, to include the animals which we see, and everything that grows or is made.

Very good.

Would you not admit that both the sections of this division have different degrees of truth, and that the copy is to the original as the sphere of opinion is to the sphere of knowledge?

Most undoubtedly.

Next proceed to consider the manner in which the sphere of the intellectual is to be divided.

In what manner?

Thus: —There are two subdivisions, in the lower of which the soul uses the figures given by the former division as images; the enquiry can only be hypothetical, and instead of going upwards to a principle descends to the other end; in the higher of the two, the soul passes out of hypotheses, and goes up to a principle which is above hypotheses, making no use of images as in the former case, but proceeding only in and through the ideas themselves.

I do not quite understand your meaning, he said.

Then I will try again; you will understand me better when I have made some preliminary remarks. You are aware that students of geometry, arithmetic, and the kindred sciences assume the odd and the even and the figures and three kinds of angles and the like in their several branches of science; these are their hypotheses, which they and every body are supposed to know, and therefore they do not deign to give any account of them either to themselves or others; but they begin with them, and go on until they arrive at last, and in a consistent manner, at their conclusion?

Yes, he said, I know.

And do you not know also that although they make use of the visible forms and reason about them, they are thinking not of these but of the ideals which they resemble; not of the figures which they draw, but of the absolute square and the absolute diameter, and so on — the forms which they draw or make, and which have shadows and reflections in water of their own, are converted by them into images, but they are really seeking to behold the things themselves, which can only be seen with the eye of the mind?

That is true.

And of this kind I spoke as the intelligible, although in the search after it the soul is compelled to use hypotheses; not ascending to a first principle, because she is unable to rise above the region of hypothesis, but employing the objects of which the shadows below are resemblances in their turn as images, they having in relation to the shadows and reflections of them a greater distinctness, and therefore a higher value.

I understand, he said, that you are speaking of the province of geometry and the sister arts.

And when I speak of the other division of the intelligible, you will understand me to speak of that other sort of knowledge which reason herself attains by the power of dialectic, using the hypotheses not as first principles, but only as hypotheses—that is to say, as steps and points of departure into a world which is above hypotheses, in order that she may soar beyond them to the first principle of the whole; and clinging to this and then to that which depends on this, by successive steps she descends again without the aid of any sensible object, from ideas, through ideas, and in ideas she ends.

I understand you, he replied; not perfectly, for you seem to me to be describing a task which is really tremendous; but, at any rate, I understand you to say that knowledge and being, which the science of dialectic contemplates, are clearer than the notions of the arts, as they are termed, which proceed from hypotheses only: these are also contemplated by the understanding, and not by the senses: yet, because they start from hypotheses and do not ascend to a principle, those who contemplate them appear to you not to exercise the higher reason upon them, although when a first principle is added to them they are cognizable by the higher reason. And the habit which is concerned with geometry and the cognate sciences I suppose that you would term understanding and not reason, as being intermediate between opinion and reason.

You have quite conceived my meaning, I said; and now, corresponding to these four divisions, let there be four faculties in the soul—reason answering to the highest, understanding to the second, faith (or conviction) to the third, and perception of shadows to the last—and let there be a scale of them, and let us suppose that the several faculties have clearness in the same degree that their objects have truth.

I understand, he replied, and give my assent, and accept your arrangement.

◆ ◆ ◆

And now, I said, let me show in a figure how far our nature is enlightened or unenlightened:—Behold! human beings living in an underground den, which has a mouth open towards the light and reaching all along the den; here they have been from their childhood, and have their legs and necks chained so that they cannot move, and can only see before them, being prevented by the chains from turning round their heads. Above and behind them a fire is blazing at a distance, and between the fire and the prisoners there is a raised way; and you will see, if you look, a low wall built along the way, like the screen which marionette players have in front of them, over which they show the puppets.

I see.

And do you see, I said, men passing along the wall carrying all sorts of vessels, and statues and figures of animals made of wood and stone and various materials, which appear over the wall? Some of them are talking, others silent.

You have shown me a strange image, and they are strange prisoners.

Like ourselves, I replied; and they see only their own shadows, or the shadows of one another, which the fire throws on the opposite wall of the cave?

True, he said; how could they see anything but the shadows if they were never allowed to move their heads?

And of the objects which are being carried in like manner they would only see the shadows?

Yes, he said.

And if they were able to converse with one another, would they not suppose that they were naming what was actually before them?

Very true.

And suppose further that the prison had an echo which came from the other side, would they not be sure to fancy when one of the passers-by spoke that the voice which they heard came from the passing shadow?

No question, he replied.

To them, I said, the truth would be literally nothing but the shadows of the images.

That is certain.

And now look again, and see what will naturally follow if the prisoners are released and disabused of their error. At first, when any of them is liberated and compelled suddenly to stand up and turn his neck round and walk and look towards the light, he will suffer sharp pains; the glare will distress him, and he will be unable to see the realities of which in his former state he had seen the shadows; and then conceive some one saying to him, that what he saw before was an illusion, but that now, when he is approaching nearer to being and his eye is turned towards more real existence, he has a clearer vision,—what will be his reply? And you may further imagine that his instructor is pointing to the objects as they pass and requiring him to name them,—will he not be perplexed? Will he not fancy that the shadows which he formerly saw are truer than the objects which are now shown to him?

Far truer.

And if he is compelled to look straight at the light, will he not have a pain in his eyes which will make him turn away to take refuge in the objects of vision which he can see, and which he will conceive to be in reality clearer than the things which are now being shown to him?

True, he said.

And suppose once more, that he is reluctantly dragged up a steep and rugged ascent, and held fast until he is forced into the presence of the sun himself, is he not likely to be pained and irritated? When he approaches the light his eyes will be dazzled, and he will not be able to see anything at all of what are now called realities.

Not all in a moment, he said.

He will require to grow accustomed to the sight of the upper world. And first he will see the shadows best, next the reflections of men and other objects in the water, and then the objects themselves; then he will gaze upon the light of the moon and the stars and the spangled heaven; and he will see the sky and the stars by night better than the sun or the light of the sun by day?

Certainly.

Last of all he will be able to see the sun, and not mere reflections of him in the water, but he will see him in his own proper place, and not in another; and he will contemplate him as he is.

Certainly.

He will then proceed to argue that this is he who gives the season and the years, and is the guardian of all that is in the visible world, and in a certain way the cause of all things which he and his fellows have been accustomed to behold?

Clearly, he said, he would first see the sun and then reason about him.

And when he remembered his old habitation, and the wisdom of the den and his fellow-prisoners, do you not suppose that he would felicitate himself on the change, and pity them?

Certainly, he would.

11

And if they were in the habit of conferring honours among themselves on those who were quickest to observe the passing shadows and to remark which of them went before, and which followed after, and which were together; and who were therefore best able to draw conclusions as to the future, do you think that he would care for such honours and glories, or envy the possessors of them? Would he not say with Homer,

'Better to be the poor servant of a poor master,'

and to endure anything, rather than think as they do and live after their manner?

Yes, he said, I think that he would rather suffer anything than entertain these false notions and live in this miserable manner.

Imagine once more, I said, such an one coming suddenly out of the sun to be replaced in his old situation; would he not be certain to have his eyes full of darkness?

To be sure, he said.

And if there were a contest, and he had to compete in measuring the shadows with the prisoners who had never moved out of the den, while his sight was still weak, and before his eyes had become steady (and the time which would be needed to acquire this new habit of sight might be very considerable), would he not be ridiculous? Men would say of him that up he went and down he came without his eyes; and that it was better not even to think of ascending; and if any one tried to loose another and lead him up to the light, let them only catch the offender, and they would put him to death.

No question, he said.

This entire allegory, I said, you may now append, dear Glaucon, to the previous argument; the prison-house is the world of sight, the light of the fire is the sun, and you will not misapprehend me if you interpret the journey upwards to be the ascent of the soul into the intellectual world according to my poor belief, which, at your desire, I have expressed—whether rightly or wrongly God knows. But, whether true or false, my opinion is that in the world of knowledge the idea of good appears last of all, and is seen only with an effort; and, when seen, is also inferred to be the universal author of all things beautiful and right, parent of light and of the lord of light in this visible world, and the immediate source of reason and truth in the intellectual; and that this is the power upon which he who would act rationally either in public or private life must have his eye fixed.

I agree, he said, as far as I am able to understand you.

Moreover, I said, you must not wonder that those who attain to this beatific vision are unwilling to descend to human affairs; for their souls are ever hastening into the upper world where they desire to dwell; which desire of theirs is very natural, if our allegory may be trusted.

Yes, very natural.

And is there anything surprising in one who passes from divine contemplations to the evil state of man, misbehaving himself in a ridiculous manner; if, while his eyes are blinking and before he has become accustomed to the surrounding darkness, he is compelled to fight in courts of law, or in other places, about the images or the shadows of images of justice, and is endeavouring to meet the conceptions of those who have never yet seen absolute justice?

Anything but surprising, he replied.

Any one who has common sense will remember that the bewilderments of the eyes are of two kinds, and arise from two causes, either from coming out of the light or from going into the light, which is true of the mind's eye, quite as much as of the bodily eye; and he who remembers this when he sees any one whose vision is perplexed and weak, will not be too ready to laugh; he will first ask whether that soul of man has come out of the brighter life, and is unable to see because unaccustomed to the dark, or having turned from darkness to the day is dazzled by excess of light. And he will count the one happy in his condition and state of being, and he will pity the other; or, if he have a mind to laugh at the soul which comes from below into the light, there will be more reason in this than in the laugh which greets him who returns from above out of the light into the den.

That, he said, is a very just distinction.

But then, if I am right, certain professors of education must be wrong when they say that they can put a knowledge into the soul which was not there before, like sight into blind eyes.

They undoubtedly say this, he replied.

Whereas, our argument shows that the power and capacity of learning exists in the soul already; and that just as the eye was unable to turn from darkness to light without the whole body, so too the instrument of knowledge can only by the movement of the whole soul be turned from the world of becoming into that of being, and learn by degrees to endure the sight of being, and of the brightest and best of being, or in other words, of the good.

Very true.

And must there not be some art which will effect conversion in the easiest and quickest manner; not implanting the faculty of sight, for that exists already, but has been turned in the wrong direction, and is looking away from the truth?

Yes, he said, such an art may be presumed.

And whereas the other so-called virtues of the soul seem to be akin to bodily qualities, for even when they are not originally innate they can be implanted later by habit and exercise, the virtue of wisdom more than anything else contains a divine element which always remains, and by this conversion is rendered useful and profitable; or, on the other hand, hurtful and useless. Did you never observe the narrow intelligence flashing from the keen eye of a clever rogue—how eager he is, how clearly his paltry soul sees the way to his end; he is the reverse of blind, but his keen eye-sight is forced into the service of evil, and he is mischievous in proportion to his cleverness?

Very true, he said.

But what if there had been a circumcision of such natures in the days of their youth; and they had been severed from those sensual pleasures, such as eating and drinking, which, like leaden weights were attached to them at their birth, and which drag them down and turn the vision of their souls upon the things that are below—if, I say, they had been released from these impediments and turned in the opposite direction, the very same faculty in them would have seen the truth as keenly as they see what their eyes are turned to now.

Very likely.

Yes, I said; and there is another thing which is likely, or rather a necessary inference from what has preceded, that neither the uneducated and uninformed of the truth, nor yet those who never make an end of their education, will be able ministers of State; not the former, because they have no single aim of duty which is the rule of all their actions, private as well as public; nor the latter, because they will not act at all except upon compulsion, fancying that they are already dwelling apart in the islands of the blest.

Very true, he replied.

Then, I said, the business of us who are the founders of the State will be to compel the best minds to attain that knowledge which we have already shown to be the greatest of all—they must continue to ascend until they arrive at the good; but when they have ascended and seen enough we must not allow them to do as they do now.

What do you mean?

I mean that they remain in the upper world: but this must not be allowed; they must be made to descend again among the prisoners in the den, and partake of their labours and honours, whether they are worth having or not.

But is not this unjust? he said; ought we to give them a worse life, when they might have a better?

You have again forgotten, my friend, I said, the intention of the legislator, who did not aim at making any one class in the State happy above the rest; the happiness was to be in the whole State, and he held the citizens together by persuasion and necessity, making them bene-factors of the State, and therefore benefactors of one another; to this end he created them, not to please themselves, but to be his instruments in binding up the State.

True, he said, I had forgotten.

Observe, Glaucon, that there will be no injustice in compelling our philosophers to have a care and providence of others; we shall explain to them that in other States, men of their class are not obliged to share in the toils of politics: and this is reasonable, for they grow up at their own sweet will, and the government would rather not have them. Being self-taught, they cannot be expected to show any gratitude for a culture which they have never received. But we have brought you into the world to be rulers of the hive, kings of yourselves and of the other citizens, and have educated you far better and more perfectly than they have been educated, and you are better able to share in the double duty. Wherefore each of you, when his turn comes, must go down to the general underground abode, and get the habit of seeing in the dark. When you have acquired the habit, you will see ten thousand times better than the inhabitants of the den, and you will know what the several images are, and what they represent, because you have seen the beautiful and just and good in their truth. And thus our State which is also yours will be a reality, and not a dream only, and will be administered in a spirit unlike that of other States, in which men fight with one another about shadows only and are distracted in the struggle for power, which in their eyes is a great good. Whereas the truth is that the State in which the rulers are most reluctant to govern is always the best and most quietly governed, and the State in which they are most eager, the worst.

Quite true, he replied.

And will our pupils, when they hear this, refuse to take their turn at the toils of State, when they are allowed to spend the greater part of their time with one another in the heavenly light?

Impossible, he answered; for they are just men, and the commands which we impose upon them are just; there can be no doubt that every one of them will take office as a stern necessity, and not after the fashion of our present rulers of State.

Yes, my friend, I said; and there lies the point. You must contrive for your future rulers another and a better life than that of a ruler, and then you may have a well-ordered State; for only in the State which offers this, will they rule who are truly rich, not in silver and gold, but in virtue and wisdom, which are the true blessings of life. Whereas if they go to the administration of public affairs, poor and hungering after their own private advantage, thinking that hence they are to snatch the chief good, order there can never be; for they will be fighting about office, and the civil and domestic broils which thus arise will be the ruin of the rulers themselves and of the whole State.

Creation
(*Timaeus*, 27–53)

Tim. All men, Socrates, who have any degree of right feeling, at the beginning of every enterprise, whether small or great, always call upon God. And we, too, who are going to discourse of the nature of the universe, how created or how existing without creation, if we be not altogether out of our wits, must invoke the aid of Gods and Goddesses and pray that our words may be acceptable to them and consistent with themselves. Let this, then, be our invocation of the Gods, to which I add an exhortation of myself to speak in such manner as will be most intelligible to you, and will most accord with my own intent.

First then, in my judgment, we must make a distinction and ask, What is that which always is and has no becoming; and what is that which is always becoming and never is? That which is apprehended by intelligence and reason is always in the same state; but that which is conceived by opinion with the help of sensation and without reason, is always in a process of becoming and perishing and never really is. Now everything that becomes or is created must of necessity be created by some cause, for without a cause nothing can be created. The work of the creator, whenever he looks to the unchangeable and fashions the form and nature of his work after an unchangeable pattern, must necessarily be made fair and perfect; but when he looks to the created only, and uses a created pattern, it is not fair or perfect. Was the heaven then or the world, whether called by this or by any other more appropriate name — assuming the name, I am asking a question which has to be asked at the beginning of an enquiry about anything — was the world, I say, always in existence and without beginning? or created, and had it a beginning? Created, I reply, being visible and tangible and having a body, and therefore sensible; and all sensible things are apprehended by opinion and sense and are in a process of creation and created. Now that which is created must, as we affirm, of necessity be created by a cause. But the father and maker of all this universe is past finding out; and even if we found him, to tell of him to all men would be impossible. And there is still a question to be asked about him: Which of the patterns had the artificer in view when he made the world, — the pattern of the unchangeable, or of that which is created? If the world be indeed fair and the artificer good, it is manifest that he must have looked to that which is eternal; but if what cannot be said without blasphemy is true, then to the created pattern. Every one will see that he must have looked to the eternal; for the world is the fairest of creations and he is the best of causes. And having been created in this way, the world has been framed in the likeness of that which is apprehended by reason and mind and is unchangeable, and must therefore of necessity, if this is admitted, be a copy of something. Now it is all-important that the beginning of everything should be according to nature. And in speaking of the copy and the original we may assume that words are akin to the matter which they describe; when they relate to the lasting and permanent and intelligible, they ought to be lasting and unalterable, and, as far as their nature allows, irrefutable and immovable—nothing less. But when they express only the copy or likeness and not the eternal things themselves, they need only be likely and analogous to the real words. As being is to becoming, so is truth to belief. If then, Socrates, amid the many opinions about the gods and the generation of the universe, we are not able to give notions which are altogether and in every respect exact and consistent with one another, do not be surprised. Enough, if we adduce probabilities as likely as any others; for we must remember that I who am the speaker, and you who are the judges, are only mortal men, and we ought to accept the tale which is probable and enquire no further.

Soc. Excellent, Timaeus; and we will do precisely as you bid us. The prelude is charming, and is already accepted by us—may we beg of you to proceed to the strain?

Tim. Let me tell you then why the creator made this world of generation. He was good, and the good can never have any jealousy of anything. And being free from jealousy, he desired that all things should be as like himself as they could be. This is in the truest sense the origin of creation and of the world, as we shall do well in believing on the testimony of wise men: God desired that all things should be good and nothing bad, so far as this was attainable. Wherefore also finding the whole visible sphere not at rest, but moving in an irregular and disorderly fashion, out of disorder he brought order, considering that this was in every way better than the other. Now the deeds of the best could never be or have been other than the fairest; and the creator, reflecting on the things which are by nature visible, found that no unintelligent creature taken as a whole was fairer than the intelligent taken as a whole; and that intelligence could not be present in anything which was devoid of soul. For which reason, when he was framing the universe, he put intelligence in soul, and soul in body, that he might be the creator of a work which was by nature fairest and best. Wherefore, using the language of probability, we may say that the world became a living creature truly endowed with soul and intelligence by the providence of God.

This being supposed, let us proceed to the next stage: In the likeness of what animal did the Creator make the world? It would be an unworthy thing to liken it to any nature which exists as a part only; for nothing can be beautiful which is like any imperfect thing; but let us suppose the world to be the very image of that whole of which all other animals both individually and in their tribes are portions. For the original of the universe contains in itself all intelligible beings, just as this world comprehends us and all other visible creatures. For the Deity, intending to make this world like the fairest and most perfect of intelligible beings, framed one visible animal comprehending within itself all other animals of a kindred nature. Are we right in saying that there is one world, or that they are many and infinite? There must be one only, if the created copy is to accord with the original. For that which includes all other intelligible creatures cannot have a second or companion; in that case there would be need of another living being which would include both, and of which they would be parts, and the likeness would be more truly said to resemble not them, but that other which included them. In order then that the world might be solitary, like the perfect animal, the creator made not two worlds or an infinite number of them; but there is and ever will be one only-begotten and created heaven.

Now that which is created is of necessity corporeal, and also visible and tangible. And nothing is visible where there is no fire, or tangible which has no solidity, and nothing is solid without earth. Wherefore also God in the beginning of creation made the body of the universe to consist of fire and earth. But two things cannot be rightly put together without a third; there must be some bond of union between them. And the fairest bond is that which makes the most complete fusion of itself and the things which it combines; and proportion is best adapted to effect such a union. For whenever in any three numbers, whether cube or square, there is a mean, which is to the last term what the first term is to it; and again, when the mean is to the first term as the last term is to the mean,—then the mean becoming first and last, and the first and last both becoming means, they will all of them of necessity come to be the same, and having become the same with one another will be all one. If the universal frame had been created a surface only and having no depth, a single mean would have sufficed to bind together itself and the other terms; but now, as the world must be solid, and solid bodies are always compacted not by one mean but by two, God placed water and air in the mean between fire and earth, and made them to have the same proportion so far as was possible (as fire is to air so is air to water, and as air is to water so is water to earth); and thus he bound and put together a visible and tangible heaven. And for these reasons, and out of such elements which are in number four, the body of the world was created, and it was harmonized by proportion, and therefore has the spirit of friendship; and having been reconciled to itself, it was indissoluble by the hand of any other than the framer.

Now the creation took up the whole of each of the four elements; for the Creator compounded the world out of all the fire and all the water and all the air and all the earth, leaving no part of any of them nor any power of them outside. His intention was, in the first place, that the animal should be as far as possible a perfect whole and of perfect parts: secondly, that it should be one, leaving no remnants out of which another such world might be created: and also that it should be free from old age and unaffected by disease. Considering that if heat and cold and other powerful forces which unite bodies surround and attack them from without, when they are unprepared, they decompose them, and by bringing diseases and old age upon them, make them waste away—for this cause and on these grounds he made the world one whole, having every part entire, and being therefore perfect and not liable to old age and disease. And he gave to the world the figure which was suitable and also natural. Now to the animal which was to comprehend all animals, that figure was suitable which comprehends within itself all other figures. Wherefore he made the world in the form of a globe, round as from a lathe, having its extremes in every direction equidistant from the centre, the most perfect and the most like itself of all figures; for he considered that the like is infinitely fairer than the unlike. This he finished off, making the surface smooth all around for many reasons; in the first place, because the living being had no need of eyes when there was nothing remaining outside him to be seen; nor of ears when there was nothing to be heard; and there was no surrounding atmosphere to be breathed; nor would there have been any use of organs by the help of which he might receive his food or get rid of what he had already digested, since there was nothing which went from him or came into him: for there was nothing beside him. Of design he was created thus, his own waste providing his own food, and all that he did or suffered taking place in and by himself. For the Creator conceived that a being which was self-sufficient would be far more excellent than one which lacked anything; and, as he had no need to take anything or defend himself against any one, the Creator did not think it necessary to bestow upon him hands: nor had he any need of feet, nor of the whole apparatus of walking; but the movement suited to his spherical form was assigned to him, being of all the seven that which is most appropriate to mind and intelligence; and he was made to move in the same manner and on the same spot, within his own limits revolving in a circle. All the other six motions were taken away from him, and he was made not to partake of their deviations. And as this circular movement required no feet, the universe was created without legs and without feet.

Such was the whole plan of the eternal God about the god that was to be, to whom for this reason he gave a body, smooth and even, having a surface in every direction equidistant from the centre, a body entire and perfect, and formed out of perfect bodies. And in the centre he put the soul, which he diffused throughout the body, making it also to be the exterior environment of it; and he made the universe a circle moving in a circle, one and solitary, yet by reason of its excellence able to converse with itself, and needing no other friendship or acquaintance. Having these purposes in view he created the world a blessed god.

Now God did not make the soul after the body, although we are speaking of them in this order; for having brought them together he would never have allowed that the elder should be ruled by the younger; but this is a random manner of speaking which we have, because somehow we ourselves too are very much under the dominion of chance. Whereas he made the soul in origin and excellence prior to and older than the body, to be the ruler and mistress, of whom the body was to be the subject. And he made her out of the following elements and on this wise: Out of the indivisible and unchangeable, and also out of that which is divisible and has to do with material bodies, he compounded a third and intermediate kind of essence, partaking of the nature of the same and of the other, and this compound he placed accordingly in a mean between the indivisible, and the divisible and material. He took the three elements of the same, the other, and the essence, and mingled them into one form, compressing by force the reluctant and unsociable nature of the other into the same. When he had mingled them with the essence and out of three made one, he again divided this whole into as many portions as was fitting, each portion being a compound of the same, the other, and the essence. And he proceeded to divide after this manner: — First of all, he took away one part of the whole [1], and then he separated a second part which was double the first [2], and then he took away a third part which was half as much again as the second and three times as much as the first [3], and then he took a fourth part which was twice as much as the second [4], and a fifth part which was three times the third [9], and a sixth part which was eight times the first [8], and a seventh part which was twenty-seven times the first [27]. After this he filled up the double intervals [i. e. between 1, 2, 4, 8] and the triple [i. e. between 1, 3, 9, 27], cutting off yet other portions from the mixture and placing them in the intervals, so that in each interval there were two kinds of means, the one exceeding and exceeded by equal parts of its extremes [as for example 1, 4/3, 2, in which the mean 4/3 is one-third of 1 more than 1, and one-third of 2 less than 2], the other being that kind of mean which exceeds and is exceeded by an equal number. Where there were intervals of 3/2 and of 4/3 and of 9/8, made by the connecting terms in the former intervals, he filled up all the intervals of 4/3 with the interval of 9/8, leaving a fraction over; and the interval which this fraction expressed was in the ratio of 256 to 243. And thus the whole mixture out of which he cut these portions was all exhausted by him. This entire compound he divided lengthways into two parts, which he joined to one another at the centre like the letter X, and bent them into a circular form, connecting them with themselves and each other at the point opposite to their original meeting-point; and, comprehending them in a uniform revolution upon the same axis, he made the one the outer and the other the inner circle. Now the motion of the outer circle he called the motion of the same, and the motion of the inner circle the motion of the other or diverse. The motion of the same he carried round by the side to the right, and the motion of the diverse diagonally to the left. And he gave dominion to the motion of the same and like, for that he left single and undivided; but the inner motion he divided in six places and made seven unequal circles having their intervals in ratios of two and three, three of each, and bade the orbits proceed in a direction opposite to one another; and three [Sun, Mercury, Venus] he made to move with equal swiftness, and the remaining four [Moon, Saturn, Mars, Jupiter] to move with unequal swiftness to the three and to one another, but in due proportion.

Now when the Creator had framed the soul according to his will, he formed within her the corporeal universe, and brought the two together, and united them centre to centre. The soul, interfused everywhere from the centre to the circumference of heaven, of which also she is the external envelopment, herself turning in herself, began a divine beginning of never-ceasing and rational life enduring throughout all time. The body of heaven is visible, but the soul is invisible, and partakes of reason and harmony, and being made by the best of intellectual and everlasting natures, is the best of things created. And because she is composed of the same and of the other and of the essence, these three, and is divided and united in due proportion, and in her revolutions returns upon herself, the soul, when touching anything which has essence, whether dispersed in parts or undivided, is stirred through all her powers, to declare the sameness or difference of that thing and some other; and to what individuals are related, and by what affected, and in what way and how and when, both in the world of generation and in the world of immutable being. And when reason, which works with equal truth, whether she be in the circle of the diverse or of the same—in voiceless silence holding her onward course in the sphere of the self-moved—when reason, I say, is hovering around the sensible world and when the circle of the diverse also moving truly imparts the intimations of sense to the whole soul, then arise opinions and beliefs sure and certain. But when reason is concerned with the rational, and the circle of the same moving smoothly declares it, then intelligence and knowledge are necessarily perfected. And if any one affirms that in which these two are found to be other than the soul, he will say the very opposite of the truth.

When the father and creator saw the creature which he had made moving and living, the created image of the eternal gods, he rejoiced, and in his joy determined to make the copy still more like the original; and as this was eternal, he sought to make the universe eternal, so far as might be. Now the nature of the ideal being was everlasting, but to bestow this attribute in its fulness upon a creature was impossible. Wherefore he resolved to have a moving image of eternity, and when he set in order the heaven, he made this image eternal but moving according to number, while eternity itself rests in unity; and this image we call time. For there were no days and nights and months and years before the heaven was created, but when he constructed the heaven he created them also. They are all parts of time, and the past and future are created species of time, which we unconsciously but wrongly transfer to the eternal essence; for we say that he 'was,' he 'is,' he 'will be,' but the truth is that 'is' alone is properly attributed to him, and that 'was'

23

and 'will be' are only to be spoken of becoming in time, for they are motions, but that which is immovably the same cannot become older or younger by time, nor ever did or has become, or hereafter will be, older or younger, nor is subject at all to any of those states which affect moving and sensible things and of which generation is the cause. These are the forms of time, which imitates eternity and revolves according to a law of number. Moreover, when we say that what has become *is* become and what becomes *is* becoming, and that what will become is about to become and that the non-existent *is* non-existent,—all these are inaccurate modes of expression. But perhaps this whole subject will be more suitably discussed on some other occasion.

Time, then, and the heaven came into being at the same instant in order that, having been created together, if ever there was to be a dissolution of them, they might be dissolved together. It was framed after the pattern of the eternal nature, that it might resemble this as far as was possible; for the pattern exists from eternity, and the created heaven has been, and is, and will be, in all time. Such was the mind and thought of God in the creation of time. The sun and moon and five other stars, which are called the planets, were created by him in order to distinguish and preserve the numbers of time; and when he had made their several bodies, he placed them in the orbits in which the circle of the other was revolving (cp. 36 D),—in seven orbits seven stars. First, there was the moon in the orbit nearest the earth, and next the sun, in the second orbit above the earth; then came the morning star and the star sacred to Hermes, moving in orbits which have an equal swiftness with the sun, but in an opposite direction; and this is the reason why the sun and Hermes and Lucifer overtake and are overtaken by each other. To enumerate the places which he assigned to the other stars, and to give all the reasons why he assigned them, although a secondary matter, would give more trouble than the primary. These things at some future time, when we are at leisure, may have the consideration which they deserve, but not at present.

Now, when all the stars which were necessary to the creation of time had attained a motion suitable to them, and had become living creatures having bodies fastened by vital chains, and learnt their appointed task, moving in the motion of the diverse, which is diagonal, and passes through and is governed by the motion of the same, they revolved, some in a larger and some in a lesser orbit,—those which had the lesser orbit revolving faster, and those which had the larger more slowly. Now by reason of the motion of the same, those which revolved fastest appeared to be overtaken by those which moved slower although they really overtook them; for the motion of the same made them all turn in a spiral, and, because some went one way and some another, that which receded most slowly from the sphere of the same, which was the swiftest, appeared to follow it most nearly. That there might be some visible measure of their relative swiftness and slowness as they proceeded in their eight courses, God lighted a fire, which we now call the sun, in the second from the earth of these orbits, that it might give light to the whole of heaven, and that the animals, as many as nature intended, might participate in number, learning arithmetic from the revolution of the same and the like. Thus, then, and for this reason the night and the day were created, being the period of the one most intelligent revolution. And the month is accomplished when the moon has completed her orbit and overtaken the sun, and the year when the sun has completed his own orbit. Mankind, with hardly an exception, have not remarked the periods of the other stars, and they have no name for them, and do not measure them against one another by the help of number, and hence they can scarcely be said to know that their wanderings, being infinite in number and admirable for their variety, make up time. And yet there is no difficulty in seeing that the perfect number of time fulfils the perfect year when all the eight revolutions, having their relative degrees of swiftness, are accomplished together and attain their completion at the same time, measured by the rotation of the same and equally moving. After this manner, and for these reasons, came into being such of the stars as in their heavenly progress received reversals of motion, to the end that the created heaven might imitate the eternal nature, and be as like as possible to the perfect and intelligible animal.

Thus far and until the birth of time the created universe was made in the likeness of the original, but inasmuch as all animals were not yet comprehended therein, it was still unlike. What remained, the creator then proceeded to fashion after the nature of the pattern. Now as in the ideal animal the mind perceives ideas or species of a certain nature and number, he thought that this created animal ought to have species of a like nature and number. There are four such; one of them is the heavenly race of the gods; another, the race of birds whose way is in the air; the third, the watery species; and the fourth, the pedestrian and land creatures. Of the heavenly and divine, he created the greater part out of fire, that they might be the brightest of all things and fairest to behold, and he fashioned them after the likeness of the universe in the figure of a circle, and made them follow the intelligent motion of the supreme, distributing them over the whole circumference of heaven which was to be a true cosmos or glorious world spangled with them all over. And he gave to each of them two movements: the first, a movement on the same spot after the same manner, whereby they ever continue to think consistently the same thoughts about the same things; the second, a forward movement, in which they are controlled by the revolution of the same and the like; but by the other five motions they were unaffected, in order that each of them might attain the highest perfection. And for this reason the fixed stars were created, to be divine and eternal animals, ever-abiding and revolving after the same manner and on the same spot; and the other stars which reverse their motion and are subject to deviations of this kind, were created in the manner already described. The earth, which is our nurse, clinging around the pole which is extended through the universe, he framed to be the guardian and artificer of night and day, first and eldest of gods that are in the interior of heaven. Vain would be the attempt to tell all the figures of them circling as in dance, and their juxtapositions, and the return of them in their revolutions upon themselves, and their approximations, and to say which of these deities in their conjunctions meet, and which of them are in opposition, and in what order they get behind and before one another, and when they are severally eclipsed to our sight and again reappear, sending terrors and intimations of the future to those who cannot calculate their movements—to attempt to tell of all this without a visible representation of the heavenly system would be labour in vain. Enough on this head; and now let what we have said about the nature of the created and visible gods have an end.

To know or tell the origin of the other divinities is beyond us, and we must accept the traditions of the men of old time who affirm themselves to be the offspring of the gods—that is what they say—and they must surely have known their own ancestors. How can we doubt the word of the children of the gods? Although they give no probable or certain proofs, still, as they declare that they are speaking of what took place in their own family, we must conform to custom and believe them.

In this manner, then, according to them, the genealogy of these gods is to be received and set forth.

Oceanus and Tethys were the children of Earth and Heaven, and from these sprang Phorcys and Cronos and Rhea, and all that generation; and from Cronos and Rhea sprang Zeus and Herè, and all those who are said to be their brethren, and others who were the children of these.

Now, when all of them, both those who visibly appear in their revolutions as well as those other gods who are of a more retiring nature, had come into being, the creator of the universe addressed them in these words: 'Gods, children of gods, who are my works, and of whom I am the artificer and father, my creations are indissoluble, if so I will. All that is bound may be undone, but only an evil being would wish to undo that which is harmonious and happy. Wherefore, since ye are but creatures, ye are not altogether immortal and indissoluble, but ye shall certainly not be dissolved, nor be liable to the fate of death, having in my will a greater and mightier bond than those with which ye were bound at the time of your birth. And now listen to my instructions: — Three tribes of mortal beings remain to be created — without them the universe will be incomplete, for it will not contain every kind of animal which it ought to contain, if it is to be perfect. On the other hand, if they were created by me and received life at my hands, they would be on an equality with the gods. In order then that they may be mortal, and that this universe may be truly universal, do ye, according to your natures, betake yourselves to the formation of animals, imitating the power which was shown by me in creating you. The part of them worthy of the name immortal, which is called divine and is the guiding principle of those who are willing to follow justice and you — of that divine part I will myself sow the seed, and having made a beginning, I will hand the work over to you. And do ye then interweave the mortal with the immortal, and make and beget living creatures, and give them food, and make them to grow, and receive them again in death.'

Thus he spake, and once more into the cup in which he had previously mingled the soul of the universe he poured the remains of the elements, and mingled them in much the same manner; they were not, however, pure as before, but diluted to the second and third degree. And having made it he divided the whole mixture into souls equal in number to the stars, and assigned each soul to a star; and having there placed them as in a chariot, he showed them the nature of the universe, and declared to them the laws of destiny, according to which their first birth would be one and the same for all,—no one should suffer a disadvantage at his hands; they were to be sown in the instruments of time severally adapted to them, and to come forth the most religious of animals; and as human nature was of two kinds, the superior race would hereafter be called man. Now, when they should be implanted in bodies by necessity, and be always gaining or losing some part of their bodily substance, then in the first place it would be necessary that they should all have in them one and the same faculty of sensation arising out of irresistible impressions; in the second place, they must have love, in which pleasure and pain mingle; also fear and anger, and the feelings which are akin or opposite to them; if they conquered these they would live righteously, and if they were conquered by them, unrighteously. He who lived well during his appointed time was to return and dwell in his native star, and there he would have a blessed and congenial existence. But if he failed in attaining this, at the second birth he would pass into a woman, and if, when in that state of being, he did not desist from evil, he would continually be changed into some brute who resembled him in the evil nature which he had acquired, and would not cease from his toils and transformations until he followed the revolution of the same and the like within him, and overcame by the help of reason the turbulent and irrational mob of later accretions, made up of fire and air and water and earth, and returned to the form of his first and better state. Having given all these laws to his creatures, that he might be guiltless of future evil in any of them, the creator sowed some of them in the earth, and some in the moon, and some in the other instruments of time; and when he had sown them he committed to the younger gods the fashioning of their mortal bodies, and desired them to furnish what was still lacking to the human soul, and having made all the suitable additions, to rule over them, and to pilot the mortal animals in the best and wisest manner which they could, and avert from him all but self-inflicted evils.

When the creator had made all these ordinances he remained in his own accustomed nature, and his children heard and were obedient to their father's word, and receiving from him the immortal principle of a mortal creature, in imitation of their own creator they borrowed portions of fire, and earth, and water, and air from the world, which were hereafter to be restored—these they took and welded them together, not with the indissoluble chains by which they were themselves bound, but with little pegs too small to be visible, making up out of all the four elements each separate body, and fastening the courses of the immortal soul in a body which was in a state of perpetual influx and efflux. Now these courses, detained as in a vast river, neither overcame nor were overcome; but were hurrying and hurried to and fro, so that the whole animal was moved and progressed, irregularly however and irrationally and anyhow, in all the six directions of motion, wandering backwards and forwards, and right and left, and up and down, and in all the six directions. For great as was the advancing and retiring flood which provided nourishment, the affections produced by external contact caused still greater tumult—when the body of any one met and came into collision with some external fire, or with the solid earth or the gliding waters, or was caught in the tempest borne on the air, and the motions produced by any of these impulses were carried through the body to the soul. All such motions have consequently received the general name of 'sensations,' which they still retain. And they did in fact at that time create a very great and mighty movement; uniting with the everflowing stream in stirring up and violently shaking the courses of the soul, they completely stopped the revolution of the same by their opposing current, and hindered it from predominating and advancing; and they so disturbed the nature of the other or diverse, that the three double intervals [i. e. between 1, 2, 4, 8], and the three triple intervals [i. e. between 1, 3, 9, 27], together with the mean terms and connecting links which are expressed by the ratios of 3 : 2, and 4 : 3, and of 9 : 8,—these, although they cannot be wholly undone except by him who united them, were twisted by them in all sorts of ways, and the circles were broken and disordered in every possible manner, so that when they moved they were tumbling to pieces and moved irrationally, at one time in a reverse direction, and then again obliquely, and then upside down, as you might imagine a person who is upside down and has his head leaning upon the ground and his feet up against something in the air; and when he is in such a position, both he and the spectator fancy that the right of either is his left, and left right. If, when powerfully experiencing these and similar effects, the revolutions of the soul come in contact with some external thing, either of the class of the same or of the other, they speak of the same or of the other in a manner the very opposite of the truth; and they become false and foolish, and there is no course or revolution in them which has a guiding or directing power; and if again any sensations enter in violently from without and drag after them the whole vessel of the soul, then the courses of the soul, though they seem to conquer, are really conquered.

And by reason of all these affections, the soul, when encased in a mortal body, now, as in the beginning, is at first without intelligence; but when the flood of growth and nutriment abates, and the courses of the soul, calming down, go their own way and become steadier as time goes on, then the several circles return to their natural form, and their revolutions are corrected, and they call the same and the other by their right names, and make the possessor of them to become a rational being. And if these combine in him with any true nurture or education, he attains the fulness and health of the perfect man, and escapes the worst disease of all; but if he neglects education he walks lame to the end of his life, and returns imperfect and good for nothing to the world below. This, however, is a later stage; at present we must treat more exactly the subject before us, which involves a preliminary enquiry into the generation of the body and its members, and as to how the soul was created,—for what reason and by what providence of the gods; and holding fast to probability, we must pursue our way.

First, then, the gods, imitating the spherical shape of the universe, enclosed the two divine courses in a spherical body, that, namely, which we now term the head, being the most divine part of us and the lord of all that is in us: to this the gods, when they put together the body, gave all the other members to be servants, considering that it partook of every sort of motion. In order then that it might not tumble about among the high and deep places of the earth, but might be able to get over the one and out of the other, they provided the body to be its vehicle and means of locomotion; which consequently had length and was furnished with four limbs extended and flexible; these God contrived to be instruments of locomotion with which it might take hold and find support, and so be able to pass through all places, carrying on high the dwelling-place of the most sacred and divine part of us. Such was the origin of legs and hands, which for this reason were attached to every man; and the gods, deeming the front part of man to be more honourable and more fit to command than the hinder part, made us to move mostly in a forward direction. Wherefore man must needs have his front part unlike and distinguished from the rest of his body. And so in the vessel of the head, they first of all put a face in which they inserted organs to minister in all things to the providence of the soul, and they appointed this part, which has authority, to be by nature the part which is in front. And of the organs they first contrived the eyes to give light, and the principle according to which they were inserted was as follows: So much of fire as would not burn, but gave a gentle light, they formed into a substance akin to the light of every-day life; and the pure fire which is within us and related thereto they made to flow through the eyes in a stream smooth and dense, compressing the whole eye, and especially the centre part, so that it kept out everything of a coarser nature, and allowed to pass only this pure element. When the light of day surrounds the stream of vision, then like falls upon like, and they coalesce, and one body is formed by natural affinity in the line of vision, wherever the light that falls from within meets with an external object. And the whole stream of vision, being similarly affected in virtue of similarity, diffuses the motions of what it touches or what touches it over the whole body, until they reach the soul, causing that perception which we call sight. But when night comes on and the external and kindred fire departs, then the stream of vision is cut off; for going forth to an unlike element it is changed and extinguished, being no longer of one nature with the surrounding atmosphere which is now deprived of fire: and so the eye no longer sees, and we feel disposed to sleep. For when the eyelids, which the gods invented for the preservation of sight, are closed, they keep in the internal fire; and the power of the fire diffuses and equalizes the inward motions; when they are equalized, there is rest, and when the rest is profound, sleep comes over us scarce disturbed by dreams; but where the greater motions still remain, of whatever nature and in whatever locality, they engender corresponding visions in dreams, which are remembered by us when we are awake and in the external world. And now there is no longer any difficulty in understanding the creation of images in mirrors and all smooth and bright surfaces. For from the communion of the internal and external fires, and again from the union of them and their numerous transformations when they meet in the mirror, all these appearances of necessity arise, when the fire from the face coalesces with the fire from the eye on the bright and smooth surface. And right appears left and left right, because the visual rays come into contact with the rays emitted by the object in a manner contrary to the usual mode of meeting; but the right appears right, and the left left, when the position of one of the two concurring lights is reversed; and this happens when the mirror is concave and its smooth surface repels the right stream of vision to the left side, and the left to the right. Or if the mirror be turned vertically, then the concavity makes the countenance appear to be all upside down, and the lower rays are driven upwards and the upper downwards.

All these are to be reckoned among the second and co-operative causes which God, carrying into execution the idea of the best as far as possible, uses as his ministers. They are thought by most men not to be the second, but the prime causes of all things, because they freeze and heat, and contract and dilate, and the like. But they are not so, for they are incapable of reason or intellect; the only being which can properly have mind is the invisible soul, whereas fire and water, and earth and air, are all of them visible bodies. The lover of intellect and knowledge ought to explore causes of intelligent nature first of all, and, secondly, of those things which, being moved by others, are compelled to move others. And this is what we too must do. Both kinds of causes should be acknowledged by us, but a distinction should be made between those which are endowed with mind and are the workers of things fair and good, and those which are deprived of intelligence and always produce chance effects without order or design. Of the second or co-operative causes of sight, which help to give to the eyes the power which they now possess, enough has been said. I will therefore now proceed to speak of the higher use and purpose, for which God has given them to us. The sight in my opinion is the source of the greatest benefit to us, for had we never seen the stars, and the sun, and the heaven, none of the words which we have spoken about the universe would ever have been uttered. But now the sight of day and night, and the months and the revolutions of the years, have created number, and have given us a conception of time, and the power of enquiring about the nature of the universe; and from this source we have derived philosophy, than which no greater good ever was or will be given by the gods to mortal man. This is the greatest boon of sight: and of the lesser benefits why should I speak? even the ordinary man if he were deprived of them would bewail his loss, but in vain. This much let me say however: God invented and gave us sight to the end that we might behold the courses of intelligence in the heaven, and apply them to

the courses of our own intelligence which are akin to them, the un-
perturbed to the perturbed; and that we, learning them and partaking
of the natural truth of reason, might imitate the absolutely unerring
courses of God and regulate our own vagaries. The same may be
affirmed of speech and hearing: they have been given by the gods to
the same end and for a like reason. For this is the principal end of
speech, whereto it most contributes. Moreover, so much of music as
is adapted to the sound of the voice and to the sense of hearing is granted
to us for the sake of harmony; and harmony, which has motions akin
to the revolutions of our souls, is not regarded by the intelligent votary
of the Muses as given by them with a view to irrational pleasure, which
is deemed to be the purpose of it in our day, but as meant to correct
any discord which may have arisen in the courses of the soul, and to
be our ally in bringing her into harmony and agreement with herself;
and rhythm too was given by them for the same reason, on account
of the irregular and graceless ways which prevail among mankind
generally, and to help us against them.

Thus far in what we have been saying, with small exception, the
works of intelligence have been set forth; and now we must place by
the side of them in our discourse the things which come into being
through necessity—for the creation is mixed, being made up of necessity
and mind. Mind, the ruling power, persuaded necessity to bring the
greater part of created things to perfection, and thus and after this
manner in the beginning, when the influence of reason got the better
of necessity, the universe was created. But if a person will truly tell of
the way in which the work was accomplished, he must include the other
influence of the variable cause as well. Wherefore, we must return again
and find another suitable beginning, as about the former matters, so
also about these. To which end we must consider the nature of fire,
and water, and air, and earth, such as they were prior to the creation
of the heaven, and what was happening to them in this previous state;
for no one has as yet explained the manner of their generation, but
we speak of fire and the rest of them, whatever they mean, as though
men knew their natures, and we maintain them to be the first principles and letters or elements of the whole, when they cannot reasonably
be compared by a man of any sense even to syllables or first compounds.
And let me say thus much: I will not now speak of the first principle
or principles of all things, or by whatever name they are to be called,

for this reason,—because it is difficult to set forth my opinion according to the method of discussion which we are at present employing. Do not imagine, any more than I can bring myself to imagine, that I should be right in undertaking so great and difficult a task. Remembering what I said at first about probability, I will do my best to give as probable an explanation as any other,—or rather, more probable; and I will first go back to the beginning and try to speak of each thing and of all. Once more, then, at the commencement of my discourse, I call upon God, and beg him to be our saviour out of a strange and unwonted enquiry, and to bring us to the haven of probability. So now let us begin again.

This new beginning of our discussion of the universe requires a fuller division than the former; for then we made two classes, now a third must be revealed. The two sufficed for the former discussion: one, which we assumed, was a pattern intelligible and always the same; and the second was only the imitation of the pattern, generated and visible. There is also a third kind which we did not distinguish at the time, conceiving that the two would be enough. But now the argument seems to require that we should set forth in words another kind, which is difficult of explanation and dimly seen. What nature are we to attribute to this new kind of being? We reply, that it is the receptacle, and in a manner the nurse, of all generation. I have spoken the truth; but I must express myself in clearer language, and this will be an arduous task for many reasons and in particular because I must first raise questions concerning fire and the other elements, and determine what each of them is; for to say, with any probability or certitude, which of them should be called water rather than fire, and which should be called any of them rather than all or some one of them, is a difficult matter. How then, shall we settle this point, and what questions about the elements may be fairly raised?

In the first place, we see that what we just now called water, by condensation, I suppose, becomes stone and earth; and this same element, when melted and dispersed, passes into vapour and air. Air, again, when inflamed, becomes fire; and again fire, when condensed and extinguished, passes once more into the form of air; and once more, air, when collected and condensed, produces cloud and mist; and from these, when still more compressed, comes flowing water, and from water comes earth and stones once more; and thus generation appears to be transmitted from one to the other in a circle. Thus, then, as the several elements never present themselves in the same form, how can any one have the assurance to assert positively that any of them, whatever it may be, is one thing rather than another? No one can. But much the safest plan is to speak of them as follows:—Anything which we see to be continually changing, as, for example, fire, we must not call 'this' or 'that,' but rather say that it is 'of such a nature;' nor let us speak of water as 'this,' but always as 'such;' nor must we imply that there is any stability in any of those things which we indicate by the use of the words 'this' and 'that,' supposing ourselves to signify something thereby; for they are too volatile to be detained in any such expressions as 'this,' or 'that,' or 'relative to this,' or any other mode of speaking which represents them as permanent. We ought not to apply 'this' to any of them, but rather the word 'such;' which expresses the similar principle circulating in each and all of them; for example, that should be called 'fire' which is of such a nature always, and so of everything that has generation. That in which the elements severally grow up, and appear, and decay, is alone to be called by the name 'this' or 'that;' but that which is of a certain nature, hot or white, or anything which admits of opposite qualities, and all things that are compounded of them, ought not to be so denominated. Let me make another attempt to explain my meaning more clearly. Suppose a person to make all kinds of figures of gold and to be always transmuting one form into all the rest;— somebody points to one of them and asks what it is. By far the safest and truest answer is, That is gold; and not to call the triangle or any other figures which are formed in the gold 'these,' as though they had existence, since they are in process of change while he is making the assertion; but if the questioner be willing to take the safe and indefinite expression, 'such,' we should be satisfied. And the same argument applies to the universal nature which receives all bodies—that must be always called the same; for, while receiving all things, she never departs at all from her own nature, and never in any way, or at any time, assumes a form like that of any of the things which enter into her; she is the natural recipient of all impressions, and is stirred and informed by them, and appears different from time to time by reason of them. But the forms which enter into and go out of her are the likenesses of real existences modelled after their patterns in a wonderful and inexplicable manner, which we will hereafter investigate. For the present we have only to conceive of three natures: first, that which is in process of generation; secondly, that in which the generation takes place; and thirdly, that of which the thing generated is a resemblance. And we may liken the receiving principle to a mother, and the source or spring to a father, and the intermediate nature to a child; and may remark further, that if the model is to take every variety of form, then the matter in which the model is fashioned will not be duly prepared, unless it is formless, and free from the impress of any of those shapes which it is hereafter to receive from without. For if the matter were like any of the supervening forms, then whenever any opposite or entirely different nature was stamped upon its surface, it would take the impression badly, because it would intrude its own shape. Wherefore, that which is to receive all forms should have no form; as in making perfumes they first contrive that the liquid substance which is to receive the scent shall be as inodorous as possible; or as those who wish to impress figures on soft substances do not allow any previous impression to remain, but begin by making the surface as even and smooth as possible. In the same way that which is to receive perpetually and through its whole extent the resemblances of all eternal beings ought to be devoid of any particular form. Wherefore, the mother and receptacle of all created and visible and in any way sensible things, is not to be termed earth, or air, or fire, or water, or any of their compounds or any of the elements from which these are derived, but is an invisible and formless being which receives all things and in some mysterious way partakes of the intelligible, and is most incomprehensible. In saying this we shall not be far wrong; as far, however, as we can attain to a knowledge of her from the previous considerations, we may truly say that fire is that part of her nature which from time to time is inflamed, and water that which is moistened, and that the mother substance becomes earth and air, in so far as she receives the impressions of them.

Let us consider this question more precisely. Is there any self-existent fire? and do all those things which we call self-existent exist? or are only those things which we see, or in some way perceive through the bodily organs, truly existent, and nothing whatever besides them? And is all that which we call an intelligible essence nothing at all, and only a name? Here is a question which we must not leave unexamined or undetermined, nor must we affirm too confidently that there can be no decision; neither must we interpolate in our present long discourse a digression equally long, but if it is possible to set forth a great principle in a few words, that is just what we want.

Thus I state my view: — If mind and true opinion are two distinct classes, then I say that there certainly are these self-existent ideas unperceived by sense, and apprehended only by the mind; if, however, as some say, true opinion differs in no respect from mind, then everything that we perceive through the body is to be regarded as most real and certain. But we must affirm them to be distinct, for they have a distinct origin and are of a different nature; the one is implanted in us by instruction, the other by persuasion; the one is always accompanied by true reason, the other is without reason; the one cannot be overcome by persuasion, but the other can: and lastly, every man may be said to share in true opinion, but mind is the attribute of the gods and of very few men. Wherefore also we must acknowledge that there is one kind of being which is always the same, uncreated and indestructible, never receiving anything into itself from without, nor itself going out to any other, but invisible and imperceptible by any sense, and of which the contemplation is granted to intelligence only. And there is another nature of the same name with it, and like to it, perceived by sense, created, always in motion, becoming in place and again vanishing out of place, which is apprehended by opinion and sense. And there is a third nature, which is space, and is eternal, and admits not of destruction and provides a home for all created things, and is apprehended without the help of sense, by a kind of spurious reason, and is hardly real; which we beholding as in a dream, say of all existence that it must of necessity be in some place and occupy a space, but that what is neither in heaven nor in earth has no existence. Of these and other things of the same kind, relating to the true and waking reality of nature, we have only this dreamlike sense, and we are unable to cast off sleep and determine the truth about them. For an image, since the reality, after which it is modelled, does not belong to it, and it exists ever as the fleeting shadow of some other, must be inferred to be in another [i. e. in space], grasping existence in some way or other, or it could not be, at all. But true and exact reason, vindicating the nature of true being, maintains that while two things [i. e. the image and space] are different they cannot exist one of them in the other and so be one and also two at the same time.

Thus have I concisely given the result of my thoughts; and my verdict is that being and space and generation, these three, existed in their three ways before the heaven; and that the nurse of generation, moistened by water and inflamed by fire, and receiving the forms of earth and air, and experiencing all the affections which accompany these, presented a strange variety of appearances; and being full of powers which were neither similar nor equally balanced, was never in any part in a state of equipoise, but swaying unevenly hither and thither, was shaken by them, and by its motion again shook them; and the elements when moved were separated and carried continually, some one way, some another; as, when grain is shaken and winnowed by fans and other instruments used in the threshing of corn, the close and heavy particles are borne away and settle in one direction, and the loose and light particles in another. In this manner, the four kinds of elements were then shaken by the receiving vessel, which, moving like a winnowing machine, scattered far away from one another the elements most unlike, and forced the most similar elements into close contact. Wherefore also the various elements had different places before they were arranged so as to form the universe. At first, they were all without reason and measure. But when the world began to get into order, fire and water and earth and air had only certain faint traces of themselves, and were altogether such as everything might be expected to be in the absence of God; this, I say, was their nature at that time, and God fashioned them by form and number. Let it be consistently maintained by us in all that we say that God made them as far as possible the fairest and best, out of things which were not fair and good.

✦ ✦ ✦

Translated by Benjamin Jowett.

ARISTOTLE

Aristotle (384–322 B.C.) was Plato's most famous pupil and the one philosopher who arguably stands on a level with Plato. Unlike Plato, however, Aristotle did not become a major influence on Christian theology until the Middle Ages, when he gradually became known to Christian theologians through Islamic and Jewish philosophers. From that point on his influence was a clear and strong rival to his master's.

Unlike Plato, Aristotle begins with an examination of the natural world and seeks to generalize from there. This is seen admirably in the following selections. In the *Categories,* the first of Aristotle's works to become known by the Christian West, he examines the notion of substance, placing its first instance in the existing individual. He then goes on to examine the ways in which we can logically talk about substance. In the selections from the *Physics,* he gives his doctrine of the "four causes" (the four ways in which we can say "why" a thing is) and his explanation of change in nature. Finally, the selection from the *Metaphysics* is his argument for the "unmoved mover," the desire for which sets the natural world in motion. While hardly an argument for the God of Christianity, with modifications this argument and the preceding distinctions on which it is based became vital tools for medieval Christianity to fully articulate and discuss the nature of God. This is seen extremely well in Thomas Aquinas's arguments for the existence of God later in this volume.

Substance and Its Predicates
(Categories 1–8)

1.   When things have only a name in common and the definition of being which corresponds to the name is different, they are called

homonymous. Thus, for example, both a man and a picture are animals. These have only a name in common and the definition of being which corresponds to the name is different; for if one is to say what being an animal is for each of them, one will give two distinct definitions.

When things have the name in common and the definition of being which corresponds to the name is the same, they are called *synonymous*. Thus, for example, both a man and an ox are animals. Each of these is called, by a common name, an animal, and the definition of being is also the same; for if one is to give the definition of each — what being an animal is for each of them — one will give the same definition.

When things get their name from something, with a difference of ending, they are called *paronymous*. Thus, for example, the grammarian gets his name from grammar, the brave get theirs from bravery.

2. Of things that are said, some involve combination while others are said without combination. Examples of those involving combination are: man runs, man wins; and of those without combination: man, ox, runs, wins.

Of things there are: (*a*) Some are *said of* a subject but are not *in* any subject. For example, man is said of a subject, the individual man, but is not in any subject. (*b*) Some are in a subject but are not said of any subject. (By 'in a subject' I mean what is in something, not as a part, and cannot exist separately from what it is in.) For example, the individual knowledge-of-grammar is in a subject, the soul, but is not said of any subject; and the individual white is in a subject, the body (for all colour is in a body), but is not said of any subject. (*c*) Some are both said of a subject and in a subject. For example, knowledge is in a subject, the soul, and is also said of a subject, knowledge-of-grammar. (*d*) Some are neither in a subject nor said of a subject, for example, the individual man or the individual horse — for nothing of this sort is either in a subject or said of a subject. Things that are individual and numerically one are, without exception, not said of any subject, but there is nothing to prevent some of them from being in a subject — the individual knowledge-of-grammar is one of the things in a subject.

3.   Whenever one thing is predicated of another as of a subject, all things said of what is predicated will be said of the subject also. For example, man is predicated of the individual man, and animal of man; so animal will be predicated of the individual man also—for the individual man is both a man and an animal.

The differentiae of genera which are different and not subordinate one to the other are themselves different in kind. For example, animal and knowledge: footed, winged, aquatic, two-footed, are differentiae of animal, but none of these is a differentia of knowledge; one sort of knowledge does not differ from another by being two-footed. However, there is nothing to prevent genera subordinate one to the other from having the same differentiae. For the higher are predicated of the genera below them, so that all differentiae of the predicated genus will be differentiae of the subject also.

4.   Of things said without any combination, each signifies either substance or quantity or qualification or a relative or where or when or being-in-a-position or having or doing or being-affected. To give a rough idea, examples of substance are man, horse; of quantity: four-foot, five-foot; of qualification: white, grammatical; of a relative: double, half, larger; of where: in the Lyceum, in the market-place; of when: yesterday, last-year; of being-in-a-position: is-lying, is-sitting; of having: has-shoes-on, has-armour-on; of doing: cutting, burning; of being-affected: being-cut, being-burned.

None of the above is said just by itself in any affirmation, but by the combination of these with one another an affirmation is produced. For every affirmation, it seems, is either true or false; but of things said without any combination none is either true or false (e.g. man, white, runs, wins).

5.   A *substance*—that which is called a substance most strictly, primarily, and most of all—is that which is neither said of a subject nor in a subject, e.g. the individual man or the individual horse. The species in which the things primarily called substances are, are called *secondary substances,* as also are the genera of these species. For example, the individual man belongs in a species, man, and animal is a genus of the species; so these—both man and animal—are called secondary substances.

It is clear from what has been said that if something is said of a subject both its name and its definition are necessarily predicated of the subject. For example, man is said of a subject, the individual man, and the name is of course predicated (since you will be predicating man of the individual man), and also the definition of man will be predicated of the individual man (since the individual man is also a man). Thus both the name and the definition will be predicated of the subject. But as for things which are in a subject, in most cases neither the name nor the definition is predicated of the subject. In some cases there is nothing to prevent the name from being predicated of the subject, but it is impossible for the definition to be predicated. For example, white, which is in a subject (the body), is predicated of the subject; for a body is called white. But the definition of white will never be predicated of the body.

All the other things are either said of the primary substances as subjects or in them as subjects. This is clear from an examination of cases. For example, animal is predicated of man and therefore also of the individual man; for were it predicated of none of the individual men it would not be predicated of man at all. Again, colour is in body and therefore also in an individual body; for were it not in some individual body it would not be in body at all. Thus all the other things are either said of the primary substances as subjects or in them as subjects. So if the primary substances did not exist it would be impossible for any of the other things to exist.

Of the secondary substances the species is more a substance than the genus, since it is nearer to the primary substance. For if one is to say of the primary substance what it is, it will be more informative and apt to give the species than the genus. For example, it would be more informative to say of the individual man that he is a man than that he is an animal (since the one is more distinctive of the individual man while the other is more general); and more informative to say of the individual tree that it is a tree than that it is a plant. Further, it is because the primary substances are subjects for all the other things and all the other things are predicated of them or are in them, that they are called substances most of all. But as the primary substances stand to the other things, so the species stands to the genus: the species is a subject for the genus (for the genera are predicated of the species

42

but the species are not predicated reciprocally of the genera). Hence for this reason too the species is more a substance than the genus.

But of the species themselves—those which are not genera—one is no more a substance than another: it is no more apt to say of the individual man that he is a man than to say of the individual horse that it is a horse. And similarly of the primary substances one is no more a substance than another: the individual man is no more a substance than the individual ox.

It is reasonable that, after the primary substances, their species and genera should be the only other things called secondary substances. For only they, of things predicated, reveal the primary substance. For if one is to say of the individual man what he is, it will be in place to give the species or the genus (though more informative to give man than animal); but to give any of the other things would be out of place—for example, to say white or runs or anything like that. So it is reasonable that these should be the only other things called substances. Further, it is because the primary substances are subjects for everything else that they are called substances most strictly. But as the primary substances stand to everything else, so the species and genera of the primary substances stand to all the rest: all the rest are predicated of these. For if you will call the individual man grammatical, then you will call both a man and an animal grammatical; and similarly in other cases.

It is a characteristic common to every substance not to be in a subject. For a primary substance is neither said of a subject nor in a subject. And as for secondary substances, it is obvious at once that they are not in a subject. For man is said of the individual man as subject but is not in a subject: man is not *in* the individual man. Similarly, animal also is said of the individual man as subject, but animal is not *in* the individual man. Further, while there is nothing to prevent the name of what is in a subject from being sometimes predicated of the subject, it is impossible for the definition to be predicated. But the definition of the secondary substances, as well as the name, is predicated of the subject: you will predicate the definition of man of the individual man, and also that of animal. No substance, therefore, is in a subject.

This is not, however, peculiar to substance, since the differentia also is not in a subject. For footed and two-footed are said of man as subject but are not in a subject; neither two-footed nor footed is *in* man.

43

Moreover, the definition of the differentia is predicated of that of which the differentia is said. For example, if footed is said of man the definition of footed will also be predicated of man; for man is footed.

We need not be disturbed by any fear that we may be forced to say that the parts of a substance, being in a subject (the whole substance), are not substances. For when we spoke of things *in a subject* we did not mean things belonging in something as *parts*.

It is a characteristic of substances and differentiae that all things called from them are so called synonymously. For all the predicates from them are predicated either of the individuals or of the species. (For from a primary substance there is no predicate, since it is said of no subject; and as for secondary substances, the species is predicated of the individual, the genus both of the species and of the individual. Similarly, differentiae too are predicated both of the species and of the individuals.) And the primary substances admit the definition of the species and of the genera, and the species admits that of the genus; for everything said of what is predicated will be said of the subject also. Similarly, both the species and the individuals admit the definition of the differentiae. But synonymous things were precisely those with both the name in common and the same definition. Hence all the things called from substances and differentiae are so called synonymously.

Every substance seems to signify a certain 'this'. As regards the primary substances, it is indisputably true that each of them signifies a certain 'this'; for the thing revealed is individual and numerically one. But as regards the secondary substances, though it appears from the form of the name—when one speaks of man or animal—that a secondary substance likewise signifies a certain 'this', this is not really true; rather, it signifies a certain qualification—for the subject is not, as the primary substance is, one, but man and animal are said of many things. However, it does not signify simply a certain qualification, as white does. White signifies nothing but a qualification, whereas the species and the genus mark off the qualification of substance—they signify substance of a certain qualification. (One draws a wider boundary with the genus than with the species, for in speaking of animal one takes in more than in speaking of man.)

Another characteristic of substances is that there is nothing contrary to them. For what would be contrary to a primary substance? For example, there is nothing contrary to an individual man, nor yet is there anything contrary to man or to animal. This, however, is not peculiar to substance but holds of many other things also, for example, of quantity. For there is nothing contrary to four-foot or to ten or to anything of this kind—unless someone were to say that many is contrary to few or large to small; but still there is nothing contrary to any *definite* quantity.

Substance, it seems, does not admit of a more and a less. I do not mean that one substance is not more a substance than another (we have said that it is), but that any given substance is not called more, or less, that which it is. For example, if this substance is a man, it will not be more a man or less a man either than itself or than another man. For one man is not more a man than another, as one pale thing is more pale than another and one beautiful thing more beautiful than another. Again, a thing is called more, or less, such-and-such than itself; for example, the body that is pale is called more pale now than before, and the one that is hot is called more, or less, hot. Substance, however, is not spoken of thus. For a man is not called more a man now than before, nor is anything else that is a substance. Thus substance does not admit of a more and a less.

It seems most distinctive of substance that what is numerically one and the same is able to receive contraries. In no other case could one bring forward anything, numerically one, which is able to receive contraries. For example, a colour which is numerically one and the same will not be black and white, nor will numerically one and the same action be bad and good; and similarly with everything else that is not substance. A substance, however, numerically one and the same, is able to receive contraries. For example, an individual man—one and the same—becomes pale at one time and dark at another, and hot and cold, and bad and good.

Nothing like this is to be seen in any other case, unless perhaps someone might object and say that statements and beliefs are like this. For the same statement seems to be both true and false. Suppose, for example, that the statement that somebody is sitting is true; after he has got up this same statement will be false. Similarly with beliefs. Suppose you believe truly that somebody is sitting; after he has got up you will believe falsely if you hold the same belief about him. However, even if we were to grant this, there is still a difference in the *way* contraries are received. For in the case of substances it is by themselves changing that they are able to receive contraries. For what has become cold instead of hot, or dark instead of pale, or good instead of bad, has changed (has altered); similarly in other cases too it is by itself undergoing change that each thing is able to receive contraries. Statements and beliefs, on the other hand, themselves remain completely unchangeable in every way; it is because the *actual thing* changes that the contrary comes to belong to them. For the statement that somebody is sitting remains the same; it is because of a change in the actual thing that it comes to be true at one time and false at another. Similarly with beliefs. Hence at least the *way* in which it is able to receive contraries — through a change in itself — would be distinctive of substance, even if we were to grant that beliefs and statements are able to receive contraries. However, this is not true. For it is not because they themselves receive anything that statements and beliefs are said to be able to receive contraries, but because of what has happened to something else. For it is because the actual thing exists or does not exist that the statement is said to be true or false, not because it is able itself to receive contraries. No statement, in fact, or belief is changed at all by anything. So, since nothing happens in them, they are not able to receive contraries. A substance, on the other hand, is said to be able to receive contraries because it itself receives contraries. For it receives sickness and health, and paleness and darkness; and because it itself receives the various things of this kind it is said to be able to receive contraries. It is, therefore, distinctive of substance that what is numerically one and the same is able to receive contraries. This brings to an end our discussion of substance.

6. Of quantities some are discrete, others continuous; and some are composed of parts which have position in relation to one another, others are not composed of parts which have position.

Discrete are number and language; continuous are lines, surfaces, bodies, and also, besides these, time and place. For the parts of a number have no common boundary at which they join together. For example, if five is a part of ten the two fives do not join together at any common boundary but are separate; nor do the three and the seven join together at any common boundary. Nor could you ever in the case of a number find a common boundary of its parts, but they are always separate. Hence number is one of the discrete quantities. Similarly, language also is one of the discrete quantities (that language is a quantity is evident, since it is measured by long and short syllables; I mean here language that is *spoken*). For its parts do not join together at any common boundary. For there is no common boundary at which the syllables join together, but each is separate in itself. A line, on the other hand, is a continuous quantity. For it is possible to find a common boundary at which its parts join together, a point. And for a surface, a line; for the parts of a plane join together at some common boundary. Similarly in the case of a body one could find a common boundary—a line or a surface—at which the parts of the body join together. Time also and place are of this kind. For present time joins on to both past time and future time. Place, again, is one of the continuous quantities. For the parts of a body occupy some place, and they join together at a common boundary. So the parts of the place occupied by the various parts of the body, themselves join together at the same boundary at which the parts of the body do. Thus place also is a continuous quantity, since its parts join together at one common boundary.

Further, some quantities are composed of parts which have position in relation to one another, others are not composed of parts which have position. For example, the parts of a line have position in relation to one another: each of them is situated somewhere, and you could distinguish them and say where each is situated in the plane and which one of the other parts it joins on to. Similarly, the parts of a plane have some position here again: one could say where each is situated and which join on to one another. So, too, with the parts of a solid and the parts of a place. With a number, on the other hand, one could not observe that the parts have some position in relation to one another or are situated somewhere, nor see which of the parts join on to one another. Nor with the parts of a time either; for none of the parts of a time endures, and how could what is not enduring have any position? Rather might you say that they have a certain *order* in that one part of a time is before and another after. Similarly with a number also, in that one is counted before two and two before three; in this way they may have a certain order, but you would certainly not find position. And language similarly. For none of its parts endures, once it has been uttered it can no longer be recaptured; and so its parts cannot have position, seeing that none of them endures. Some quantities then are composed of parts which have position, others are not composed of parts which have position.

Only these we have mentioned are called quantities strictly, all the others derivatively; for it is to these we look when we call the others quantities. For example, we speak of a large amount of white because the *surface* is large, and an action or a change is called long because the *time* is long. For it is not in its own right that each of these others is called a quantity. For example, if one is to say how long an action is, one will determine this by the time, saying that it is a-year-long or something of that sort; and in saying how much white one will determine it by the surface—whatever the size of the surface one will say that the white too is that size. Thus only those we mentioned are called quantities strictly and in their own right, while nothing else is so in its own right but, if at all, derivatively.

Next, a quantity has no contrary. In the case of definite quantities it is obvious that there is no contrary; there is, for example, no contrary to four-foot or five-foot or to a surface or anything like that. But might someone say that many is contrary to few or large to small? None of these, however, is a quantity; they are relatives. For nothing is called large or small just in itself, but by reference to something else. For example, a mountain is called small yet a grain of millet large—because one is larger than other things of its kind while the other is smaller than other things of its kind. Thus the reference is to something else, since if a thing were called small or large in itself the mountain would never be called small yet the grain of millet large. Again, we say that there are many people in the village but few in Athens—though there are many times more here than there; and that there are many in the house but few in the theatre—though there are many more here than there. Further, 'four-foot', 'five-foot', and the like all signify a quantity, but 'large' or 'small' does not signify a quantity but rather a relative, since the large and the small are looked at in relation to something else. So it is clear that these are relatives.

Moreover, whether one counts them as quantities or does not, they have no contrary. For how could there be any contrary to what cannot be grasped just in itself but only by reference to something else? Further, if large and small are to be contraries it will turn out that the same thing admits contraries at the same time, and that things are their own contraries. For the same thing turns out to be at the same time both large and small—since in relation to this thing it is small but in relation to another this same thing is large; so the same thing turns out to be both large and small at the same time and thus to admit contraries at the same time. But nothing seems to admit contraries at the same time. In the case of a substance, for example, while it seems to be able to receive contraries, yet it is certainly not at the same time ill and well nor is it at the same time pale and dark; nor does anything else admit contraries at the same time. It turns out also that things are their own contraries. For if large is contrary to small, and the same thing is at the same time large and small, a thing would be its own contrary. But it is impossible for a thing to be its own contrary. Large, therefore, is not contrary to small, nor many to few. So that even if someone says that these belong not to relatives but to quantity, it will still have no contrary.

But it is most of all with regard to place that there seems to be contrariety of a quantity. For people regard up as contrary to down—meaning by 'down' the region towards the centre—because the centre is at the greatest distance from the limits of the world. And they probably derive from these their definition of the other contraries also; for they define as contraries those things in the same genus which are most distant from one another.

A quantity does not seem to admit of a more and a less. Four-foot for example: one thing is not more four-foot than another. Or take number: we do not speak of a three as more three than a five, nor of one three as more three than another three. Nor yet is one time called more a time than another. Nor is there a single one, among those we listed, as to which a more and a less is spoken of. Hence a quantity does not admit of a more and a less.

Most distinctive of a quantity is its being called both equal and unequal. For each of the quantities we spoke of is called both equal and unequal. For example, a body is called both equal and unequal, and a number is called both equal and unequal, and so is a time; so also with the others we spoke of, each is called both equal and unequal. But anything else—whatever is not a quantity—is certainly not, it would seem, called equal and unequal. For example, a condition is certainly not called equal and unequal, but, rather, similar; and white is certainly not equal and unequal, but similar. Thus most distinctive of a quantity would be its being called both equal and unequal.

7. We call *relatives* all such things as are said to be just what they are, *of* or *than* other things, or in some other way *in relation to* something else. For example, what is larger is called what it is *than* something else (it is called larger than something); and what is double is called what it is *of* something else (it is called double of something); similarly with all other such cases. The following, too, and their like, are among relatives: state, condition, perception, knowledge, position. For each of these is called what it is (and not something different) *of* something else. A state is called a state of something, knowledge knowledge of something, position position of something, and the rest similarly. All things then are relative which are called just what they are, *of* or *than* something else — or in some other way *in relation to* something else. Thus a mountain is called large in relation to something else (the mountain is called large in relation to something); and what is similar is called similar to something; and the others of this kind are in the same way spoken of in relation to something.

Lying, standing, and sitting are particular positions; position is a relative. To-be-lying, to-be-standing, or to-be-sitting are themselves not positions, but they get their names paronymously from the aforesaid positions.

There is contrariety in relatives, e.g. virtue is contrary to vice (and each of them is relative), and knowledge to ignorance. But there is not a contrary to every relative; there is no contrary to what is double or treble or anything like that.

Relatives seem also to admit of a more and a less. For a thing is called more similar and less similar, and more unequal and less unequal; and each of these is relative, since what is similar is called similar *to* something and what is unequal unequal *to* something. But not all admit of a more and less; for what is double, or anything like that, is not called more double or less double.

All relatives are spoken of in relation to correlatives that reciprocate. For example, the slave is called slave of a master and the master is called master of a slave; the double double of a half, and the half half of a double; the larger larger than a smaller, and the smaller smaller than a larger; and so for the rest too. Sometimes, however, there will be a verbal difference, of ending. Thus knowledge is called knowledge *of* what is knowable, and what is knowable knowable *by* knowledge;

perception perception *of* the perceptible, and the perceptible perceptible *by* perception.

Sometimes, indeed, they will not seem to reciprocate — if a mistake is made and that in relation to which something is spoken of is not given properly. For example, if a wing is given as *of a bird, bird of a wing* does not reciprocate; for it has not been given properly in the first place as wing of a bird. For it is not as being a bird that a wing is said to be of it, but as being a winged, since many things that are not birds have wings. Thus if it is given properly there is reciprocation; for example, a wing is wing of a winged and a winged is winged with a wing.

It may sometimes be necessary even to invent names, if no name exists in relation to which a thing would be given properly. For example, if a rudder is given as *of a boat,* that is not to give it properly (for it is not as being a boat that a rudder is said to be of it, since there are boats which have not got rudders); and so there is not reciprocation — a boat is not called boat of a rudder. But perhaps it would be given more properly if given thus, that a rudder is rudder of (or somehow else related to) a 'ruddered' (since there is no established name); and now there *is* reciprocation, if it is given properly — a ruddered is ruddered by a rudder. Similarly in other cases. For example, a head would be more properly given as of a headed than as of an animal, because it is not as being an animal that a thing has a head, since many animals have not got a head. This is perhaps the easiest way to lay hold of things for which there are no established names — if names derived from the original relatives are assigned to their reciprocating correlatives, as in the above case 'winged' was derived from 'wing' and 'ruddered' from 'rudder'.

All relatives, then, are spoken of in relation to correlatives that reciprocate, provided they are properly given. For, of course, if a relative is given as related to some chance thing and not to just that thing in relation to which it is spoken of, there is not reciprocation. I mean that even with relatives that are admittedly spoken of in relation to correlatives that reciprocate and for which names exist, none reciprocates if a relative is given as related to something accidental and not to just that thing in relation to which it is spoken of. For example, if a slave is given as of — not a master, but — a man or a biped or anything else like that, there is not reciprocation; for it has not been given properly.

Again, if that in relation to which a thing is spoken of is properly given, then, when all the other things that are accidental are stripped off and that alone is left to which it was properly given as related, it will always be spoken of in relation to that. For example, if a slave is spoken of in relation to a master, then, when everything accidental to a master is stripped off—like being a biped, capable of knowledge, a man—and there is left only being a master, a slave will always be spoken of in relation to that. For a slave is called slave of a master. On the other hand, if that in relation to which a thing is spoken of is not properly given, then, when the other things are stripped off and that alone is left to which it was given as related, it will not be spoken of in relation to that. Suppose a slave is given as *of a man* and a wing as *of a bird,* and strip off from man his being a master; a slave will no longer be spoken of in relation to a man, for if there is no master there is no slave either. Similarly, strip off from bird its being winged; a wing will no longer be a relative, for if there is nothing winged neither will there be a wing of anything.

One must therefore give as correlative whatever it is properly spoken of in relation to; and if a name already exists it is easy to give this, but if it does not it may be necessary to invent a name. When correlatives are given thus it is clear that all relatives will be spoken of in relation to correlatives that reciprocate.

Relatives seem to be simultaneous by nature; and in most cases this is true. For there is at the same time a double and a half, and when there is a half there is a double, and when there is a slave there is a master; and similarly with the others. Also, each carries the other to destruction; for if there is not a double there is not a half, and if there is not a half there is not a double. So too with other such cases.

Yet it does not seem to be true of all relatives that they are simultaneous by nature. For the knowable would seem to be prior to knowledge. For as a rule it is of actual things already existing that we acquire knowledge; in few cases, if any, could one find knowledge coming into existence at the same time as what is knowable. Moreover, destruction of the knowable carries knowledge to destruction, but knowledge does not carry the knowable to destruction. For if there is not a knowable there is not knowledge—there will no longer be anything for knowledge to be of—but if there is not knowledge there is nothing to prevent there being a knowable. Take, for example, the squaring of the circle, supposing it to be knowable; knowledge of it does not yet exist but the knowable itself exists. Again, if animal is destroyed there is no knowledge, but there may be many knowables.

The case of perception is similar to this; for the perceptible seems to be prior to perception. For the destruction of the perceptible carries perception to destruction, but perception does not carry the perceptible to destruction. For perceptions are to do with body and in body, and if the perceptible is destroyed, body too is destroyed (since body is itself a perceptible), and if there is not body, perception too is destroyed; hence the perceptible carries perception to destruction. But perception does not carry the perceptible. For if animal is destroyed perception is destroyed, but there will be something perceptible, such as body, hot, sweet, bitter, and all the other perceptibles. Moreover, perception comes into existence at the same time as what is capable of perceiving—an animal and perception come into existence at the same time—but the perceptible exists even before perception exists; fire and water and so on, of which an animal is itself made up, exist even before there exists an animal at all, or perception. Hence the perceptible would seem to be prior to perception.

It is a problem whether (as one would think) *no* substance is spoken of as a relative, or whether this is possible with regard to some secondary substances. In the case of primary substances it is true; neither wholes nor parts are spoken of in relation to anything. An individual man is not called someone's individual man, nor an individual ox someone's individual ox. Similarly with parts; an individual hand is not called someone's individual hand (but someone's hand), and an individual head is not called someone's individual head (but someone's head). Similarly with secondary substances, at any rate most of them. For example, a man is not called someone's man nor an ox someone's ox nor a log someone's log (but it is called someone's property). With such cases, then, it is obvious that they are not relatives, but with some secondary substances there is room for dispute. For example, a head is called someone's head and a hand is called someone's hand, and so on; so that these would seem to be relatives.

Now if the definition of relatives given above was adequate, it is either exceedingly difficult or impossible to reach the solution that no substance is spoken of as a relative. But if it was not adequate, and if those things are relatives for which *being is the same as being somehow related*

53

to something, then perhaps some answer may be found. The previous definition does, indeed, apply to all relatives, yet this—their being called what they are, of other things—is not what their being relatives is.

It is clear from this that if someone knows any relative definitely he will also know definitely that in relation to which it is spoken of. This is obvious on the face of it. For if someone knows of a certain 'this' that it is a relative, and being for relatives is the same as being somehow related to something, he knows that also to which this is somehow related. For if he does not in the least know that to which this is somehow related, neither will he know whether it is somehow related to something. The same point is clear also in particular cases. For example, if someone knows definitely of a certain 'this' that it is double he also, by the same token, knows definitely what it is double of; for if he does not know it to be double anything definite neither does he know whether it is double at all. Similarly, if he knows of a certain 'this' that it is more beautiful, he must also, because of this, know definitely what it is more beautiful than. (He is not to know *indefinitely* that this is more beautiful than an inferior thing. For that sort of thing is supposition, not knowledge. For he will no longer strictly *know* that it is more beautiful than an inferior thing, since it may so happen that there is nothing inferior to it.) It is plain, therefore, that anyone who knows any relative definitely must know definitely that also in relation to which it is spoken of.

But as for a head or a hand or any such substance, it is possible to know it—what it itself is—definitely, without necessarily knowing definitely that in relation to which it is spoken of. For whose this head is, or whose the hand, it is not necessary to know definitely. So these would not be relatives. And if they are not relatives it would be true to say that no substance is a relative.

It is perhaps hard to make firm statements on such questions without having examined them many times. Still, to have gone through the various difficulties is not unprofitable.

8. By a *quality* I mean that in virtue of which things are said to be qualified somehow. But quality is one of the things spoken of in a number of ways.

One kind of quality let us call *states* and *conditions.* A state differs from a condition in being more stable and lasting longer. Such are the branches of knowledge and the virtues. For knowledge seems to be something permanent and hard to change if one has even a moderate grasp of a branch of knowledge, unless a great change is brought about by illness or some other such thing. So also virtue; justice, temperance, and the rest seem to be not easily changed. It is what are easily changed and quickly changing that we call conditions, e.g. hotness and chill and sickness and health and the like. For a man is in a certain condition in virtue of these but he changes quickly from hot to cold and from being healthy to being sick. Similarly with the rest, unless indeed even one of these were eventually to become through length of time part of a man's nature and irremediable or exceedingly hard to change — and *then* one would perhaps call this a state. It is obvious that by a state people do mean what is more lasting and harder to change. For those who lack full mastery of a branch of knowledge and are easily changed are not said to be in a state of knowledge, though they are of course in some condition, a better or a worse, in regard to that knowledge. Thus a state differs from a condition in that the one is easily changed while the other lasts longer and is harder to change.

States are also conditions but conditions are not necessarily states. For people in a state are, in virtue of this, also in some condition, but people in a condition are not in every case also in a state.

Another kind of quality is that in virtue of which we call people boxers or runners or healthy or sickly — anything, in short, which they are called in virtue of a natural capacity or incapacity. For it is not because one is in some condition that one is called anything of this sort, but because one has a natural capacity for doing something easily or for being unaffected. For example, people are called boxers or runners not because they are in some condition but because they have a natural capacity to do something easily; they are called healthy because they have a natural capacity not to be affected easily by what befalls them, and sickly because they have an incapacity to be unaffected. Similarly with the hard and the soft: the hard is so called because it has a capacity not to be divided easily, the soft because it has an incapacity for this same thing.

A third kind of quality consists of *affective qualities* and *affections*. Examples of such are sweetness, bitterness, sourness, and all their kin, and also hotness and coldness and paleness and darkness. That these are qualities is obvious, for things that possess them are said to be qualified in virtue of them. Thus honey because it possesses sweetness is called sweet, and a body pale because it possesses paleness, and similarly with the others. They are called *affective* qualities not because the things that possess them have themselves been affected somehow—for honey is not called sweet because it has been affected somehow nor is any other such thing. Similarly, hotness and coldness are not called affective qualities because the things that possess them have themselves been affected somehow, but it is because each of the qualities mentioned is productive of an affection of the senses that they are called affective qualities. For sweetness produces a certain affection of taste, hotness one of touch, and the rest likewise.

Paleness and darkness, however, and other colourings are not called affective qualities in the same way as those just mentioned, but because they themselves have been brought about by an affection. That many changes of colour do come about through an affection is clear; when ashamed one goes red, when frightened one turns pale, and so on. And so if somebody suffers by nature from some such affection it is reasonable that he should have the corresponding colouring. For the very same bodily condition which occurs now when one is ashamed might occur also in virtue of a man's natural make-up, so that the corresponding colouring too would come about by nature.

When such circumstances have their origin in affections that are hard to change and permanent they are called qualities. For if pallor or darkness have come about in the natural make-up they are called qualities (for in virtue of them we are said to be qualified); and if pallor or darkness have resulted from long illness or from sunburn, and do not easily give way—or even last for a lifetime—these too are called qualities (since, as before, in virtue of them we are said to be qualified). But those that result from something that easily disperses and quickly gives way are called affections; for people are not, in virtue of them, said to be qualified somehow. Thus a man who reddens through shame is not called ruddy, nor one who pales in fright pallid; rather he is said to have been affected somehow. Hence such things are called affections but not qualities.

Similarly with regard to the soul also we speak of affective qualities and affections. Those which are present right from birth as a result of certain affections are called qualities, for example, madness and irascibility and the like; for in virtue of these people are said to be qualified, being called irascible and mad. Similarly with any aberrations that are not natural but result from some other circumstances, and are hard to get rid of or even completely unchangeable; such things, too, are qualities, for in virtue of them people are said to be qualified. But those which result from things that quickly subside are called affections, e.g. if a man in distress is rather bad-tempered; for the man who in such an affection is rather bad-tempered is not said to be bad-tempered, but rather he is said to have been affected somehow. Hence such things are called affections but not qualities.

A fourth kind of quality is shape and the external form of each thing, and in addition straightness and curvedness and anything like these. For in virtue of each of these a thing is said to be qualified somehow; because it is a triangle or square it is said to be qualified somehow, and because it is straight or curved. And in virtue of its form each thing is said to be qualified somehow.

'Rare' and 'dense' and 'rough' and 'smooth' might be thought to signify a qualification; they seem, however, to be foreign to the classification of qualifications. It seems rather to be a certain position of the parts that each of them reveals. For a thing is dense because its parts are close together, rare because they are separated from one another; smooth because its parts lie somehow on a straight line, rough because some stick up above others.

Perhaps some other manner of quality might come to light, but we have made a pretty complete list of those most spoken of.

These, then, that we have mentioned are *qualities,* while things called paronymously because of these or called in some other way from them are *qualified.* Now in most cases, indeed in practically all, things are called paronymously, as the pale man from paleness, the grammatical from grammar, the just from justice, and so on. But in some cases, because there are no names for the qualities, it is impossible for things to be called paronymously from them. For example, the runner or the boxer, so called in virtue of a natural capacity, is not called paronymously from any quality; for there are no names for the capacities in virtue of which these men are said to be qualified — as there *are* for the branches of knowledge in virtue of which men are called boxers or wrestlers with reference to their condition (for we speak of boxing and of wrestling as branches of knowledge, and it is paronymously from them that those in the condition are said to be qualified). Sometimes, however, even when there is a name for a quality, that which is said to be qualified in virtue of it is not so called paronymously. For example, the good man is so called from virtue, since it is because he has virtue that he is called good; but he is not called paronymously from virtue. This sort of case is, however, rare. Things then that are called paronymously from the qualities we mentioned, or called from them in some other way, are said to be qualified.

There is contrariety in regard to qualification. For example, justice is contrary to injustice and whiteness to blackness, and so on; also things said to be qualified in virtue of them—the unjust to the just and the white to the black. But this is not so in all cases; for there is no contrary to red or yellow or such colours though they are qualifications.

Further, if one of a pair of contraries is a qualification, the other too will be a qualification. This is clear if one examines the other predicates. For example, if justice is contrary to injustice and justice is a qualification, then injustice too is a qualification. For none of the other predicates fits injustice, neither quantity nor relative nor where nor in fact any other such predicate except qualification. Similarly with the other contraries that involve qualification.

Qualifications admit of a more and a less; for one thing is called more pale or less pale than another, and more just than another. Moreover, it itself sustains increase (for what is pale can still become paler)—not in all cases though, but in most. It might be questioned whether one justice is called more a justice than another, and similarly for the other conditions. For some people dispute about such cases. They utterly deny that one justice is called more or less a justice than another, or one health more or less a health, though they say that one person has health less than another, justice less than another, and similarly with grammar and the other conditions. At any rate things spoken of in virtue of these unquestionably admit of a more and a less: one man is called more grammatical than another, juster, healthier, and so on.

Triangle and square do not seem to admit of a more, nor does any other shape. For things which admit the definition of triangle or circle are all equally triangles or circles, while of things which do not admit it none will be called *more that* than another—a square is not more a circle than an oblong is, for neither admits the definition of circle. In short, unless both admit the definition of what is under discussion neither will be called more that than the other. Thus not all qualifications admit of a more and a less.

Nothing so far mentioned is distinctive of quality, but it is in virtue of qualities only that things are called *similar* and *dissimilar;* a thing is not similar to another in virtue of anything but that in virtue of which it is qualified. So it would be distinctive of quality that a thing is called similar or dissimilar in virtue of it.

We should not be disturbed lest someone may say that though we proposed to discuss quality we are counting in many relatives (since states and conditions are relatives). For in pretty well all such cases the genera are spoken of in relation to something, but none of the particular cases is. For knowledge, a genus, is called just what it is, of something else (it is called knowledge of something); but none of the particular cases is called just what it is, of something else. For example, grammar is not called grammar of something nor music music of something. If at all it is in virtue of the genus that these too are spoken of in relation to something: grammar is called knowledge of something (not grammar of something) and music knowledge of something (not music of something). Thus the particular cases are not relatives. But it is with the particular cases that we are said to be qualified, for it is these which we possess (it is because we have some particular knowledge that we are called knowledgeable). Hence these — the particular cases, in virtue of which we are on occasion said to be qualified — would indeed be qualities; and these are not relatives.

Moreover, if the same thing really is a qualification and a relative there is nothing absurd in its being counted in both the genera.

Nature and the Four Causes
(*Physics* II.1–3)

BOOK II

1. Of things that exist, some exist by nature, some from other causes. By nature the animals and their parts exist, and the plants and the simple bodies (earth, fire, air, water) — for we say that these and the like exist by nature.

All the things mentioned plainly differ from things which are *not* constituted by nature. For each of them has within itself a principle of motion and of stationariness (in respect of place, or of growth and decrease, or by way of alteration). On the other hand, a bed and a coat and anything else of that sort, *qua* receiving these designations — i.e. in so far as they are products of art — have no innate impulse to change. But in so far as they happen to be composed of stone or of earth or of a mixture of the two, they *do* have such an impulse, and just to that extent — which seems to indicate that nature is a principle or cause of being moved and of being at rest in that to which it belongs primarily, in virtue of itself and not accidentally.

I say 'not accidentally', because (for instance) a man who is a doctor might himself be a cause of health to himself. Nevertheless it is not in so far as he is a patient that he possesses the art of medicine: it merely has happened that the same man is doctor and patient — and that is why these attributes are not always found together. So it is with all other artificial products. None of them has in itself the principle of its own production. But while in some cases (for instance houses and the other products of manual labour) that principle is in something else external to the thing, in others — those which may cause a change in themselves accidentally — it lies in the things themselves (but not in virtue of what they are).

Nature then is what has been stated. Things have a nature which have a principle of this kind. Each of them is a substance; for it is a subject, and nature is always in a subject.

The term 'according to nature' is applied to all these things and also to the attributes which belong to them in virtue of what they are, for instance the property of fire to be carried upwards — which is not a nature nor has a nature but is by nature or according to nature.

What nature is, then, and the meaning of the terms 'by nature' and 'according to nature', has been stated. *That* nature exists, it would be absurd to try to prove; for it is obvious that there are many things of this kind, and to prove what is obvious by what is not is the mark of a man who is unable to distinguish what is self-evident from what is not. (This state of mind is clearly possible. A man blind from birth might reason about colours.) Presumably therefore such persons must be talking about words without any thought to correspond.

Some identify the nature or substance of a natural object with that immediate constituent of it which taken by itself is without arrangement, e.g. the wood is the nature of the bed, and the bronze the nature of the statue.

As an indication of this Antiphon points out that if you planted a bed and the rotting wood acquired the power of sending up a shoot, it would not be a bed that would come up, but *wood* which shows that the arrangement in accordance with the rules of the art is merely an accidental attribute, whereas the substance is the other, which, further, persists continuously through the process.

But if the material of each of these objects has itself the same relation to something else, say bronze (or gold) to water, bones (or wood) to earth and so on, *that* (they say) would be their nature and substance. Consequently some assert earth, others fire or air or water or some or all of these, to be the nature of the things that are. For whatever any one of them supposed to have this character—whether one thing or more than one thing—this or these he declared to be the whole of substance, all else being its affections, states, or dispositions. Every such thing they held to be eternal (for it could not pass into anything else), but other things to come into being and cease to be times without number.

This then is one account of nature, namely that it is the primary underlying matter of things which have in themselves a principle of motion or change.

Another account is that nature is the shape or form which is specified in the definition of the thing.

For the word 'nature' is applied to what is according to nature and the natural in the same way as 'art' is applied to what is artistic or a work of art. We should not say in the latter case that there is anything artistic about a thing, if it is a bed only potentially, not yet having the form of a bed; nor should we call it a work of art. The same is true of natural compounds. What is potentially flesh or bone has not yet its own nature, and does not exist by nature, until it receives the form specified in the definition, which we name in defining what flesh or bone is. Thus on the second account of nature, it would be the shape or form (not separable except in statement) of things which have in themselves a principle of motion. (The combination of the two, e.g. man, is not nature but by nature.)

The form indeed is nature rather than the matter; for a thing is more properly said to be what it is when it exists in actuality than when it exists potentially. Again man is born from man but not bed from bed. That is why people say that the shape is not the nature of a bed, but the wood is—if the bed sprouted, not a bed but wood would come up. But even if the shape *is* art, then on the same principle the shape of man is his nature. For man is born from man.

Again, nature in the sense of a coming-to-be proceeds towards nature. For it is not like doctoring, which leads not to the art of doctoring but to health. Doctoring must start from the art, not lead to it. But it is not in this way that nature is related to nature. What grows *qua* growing grows from something into something. Into what then does it grow? Not into that from which it arose but into that to which it tends. The shape then is nature.

Shape and nature are used in two ways. For the privation too is in a way form. But whether in unqualified coming to be there is privation, i.e. a contrary, we must consider later.

2. We have distinguished, then, the different ways in which the term 'nature' is used.

The next point to consider is how the mathematician differs from the student of nature; for natural bodies contain surfaces and volumes, lines and points, and these are the subject-matter of mathematics.

Further, is astronomy different from natural science or a department of it? It seems absurd that the student of nature should be supposed to know the nature of sun or moon, but not to know any of their essential attributes, particularly as the writers on nature obviously do discuss their shape and whether the earth and the world are spherical or not.

Now the mathematician, though he too treats of these things, nevertheless does not treat of them as the limits of a natural body; nor does he consider the attributes indicated as the attributes of such bodies. That is why he separates them; for in thought they are separable from motion, and it makes no difference, nor does any falsity result, if they are separated. The holders of the theory of Forms do the same, though they are not aware of it; for they separate the objects of natural science, which are less separable than those of mathematics. This becomes plain if one tries to state in each of the two cases the definitions of the things and of their attributes. Odd and even, straight and curved, and likewise number, line, and figure, do not involve motion; not so flesh and bone and man — *these* are defined like snub nose, not like curved.

Similar evidence is supplied by the more natural of the branches of mathematics, such as optics, harmonics, and astronomy. These are in a way the converse of geometry. While geometry investigates natural lines but not *qua* natural, optics investigates mathematical lines, but *qua* natural, not *qua* mathematical.

Since two sorts of thing are called nature, the form and the matter, we must investigate its objects as we would the essence of snubness, that is neither independently of matter nor in terms of matter only. Here too indeed one might raise a difficulty. Since there are two natures, with which is the student of nature concerned? Or should he investigate the combination of the two? But if the combination of the two, then also each severally. Does it belong then to the same or to different sciences to know each severally?

If we look at the ancients, natural science would seem to be concerned with the *matter*. (It was only very slightly that Empedocles and Democritus touched on form and essence.)

But if on the other hand art imitates nature, and it is the part of the same discipline to know the form and the matter up to a point (e.g. the doctor has a knowledge of health and also of bile and phlegm, in which health is realized and the builder both of the form of the house and of the matter, namely that it is bricks and beams, and so forth): if this is so, it would be the part of natural science also to know nature in both its senses.

Again, that for the sake of which, or the end, belongs to the same department of knowledge as the means. But the nature is the end or that for the sake of which. For if a thing undergoes a continuous change toward some end, that last stage is actually that for the sake of which. (That is why the poet was carried away into making an absurd statement when he said 'he has the end for the sake of which he was born'. For not every stage that is last claims to be an end, but only that which is best.)

For the arts make their material (some simply make it, others make it serviceable), and we use everything as if it was there for our sake. (We also are in a sense an end. 'That for the sake of which' may be taken in two ways, as we said in our work *On Philosophy*.) The arts, therefore, which govern the matter and have knowledge are two, namely the art which uses the product and the art which directs the production of it. That is why the using art also is in a sense directive; but it differs in that it knows the form, whereas the art which is directive as being concerned with production knows the matter. For the helmsman knows and prescribes what sort of form a helm should have, the other from what wood it should be made and by means of what operations. In the products of art, however, we make the material with a view to the function, whereas in the products of nature the matter is there all along.

Again, matter is a relative thing—for different forms there is different matter.

How far then must the student of nature know the form or essence? Up to a point, perhaps, as the doctor must know sinew or the smith bronze (i.e. until he understands the purpose of each); and the student of nature is concerned only with things whose forms are separable indeed, but do not exist apart from matter. Man is begotten by man and by the sun as well. The mode of existence and essence of the separable it is the business of first philosophy to define.

3. Now that we have established these distinctions, we must proceed to consider causes, their character and number. Knowledge is the object of our inquiry, and men do not think they know a thing till they have grasped the 'why' of it (which is to grasp its primary cause). So clearly we too must do this as regards both coming to be and passing away and every kind of natural change, in order that, knowing their principles, we may try to refer to these principles each of our problems.

In one way, then, that out of which a thing comes to be and which persists, is called a cause, e.g. the bronze of the statue, the silver of the bowl, and the genera of which the bronze and the silver are species.

In another way, the form or the archetype, i.e. the definition of the essence, and its genera, are called causes (e.g. of the octave the relation of 2:1, and generally number), and the parts in the definition.

Again, the primary source of the change or rest; e.g. the man who deliberated is a cause, the father is cause of the child, and generally what makes of what is made and what changes of what is changed.

Again, in the sense of end or that for the sake of which a thing is done, e.g. health is the cause of walking about. ('Why is he walking about?' We say: 'To be healthy', and, having said that, we think we have assigned the cause.) The same is true also of all the intermediate steps which are brought about through the action of something else as means towards the end, e.g. reduction of flesh, purging, drugs, or surgical instruments are means towards health. All these things are for the sake of the end, though they differ from one another in that some are activities, others instruments.

This then perhaps exhausts the number of ways in which the term 'cause' is used.

As things are called causes in many ways, it follows that there are several causes of the same thing (not merely accidentally), e.g. both the art of the sculptor and the bronze are causes of the statue. These are causes of the statue *qua* statue, not in virtue of anything else that it may be—only not in the same way, the one being the material cause, the other the cause whence the motion comes. Some things cause each other reciprocally, e.g. hard work causes fitness and *vice versa,* but again not in the same way, but the one as end, the other as the principle of motion. Further the same thing is the cause of contrary results. For that which by its presence brings about one result is sometimes blamed for bringing about the contrary by its absence. Thus we ascribe the wreck of a ship to the absence of the pilot whose presence was the cause of its safety.

All the causes now mentioned fall into four familiar divisions. The letters are the causes of syllables, the material of artificial products, fire and the like of bodies, the parts of the whole, and the premisses of the conclusion, in the sense of 'that from which'. Of these pairs the one set are causes in the sense of what underlies, e.g. the parts, the other set in the sense of essence—the whole and the combination and the form. But the seed and the doctor and the deliberator, and generally the maker, are all sources whence the change or stationariness originates, which the others are causes in the sense of the end or the good of the rest; for that for the sake of which tends to be what is best and the end of the things that lead up to it. (Whether we call it good or apparently good makes no difference.)

Such then is the number and nature of the kinds of cause.

Now the modes of causation are many, though when brought under heads they too can be reduced in number. For things are called causes in many ways and even within the same kind one may be prior to another: e.g. the doctor and the expert are causes of health, the relation

2:1 and number of the octave, and always what is inclusive to what is particular. Another mode of causation is the accidental and its genera, e.g. in one way Polyclitus, in another a sculptor is the cause of a statue, because being Polyclitus and a sculptor are accidentally conjoined. Also the classes in which the accidental attribute is included; thus a man could be said to be the cause of a statue or, generally, a living creature. An accidental attribute too may be more or less remote, e.g. suppose that a pale man or a musical man were said to be the cause of the statue.

All causes, both proper and accidental, may be spoken of either as potential or as actual; e.g. the cause of a house being built is either a house-builder or a house-builder building.

Similar distinctions can be made in the things of which the causes are causes, e.g. of this statue or of a statue or of an image generally, of this bronze or of bronze or of material generally. So too with the accidental attributes. Again we may use a complex expression for either and say, e.g., neither 'Polyclitus' nor a 'sculptor' but 'Polyclitus, the sculptor'.

All these various uses, however, come to six in number, under each of which again the usage is twofold. It is either what is particular or a genus, or an accidental attribute or a genus of that, and these either as a complex or each by itself; and all either as actual or as potential. The difference is this much, that causes which are actually at work and particular exist and cease to exist simultaneously with their effect, e.g. this healing person with this being-healed person and that house-building man with that being-built house; but this is not always true of potential causes — the house and the housebuilder do not pass away simultaneously.

In investigating the cause of each thing it is always necessary to seek what is most precise (as also in other things): thus a man builds because he is a builder, and a builder builds in virtue of his art of building. This last cause then is prior; and so generally.

Further, generic effects should be assigned to generic causes, particular effects to particular causes, e.g. statue to sculptor, this statue to this sculptor; and powers are relative to possible effects, actually operating causes to things which are actually being effected.

This must suffice for our account of the number of causes and the modes of causation.

Motion
(*Physics* III.1–3)

BOOK III

1. Nature is a principle of motion and change, and it is the subject of our inquiry. We must therefore see that we understand what motion is; for if it were unknown, nature too would be unknown.

When we have determined the nature of motion, our task will be to attack in the same way the terms which come next in order. Now motion is supposed to belong to the class of things which are continuous; and the infinite presents itself first in the continuous—that is how it comes about that the account of the infinite is often used in definitions of the continuous; for what is infinitely divisible is continuous. Besides these, place, void, and time are thought to be necessary conditions of motion.

Clearly, then, for these reasons and also because the attributes mentioned are common to everything and universal, we must first take each of them in hand and discuss it. For the investigation of special attributes comes after that of the common attributes.

To begin then, as we said, with motion.

Some things are in fulfilment only, others in potentiality and in fulfilment—one being a 'this', another so much, another such and such, and similarly for the other categories of being. The term 'relative' is applied sometimes with reference to excess and defect, sometimes to agent and patient, and generally to what can move and what can be moved. For what can cause movement is relative to what can be moved, and *vice versa*.

There is no such thing as motion over and above the things. It is always with respect to substance or to quantity or to quality or to place that what changes changes. But it is impossible, as we assert, to find anything common to these which is neither 'this' nor quantity nor quality nor any of the other predicates. Hence neither will motion and change have reference to something over and above the things mentioned; for there *is* nothing over and above them.

Now each of these belongs to all its subjects in either of two ways: namely, substance—the one is its form, the other privation; in quality, white and black; in quantity, complete and incomplete. Similarly, in respect of locomotion, upwards and downwards or light and heavy. Hence there are as many types of motion or change as there are of being.

We have distinguished in respect of each class between what is in fulfilment and what is potentially; thus the fulfilment of what is potentially, as such, is motion—e.g. the fulfilment of what is alterable, as alterable, is alteration; of what is increasable and its opposite, decreasable (there is no common name for both), increase and decrease; of what can come to be and pass away, coming to be and passing away; of what can be carried along, locomotion.

That this is what motion is, is clear from what follows: when what is buildable, in so far as we call it such, is in fulfilment, it is being built, and that is building. Similarly with learning, doctoring, rolling, jumping, ripening, aging.

The same thing can be both potential and fulfilled, not indeed at the same time or not in the same respect, but e.g. potentially hot and actually cold. Hence such things will act and be acted on by one another in many ways: each of them will be capable at the same time of acting and of being acted upon. Hence, too, what effects motion as a natural agent can be moved: when a thing of this kind causes motion, it is itself also moved. This, indeed, has led some people to suppose that every mover is moved. But this question depends on another set of arguments, and the truth will be made clear later. It *is* possible for a thing to cause motion, though it is itself incapable of being moved.

It is the fulfilment of what is potential when it is already fulfilled and operates not as itself but as movable, that is motion. What I mean by 'as' is this: bronze is potentially a statue. But it is not the fulfilment of bronze as *bronze* which is motion. For to be bronze and to be a certain potentiality are not the same. If they were identical without qualification, i.e. in definition, the fulfilment of bronze as bronze *would* be motion. But they are not the same, as has been said. (This is obvious in contraries. To be capable of health and to be capable of illness are not the same; for if they were there would be no difference between being ill and being well. Yet the subject both of health and of sickness— whether it is humour or blood—is one and the same.)

We can distinguish, then, between the two—just as colour and visible are different—and clearly it is the fulfilment of what is potential as potential that is motion.

It is evident that this is motion, and that motion occurs just when the fulfilment itself occurs and neither before nor after. For each thing is capable of being at one time actual, at another not. Take for instance the buildable: the actuality of the buildable as buildable is the process of building. For the actuality must be either this or the house. But when there is a house, the buildable is no longer there. On the other hand, it *is* the buildable which is *being* built. Necessarily, then, the actuality is the process of building. But building is a kind of motion, and the same account will apply to the other kinds also.

2. The soundness of this definition is evident both when we consider the accounts of motion that the others have given, and also from the difficulty of defining it otherwise.

One could not easily put motion and change in another genus—this is plain if we consider where some people put it: they identify motion with difference or inequality or not being; but such things are not necessarily moved, whether they are different or unequal or non-existent. Nor is change either to or from *these* rather than to or from their opposites.

The reason why they put motion into these genera is that it is thought to be something indefinite, and the principles in the second column are indefinite because they are privative: none of them is either a 'this' or such or comes under any of the other categories. The reason why motion is thought to be indefinite is that it cannot be classed as a potentiality or as an actuality—a thing that is merely *capable* of having a certain size is not necessarily undergoing change, nor yet a thing that is *actually* of a certain size, and motion is thought to be a sort of *actuality*, but incomplete, the reason for this view being that the potential whose actuality it is is incomplete. This is why it is hard to grasp what motion is. It is necessary to class it with privation or with potentiality or with simple actuality, yet none of these seems possible. There remains then the suggested mode of definition, namely that it is a sort of actuality, or actuality of the kind described, hard to grasp, but not incapable of existing.

Every mover too is moved, as has been said—every mover, that is, which is capable of motion, and whose immobility is rest (for when a thing is subject to motion its immobility is rest). For to act on the movable as such is just to move it. But this it does by contact, so that at the same time it is also acted on. Hence motion is the fulfilment of the movable as movable, the cause being contact with what can move, so that the mover is also acted on. The mover will always transmit a form either a 'this' or such or so much, which, when it moves, will be the principle and cause of the motion, e.g. the actual man begets man from what is potentially man.

3. The solution of the difficulty is plain: motion is in the movable. It is the fulfilment of this potentiality by the action of that which has the power of causing motion; and the actuality of that which has the power of causing motion is not other than the actuality of the movable; for it must be the fulfilment of *both*. A thing is capable of causing motion because it *can* do this, it is a mover because it actually *does* it. But it is on the movable that it is capable of acting. Hence there is a single actuality of both alike, just as one to two and two to one are the same interval, and the steep ascent and the steep descent are one — for these are one and the same, although their definitions are not one. So it is with the mover and the moved.

This view has a dialectical difficulty. Perhaps it is necessary that there should be an actuality of the agent and of the patient. The one is agency and the other patiency; and the outcome and end of the one is an action, that of the other a passion. Since then they are both motions, we may ask: *in* what are they, if they are different?

Either both are in what is acted on and moved, or the agency is in the agent and the patiency in the patient. (If we ought to call the latter also 'agency', the word would be used in two senses.)

Now, in the latter case, the motion will be in the mover, for the same account will hold of mover and moved. Hence either *every* mover will be moved, or, though having motion, it will not be moved.

If on the other hand both are in what is moved and acted on — both the agency and the patiency (e.g. both teaching and learning, though they are two, in the learner), then, first, the actuality of each will not be present *in* each, and, a second absurdity, a thing will have two motions at the same time. How will there be two alterations of quality in *one* subject towards *one* form? The thing is impossible: the actualization will be one.

But (someone will say) it is contrary to reason to suppose that there should be one identical actualization of two things which are different in kind. Yet there will be, if teaching and learning are the same, and agency and patiency. To teach will be the same as to learn, and to act the same as to be acted on — the teacher will necessarily be learning everything that he teaches, and the agent will be acted on.

It is not absurd that the actualization of one thing should be in another. Teaching is the activity of a person who can teach, yet the operation is performed in something — it is not cut adrift from a subject, but is of one thing in another.

There is nothing to prevent two things having one and the same actualization (not the same in being, but related as the potential is to the actual).

Nor is it necessary that the teacher should learn, even if to act and to be acted on are one and the same, provided they are not the same in respect of the account which states their essence (as raiment and dress), but are the same in the sense in which the road from Thebes to Athens and the road from Athens to Thebes are the same, as has been explained above. For it is not things which are in any way the same that have all their attributes the same, but only those to be which is the same. But indeed it by no means follows from the fact that teaching is the same as learning, that to learn is the same as to teach, any more than it follows from the fact that there is one distance between two things which are at a distance from each other, that being here at a distance from there and being there at a distance from here are one and the same. To generalize, teaching is not the same as learning, or agency as patiency, in the full sense, though they belong to the same subject, the motion; for the actualization of this in that and the actualization of that through the action of this differ in definition.

What then motion is, has been stated both generally and particularly. It is not difficult to see how each of its types will be defined — alteration is the fulfilment of the alterable as alterable (or, more scientifically, the fulfilment of what can act and what can be acted on, as such) — generally and again in each particular case, building, healing. A similar definition will apply to each of the other kinds of motion.

The Unmoved Mover
(*Metaphysics* XII.6–10)

6. Since there were three kinds of substance, two of them natural and one unmovable, regarding the latter we must assert that it is necessary that there should be an eternal unmovable substance. For substances are the first of existing things, and if they are all destructible, all things are destructible. But it is impossible that movement should either come into being or cease to be; for it must always have existed. Nor can time come into being or cease to be; for there could not be a before and an after if time did not exist. Movement also is continuous, then, in the sense in which time is; for time is either the same thing as movement or an attribute of movement. And there is no continuous movement except movement in place, and of this only that which is circular is continuous.

But if there is something which is capable of moving things or acting on them, but is not actually doing so, there will not be movement; for that which has a capacity need not exercise it. Nothing, then, is gained even if we suppose eternal substances, as the believers in the Forms do, unless there is to be in them some principle which can cause movement; and even this is not enough, nor is another substance besides the Forms enough; for if it does not *act,* there will be no movement. Further, even if it acts, this will not be enough, if its substance is potentiality; for there will not be *eternal* movement; for that which is potentially may possibly not be. There must, then, be such a principle, whose very substance is actuality. Further, then, these substances must be without matter; for they must be eternal, at least if anything else is eternal. Therefore they must be actuality.

Yet there is a difficulty; for it is thought that everything that acts is able to act, but that not everything that is able to act acts, so that the potentiality is prior. But if this is so, nothing at all will exist; for it is possible for things to be capable of existing but not yet to exist. Yet if we follow the mythologists who generate the world from night, or the natural philosophers who say that all things were together, the same impossible result ensues. For how will there be movement, if there is no actual cause? Matter will surely not move itself—the carpenter's art must act on it; nor will the menstrual fluids nor the earth set themselves in motion, but the seeds and the semen must act on them.

This is why some suppose eternal actuality—e.g. Leucippus and Plato; for they say there is always movement. But why and what this movement is they do not say, nor, if the world moves in this way or that, do they tell us the cause of its doing so. Now nothing is moved at random, but there must always be something present, e.g. as a matter of fact a thing moves in one way by nature, and in another by force or through the influence of thought or something else. Further, what sort of movement is primary? This makes a vast difference. But again Plato, at least, cannot even say what it is that he sometimes supposes to be the source of movement—that which moves itself; for the *soul* is later, and simultaneous with the heavens, according to his account. To suppose potentiality prior to actuality, then, is in a sense right, and in a sense not; and we have specified these senses.

That actuality is prior is testified by Anaxagoras (for his thought is actuality) and by Empedocles in his doctrine of love and strife, and by those who say that there is always movement, e.g. Leucippus.

Therefore chaos or night did not exist for any infinite time, but the same things have always existed (either passing through a cycle of changes or in some other way), since actuality is prior to potentiality. If, then, there is a constant cycle, something must always remain, acting in the same way. And if there is to be generation and destruction, there must be something else which is always acting in different ways. This must, then, act in one way in virtue of itself, and in another in virtue of something else—either of a third agent, therefore, or of the first. But it must be in virtue of the first. For otherwise this again causes the motion both of the third agent and of the second. Therefore it is better to say the first. For it was the cause of eternal movement; and something else is the cause of variety, and evidently both together are the cause of eternal variety. This, accordingly, is the character which the motions actually exhibit. What need then is there to seek for other principles?

7. Since this is a possible account of the matter, and if it were not true, the world would have proceeded out of night and 'all things together' and out of non-being, these difficulties may be taken as solved. There is, then, something which is always moved with an unceasing

motion, which is motion in a circle; and this is plain not in theory only but in fact. Therefore the first heavens must be eternal. There is therefore also something which moves them. And since that which is moved and moves is intermediate, there is a mover which moves without being moved, being eternal, substance, and actuality. And the object of desire and the object of thought move in this way; they move without being moved. The primary objects of desire and of thought are the same. For the apparent good is the object of appetite, and the real good is the primary object of wish. But desire is consequent on opinion rather than opinion on desire; for the thinking is the starting-point. And thought is moved by the object of thought, and one side of the list of opposites is in itself the object of thought; and in this, substance is first, and in substance, that which is simple and exists actually. (The one and the simple are not the same; for 'one' means a measure, but 'simple' means that the thing itself has a certain nature.) But the good, also, and that which is in itself desirable are on this same side of the list; and the first in any class is always best, or analogous to the best.

That that for the sake of which is found among the unmovables is shown by making a distinction; for that for the sake of which is both that *for* which and that *towards* which, and of these the one is unmovable and the other is not. Thus it produces motion by being loved, and it moves the other moving things. Now if something is moved it is capable of being otherwise than as it is. Therefore if the actuality of the heavens is primary motion, then in so far as they are in motion, in *this* respect they are capable of being otherwise,—in place, even if not in substance. But since there is something which moves while itself unmoved, existing actually, this can in no way be otherwise than as it is. For motion in space is the first of the kinds of change, and motion in a circle the first kind of spatial motion; and this the first mover *produces*. The first mover, then, of necessity exists; and in so far as it is necessary, it is good, and in this sense a first principle. For the necessary has all these senses—that which is necessary perforce because it is contrary to impulse, that without which the good is impossible, and that which cannot be otherwise but is *absolutely* necessary.

On such a principle, then, depend the heavens and the world of nature. And its life is such as the best which we enjoy, and enjoy for but a short time. For it is ever in this state (which we cannot be), since its actuality is also pleasure. (And therefore waking, perception, and thinking are most pleasant, and hopes and memories are so because of their reference to these.) And thought in itself deals with that which is best in itself, and that which is thought in the fullest sense with that which is best in the fullest sense. And thought thinks itself because it shares the nature of the object of thought; for it becomes an object of thought in coming into contact with and thinking its objects, so that thought and object of thought are the same. For that which is *capable* of receiving the object of thought, i.e. the substance, is thought. And it is *active* when it *possesses* this object. Therefore the latter rather than the former is the divine element which thought seems to contain, and the act of contemplation is what is most pleasant and best. If, then, God is always in that good state in which we sometimes are, this compels our wonder; and if in a better this compels it yet more. And God *is* in a better state. And life also belongs to God; for the actuality of thought is life, and God is that actuality; and God's essential actuality is life most good and eternal. We say therefore that God is a living being, eternal, most good, so that life and duration continuous and eternal belong to God; for this *is* God.

Those who suppose, as the Pythagoreans and Speusippus do, that supreme beauty and goodness are not present in the beginning, because the beginnings both of plants and of animals are *causes,* but beauty and completeness are in the *effects* of these, are wrong in their opinion. For the seed comes from other individuals which are prior and complete, and the first thing is not seed but the complete being, e.g. we must say that before the seed there is a man,—not the man produced from the seed, but another from whom the seed comes.

It is clear then from what has been said that there is a substance which is eternal and unmovable and separate from sensible things. It has been shown also that this substance cannot have any magnitude, but is without parts and indivisible. For it produces movement through infinite time, but nothing finite has infinite power. And, while every magnitude is either infinite or finite, it cannot, for the above reason, have finite magnitude, and it cannot have infinite magnitude because there is no infinite magnitude at all. But it is also clear that it is impassive and unalterable; for all the other changes are posterior to change of place. It is clear, then, why the first mover has these attributes.

8. We must not ignore the question whether we have to suppose one such substance or more than one, and if the latter, how many; we must

also mention, regarding the opinions expressed by others, that they have said nothing that can even be clearly stated about the number of the substances. For the theory of Ideas has no special discussion of the subject; for those who believe in Ideas say the Ideas are numbers, and they speak of numbers now as unlimited, now as limited by the number 10; but as for the reason why there should be just so many numbers, nothing is said with any demonstrative exactness.

We however must discuss the subject, starting from the presuppositions and distinctions we have mentioned. The first principle or primary being is not movable either in itself or accidentally, but produces the primary eternal and single movement. And since that which is moved must be moved by something, and the first mover must be in itself unmovable, and eternal movement must be produced by something eternal and a single movement by a single thing, and since we see that besides the simple spatial movement of the universe, which we say the first and unmovable substance produces, there are other spatial movements—those of the planets—which are eternal (for the body which moves in a circle is eternal and unresting; we have proved these points in the *Physics*), each of *these* movements also must be caused by a substance unmovable in itself and eternal. For the nature of the stars is eternal, being a kind of substance, and the mover is eternal and prior to the moved, and that which is prior to a substance must be a substance. Evidently, then, there must be substances which are of the same number as the movements of the stars, and in their nature eternal, and in themselves unmovable, and without magnitude, for the reason before mentioned.

That the movers are substances, then, and that one of these is first and another second according to the same order as the movements of the stars, is evident. But in the number of movements we reach a problem which must be treated from the standpoint of that one of the mathematical sciences which is most akin to philosophy—viz. of astronomy; for this science speculates about substance which is perceptible but eternal, but the other mathematical sciences, i.e. arithmetic and geometry, treat of no substance. That the movements are more numerous than the bodies that are moved, is evident to those who have given even moderate attention to the matter; for each of the planets has more than one movement. But as to the actual number of these movements, we now—to give some notion of the subject—quote what some of the mathematicians say, that our thought may have some definite number to grasp; but, for the rest, we must partly investigate for ourselves, partly learn from other investigators, and if those who study this subject form an opinion contrary to what we have now stated, we must esteem both parties indeed, but follow the more accurate.

Eudoxus supposed that the motion of the sun or of the moon involves, in either case, three spheres, of which the first is the sphere of the fixed stars, and the second moves in the circle which runs along the middle of the zodiac, and the third in the circle which is inclined across the breadth of the zodiac; but the circle in which the moon moves is inclined at a greater angle than that in which the sun moves. And the motion of the planets involves, in each case, four spheres, and of these also the first and second are the same as the first two mentioned above (for the sphere of the fixed stars is that which moves all the other spheres, and that which is placed beneath this and has its movement in the circle which bisects the zodiac is common to all), but the *poles* of the third sphere of each planet are in the circle which bisects the zodiac, and the motion of the fourth sphere is in the circle which is inclined at an angle to the equator of the third sphere; and the poles of the third spheres are different for the other planets, but those of Venus and Mercury are the same.

Callippus made the position of the spheres the same as Eudoxus did, but while he assigned the same number as Eudoxus did to Jupiter and to Saturn, he thought two more spheres should be added to the sun and two to the moon, if we were to explain the phenomena, and one more to each of the other planets.

But it is necessary, if all the spheres combined are to explain the phenomena, that for each of the planets there should be other spheres (one fewer than those hitherto assigned) which counteract those already mentioned and bring back to the same position the first sphere of the star which in each case is situated below the star in question; for only thus can all the forces at work produce the motion of the planets. Since, then, the spheres by which the planets themselves are moved are eight and twenty-five, and of these only those by which the lowest-situated planet is moved need not be counteracted, the spheres which counteract those of the first two planets will be six in number, and the spheres which counteract those of the next four planets will be sixteen, and the number of all the spheres — those which move the planets and those which counteract these—will be fifty-five. And if one were not to add to the moon and to the sun the movements we mentioned, all the spheres will be forty-nine in number.

Let this then be taken as the number of the spheres, so that the unmovable substances and principles may reasonably be taken as just so many; the assertion of *necessity* must be left to more powerful thinkers.

If there can be no spatial movement which does not conduce to the moving of a star, and if further every being and every substance which is immune from change and in virtue of itself has attained to the best must be considered an end, there can be no other being apart from these we have named, but this must be the number of the substances. For if there are others, they will cause change as being an end of movement, but there *cannot* be other movements besides those mentioned. And it is reasonable to infer this from a consideration of the bodies that are moved; for if everything that moves is for the sake of that which is moved, and every movement belongs to something that is moved, no movement can be for the sake of itself or of another movement, but all movements must be for the sake of the stars. For if a movement is to be for the sake of a movement, this latter also will have to be for the sake of something else; so that since there cannot be an infinite regress, the end of every movement will be one of the divine bodies which move through the heaven.

Evidently there is but one heaven. For if there are many heavens as there are many men, the moving principles, of which each heaven will have one, will be one in form but in number many. But all things that are many in number have matter. (For one and the same formula applies to *many* things, e.g. the formula of man; but Socrates is *one*.) But the primary essence has not matter; for it is fulfillment. So the unmovable first mover is one both in formula and in number; therefore also that which is moved always and continuously is one alone; therefore there is one heaven alone.

Our forefathers in the most remote ages have handed down to us their posterity a tradition, in the form of a myth, that these substances are gods and that the divine encloses the whole of nature. The rest of the tradition has been added later in mythical form with a view to the persuasion of the multitude and to its legal and utilitarian expediency; they say these gods are in the form of men or like some of the other animals, and they say other things consequent on and similar to these which we have mentioned. But if we were to separate the first point from these additions and take it alone—that they thought the first substances to be gods—we must regard this as an inspired utterance, and reflect that, while probably each art and science has often been developed as far as possible and has again perished, these opinions have been preserved like relics until the present. Only thus far, then, is the opinion of our ancestors and our earliest predecessors clear to us.

9. The nature of the divine thought involves certain problems; for while thought is held to be the most divine of phenomena, the question what it must be in order to have that character involves difficulties. For if it thinks nothing, what is there here of dignity? It is just like one who sleeps. And if it thinks, but this depends on something else, then (as that which is its substance is not the act of thinking, but a capacity) it cannot be the best substance; for it is through thinking that its value belongs to it. Further, whether its substance is the faculty of thought or the act of thinking, what does it think? Either itself or something else; and if something else, either the same always or something different. Does it matter, then, or not, whether it thinks the good or any chance thing? Are there not some things about which it is incredible that it should think? Evidently, then, it thinks that which is most divine and precious, and it does not change; for change would be change for the worse, and this would be already a movement. First, then, if it is not the act of thinking but a capacity, it would be reasonable to suppose that the continuity of its thinking is wearisome to it. Secondly, there would evidently be something else more precious than thought, viz. that which is thought. For both thinking and the act of thought will belong even to one who has the worst of thoughts. Therefore if this ought to be avoided (and it ought, for there are even some things which it is better not to see than to see), the act of thinking cannot be the best of things. Therefore it must be itself that thought thinks (since it is the most excellent of things), and its thinking is a thinking on thinking.

But evidently knowledge and perception and opinion and understanding have always something else as their object, and themselves only by the way. Further, if thinking and being thought are different, in respect of which does goodness belong to thought? For being an act of thinking and being an object of thought are not the same. We answer that in some cases the knowledge is the object. In the productive sciences (if we abstract from the matter) the substance in the sense of essence, and in the theoretical sciences the formula or the act of thinking, *is* the object. As, then, thought and the object of thought are not different in the case of things that have not matter, they will be the same, i.e. the thinking will be one with the object of its thought.

A further question is left—whether the object of the thought is composite; for if it were, thought would change in passing from part to part of the whole. We answer that everything which has not matter is indivisible. As human thought, or rather the thought of composite objects, is in a certain period of time (for it does not possess the good at this moment or at that, but its best, being something *different* from it, is attained only in a whole period of time), so throughout eternity is the thought which has *itself* for its object.

10. We must consider also in which of two ways the nature of the universe contains the good or the highest good, whether as something separate and by itself, or as the order of the parts. Probably in both ways, as an army does. For the good is found both in the order and in the leader, and more in the latter; for he does not depend on the order but it depends on him. And all things are ordered together somehow, but not all alike,—both fishes and fowls and plants; and the world is not such that one thing has nothing to do with another, but they are connected. For all are ordered together to one end. (But it is as in a house, where the freemen are least at liberty to act as they will, but all things or most things are already ordained for them, while the slaves and the beasts do little for the common good, and for the most part live at random; for this is the sort of principle that constitutes the nature of each.) I mean, for instance, that all must at least come to be dissolved into their elements, and there are other functions similarly in which all share for the good of the whole.

We must not fail to observe how many impossible or paradoxical results confront those who hold different views from our own, and what are the views of the subtler thinkers, and which views are attended by fewest difficulties. All make all things out of contraries. But neither 'all things' nor 'out of contraries' is right; nor do they tell us how the things in which the contraries are present can be made out of the contraries; for contraries are not affected by one another. Now for us this difficulty is solved naturally by the fact that there is a third factor. These thinkers however make one of the two contraries matter; this is done for instance by those who make the unequal matter for the equal, or the many matter for the one. But this also is refuted in the same way; for the matter which is one is contrary to nothing. Further, all things, except the one, will, on the view we are criticizing, partake of evil; for the bad is itself one of the two elements. But the other school does not treat the good and the bad even as principles; yet in all things the good is in the highest degree a principle. The school we first mentioned is right in saying that it is a principle, but *how* the good is a principle they do not say—whether as end or as mover or as form.

Empedocles also has a paradoxical view; for he identifies the good with love. But this is a principle both as mover (for it brings things together) and as matter (for it is part of the mixture). Now even if it happens that the same thing is a principle both as matter and as mover, still *being* them is not the same. In which respect then is love a principle? It is paradoxical also that strife should be imperishable; strife is for him the nature of the bad.

Anaxagoras makes the good a motive principle; for thought moves things, but moves them for the sake of something, which must be something other than it, except according to *our* way of stating the case; for the medical art is in a sense health. It is paradoxical also not to suppose a contrary to the good, i.e. to thought. But all who speak of the contraries make no use of the contraries, unless we bring their views into shape. And why some things are perishable and others imperishable, no one tells us; for they make all existing things out of the same principles. Further, some make existing things out of the non-existent; and others to avoid the necessity of this make all things one.

Further, why should there always be becoming, and what is the cause of becoming?—this no one tells us. And those who suppose two principles must suppose another, a superior principle, and so must those who believe in the Forms; for why did things come to participate, or why do they participate, in the Forms? And all other thinkers are confronted by the necessary consequence that there is something contrary to Wisdom, i.e. to the highest knowledge; but *we* are not. For there is nothing contrary to that which is primary (for all contraries have matter and are potentially); and the ignorance which is contrary would lead us to a contrary object; but what is primary has no contrary.

Again, if besides sensible things no others exist, there will be no first principle, no order, no becoming, no heavenly bodies, but each principle will have a principle before it, as in the accounts of the mythologists and all the natural philosophers. But if the Forms or the numbers are to exist, they will be causes of nothing; or if not that, at least not of movement.

Further, how is extension, i.e. a *continuum,* to be produced out of unextended parts? For number will not, either as mover or as form, produce a *continuum.* But again there cannot be any contrary that is also a productive or moving principle; for it would be possible for it not to be. Or at least its action would be posterior to its capacity. The world then would not be eternal. But it is; one of these premises, then, must be denied. And we have said how this must be done. Further, in virtue of what the numbers, or the soul and the body, or in general the form and the thing, are one—of this no one tells us anything; nor can any one tell, unless he says, as we do, that the mover makes them one. And those who say mathematical number is first and go on to generate one kind of substance after another and give different principles for each, make the substance of the universe a series of episodes (for one substance has no influence on another by its existence or nonexistence), and they give us many principles; but the world must not be governed badly.

'The rule of many is not good; let there be one ruler.'

Barnes, Jonathan, editor. *The Complete Works of Aristotle: Revised Oxford Translation.* Copyright © 1984 by Princeton University Press. Categories 1–8; Physics Bk. II, 1–3; Bk. III, 1–3; Metaphysics Bk. XII, 6–10. Reprinted by permission of Princeton University Press.

ST. ANSELM

Born in Italy, St. Anselm (1033–1109) became an abbot in Normandy and finally archbishop of Canterbury. He represents the blooming and ubiquity of medieval intellectual culture and also forms a bridge between ancient and scholastic forms of theology. Faithful to a tradition of biblical meditation highlighted in St. Augustine, Anselm borrows his motto "Faith seeking understanding" from that ancient church father. But Anselm is also one of the first in the Christian West to use the newly discovered tools of Aristotelian dialectic. Nowhere is this seen so well as in his famous "ontological proof" for the existence of God found in the opening chapters of his *Proslogium*. What that proof intends is much debated, for, on the one hand, if one wants to understand theologically what Anselm seeks in this proof, one needs to take into consideration not only the prayers surrounding it but also the fact that he explicitly understands God as the divinely revealed Creator throughout the meditation. On the other hand, the proof and the subsequent demonstrations of the nature of God based on it can be taken as philosophical arguments in their own right. The proof in later times was taken up and discussed by philosophers such as Descartes, Leibniz, and Kant and by theologians such as Karl Barth.

The Ontological Argument
(*Proslogium,* Chapters I–VI)

CHAPTER I

Exhortation of the mind to the contemplation of God.—It casts aside cares, and excludes all thoughts save that of God, that it may seek Him. Man was created to see God. Man by sin lost the blessedness for which he was made, and found the misery for which he was not made. He did not keep this good when he could keep it easily. Without God it is ill with us. Our labors and attempts are in vain without God. Man cannot seek God, unless God himself teaches him; nor find him, unless he reveals himself. God created man in his image, that he might be mindful of him, think of him, and love him. The believer does not seek to understand, that he may believe, but he believes that he may understand: for unless he believed he would not understand.

Up now, slight man! flee, for a little while, thy occupations; hide thyself, for a time, from thy disturbing thoughts. Cast aside, now, thy burdensome cares, and put away thy toilsome business. Yield room for some little time to God; and rest for a little time in him. Enter the inner chamber of thy mind; shut out all thoughts save that of God, and such as can aid thee in seeking him; close thy door and seek him. Speak now, my whole heart! speak now to God, saying, I seek thy face; thy face, Lord, will I seek (Psalms xxvii. 8). And come thou now, O Lord my God, teach my heart where and how it may seek thee, where and how it may find thee.

Lord, if thou art not here, where shall I seek thee, being absent? But if thou art everywhere, why do I not see thee present? Truly thou dwellest in unapproachable light. But where is unapproachable light, or how shall I come to it? Or who shall lead me to that light and into it, that I may see thee in it? Again, by what marks, under what form, shall I seek thee? I have never seen thee, O Lord my God; I do not know thy form. What, O most high Lord, shall this man do, an exile far from thee? What shall thy servant do, anxious in his love of thee, and cast out afar from thy face? He pants to see thee, and thy face is too far from him. He longs to come to thee, and thy dwelling-place is inaccessible. He is eager to find thee, and knows not thy place. He desires to seek thee, and does not know thy face. Lord, thou art my God, and thou art my Lord, and never have I seen thee. It is thou that hast made me, and hast made me anew, and hast bestowed upon me all the blessings I enjoy; and not yet do I know thee. Finally, I was created to see thee, and not yet have I done that for which I was made.

O wretched lot of man, when he hath lost that for which he was made! O hard and terrible fate! Alas, what has he lost, and what has he found? What has departed, and what remains? He has lost the blessedness for which he was made, and has found the misery for which he was not made. That has departed without which nothing is happy, and that remains which, in itself, is only miserable. Man once did eat the bread of angels, for which he hungers now; he eateth now the bread of sorrows, of which he knew not then. Alas! for the mourning of all mankind, for the universal lamentation of the sons of Hades! He choked with satiety, we sigh with hunger. He abounded, we beg. He possessed in happiness, and miserably forsook his possession; we suffer want in unhappiness, and feel a miserable longing, and alas! we remain empty.

Why did he not keep for us, when he could so easily, that whose lack we should feel so heavily? Why did he shut us away from the light, and cover us over with darkness? With what purpose did he rob us of life, and inflict death upon us? Wretches that we are, whence have we been driven out; whither are we driven on? Whence hurled? Whither consigned to ruin? From a native country into exile, from the vision of God into our present blindness, from the joy of immortality into the bitterness and horror of death. Miserable exchange of how great a good, for how great an evil! Heavy loss, heavy grief, heavy all our fate!

But alas! wretched that I am, one of the sons of Eve, far removed from God! What have I undertaken? What have I accomplished? Whither was I striving? How far have I come? To what did I aspire? Amid what thoughts am I sighing? I sought blessings, and lo! confusion. I strove toward God, and I stumbled on myself. I sought calm in privacy, and I found tribulation and grief, in my inmost thoughts. I wished to smile in the joy of my mind, and I am compelled to frown by the sorrow of my heart. Gladness was hoped for, and lo! a source of frequent sighs!

And thou too, O Lord, how long? How long, O Lord, dost thou forget us; how long dost thou turn thy face from us? When wilt thou look upon us, and hear us? When wilt thou enlighten our eyes, and show us thy face? When wilt thou restore thyself to us? Look upon us, Lord; hear us, enlighten us, reveal thyself to us. Restore thyself to us, that it may be well with us,—thyself, without whom it is so ill with us. Pity our toilings and strivings toward thee, since we can do nothing without thee. Thou dost invite us; do thou help us. I beseech thee, O Lord, that I may not lose hope in sighs, but may breathe anew in hope. Lord, my heart is made bitter by its desolation; sweeten thou it, I beseech thee, with thy consolation. Lord, in hunger I began to seek thee; I beseech thee that I may not cease to hunger for thee. In hunger I have come to thee; let me not go unfed. I have come in poverty to the Rich, in misery to the Compassionate; let me not return empty and despised.

And if, before I eat, I sigh, grant, even after sighs, that which I may eat. Lord, I am bowed down and can only look downward; raise me up that I may look upward. My iniquities have gone over my head; they overwhelm me; and, like a heavy load, they weigh me down. Free me from them; unburden me, that the pit of iniquities may not close over me.

Be it mine to look up to thy light, even from afar, even from the depths. Teach me to seek thee, and reveal thyself to me, when I seek thee, for I cannot seek thee, except thou teach me, nor find thee, except thou reveal thyself. Let me seek thee in longing, let me long for thee in seeking; let me find thee in love, and love thee in finding. Lord, I acknowledge and I thank thee that thou hast created me in this thine image, in order that I may be mindful of thee, may conceive of thee, and love thee; but that image has been so consumed and wasted away by vices, and obscured by the smoke of wrong-doing, that it cannot achieve that for which it was made, except thou renew it, and create it anew. I do not endeavor, O Lord, to penetrate thy sublimity, for in no wise do I compare my understanding with that; but I long to understand in some degree thy truth, which my heart believes and loves. For I do not seek to understand that I may believe, but I believe in order to understand. For this also I believe,—that unless I believed, I should not understand.

CHAPTER II

Truly there is a God, although the fool hath said in his heart, There is no God.

And so, Lord, do thou, who dost give understanding to faith, give me so far as thou knowest it to be profitable, to understand that thou art as we believe; and that thou art that which we believe. And, indeed, we believe that thou art a being than which nothing greater can be conceived. Or is there no such nature, since the fool hath said in his heart, there is no God? (Psalms xiv. 1). But, at any rate, this very fool, when he hears of this being of which I speak—a being than which nothing greater can be conceived—understands what he hears, and what he understands is in his understanding; although he does not understand it to exist.

For, it is one thing for an object to be in the understanding, and another to understand that the object exists. When a painter first conceives of what he will afterwards perform, he has it in his understanding, but he does not yet understand it to be, because he has not yet performed it. But after he has made the painting, he both has it in his understanding, and he understands that it exists, because he has made it.

Hence, even the fool is convinced that something exists in the understanding, at least, than which nothing greater can be conceived. For, when he hears of this, he understands it. And whatever is understood, exists in the understanding. And assuredly that, than which nothing greater can be conceived, cannot exist in the understanding alone. For, suppose it exists in the understanding alone: then it can be conceived to exist in reality; which is greater.

Therefore, if that, than which nothing greater can be conceived, exists in the understanding alone, the very being, than which nothing greater can be conceived, is one, than which a greater can be conceived. But obviously this is impossible. Hence, there is no doubt that there exists a being, than which nothing greater can be conceived, and it exists both in the understanding and in reality.

CHAPTER III

God cannot be conceived not to exist.—God is that, than which nothing greater can be conceived.—That which can be conceived not to exist is not God.

And it assuredly exists so truly, that it cannot be conceived not to exist. For, it is possible to conceive of a being which cannot be conceived not to exist; and this is greater than one which can be conceived not to exist. Hence, if that, than which nothing greater can be conceived, can be conceived not to exist, it is not that, than which nothing greater can be conceived. But this is an irreconcilable contradiction. There is, then, so truly a being than which nothing greater can be conceived to exist, that it cannot even be conceived not to exist; and this being thou art, O Lord, our God.

So truly, therefore, dost thou exist, O Lord, my God, that thou canst not be conceived not to exist; and rightly. For, if a mind could conceive of a being better than thee, the creature would rise above the

Creator; and this is most absurd. And, indeed, whatever else there is, except thee alone, can be conceived not to exist. To thee alone, therefore, it belongs to exist more truly than all other beings, and hence in a higher degree than all others. For, whatever else exists does not exist so truly, and hence in a less degree it belongs to it to exist. Why, then, has the fool said in his heart, there is no God (Psalms xiv. 1); since it is so evident, to a rational mind, that thou dost exist in the highest degree of all? Why, except that he is dull and a fool?

CHAPTER IV

How the fool has said in his heart what cannot be conceived.—A thing may be conceived in two ways: (1) when the word signifying it is conceived; (2) when the thing itself is understood. As far as the word goes, God can be conceived not to exist; in reality he cannot.

But how has the fool said in his heart what he could not conceive; or how is it that he could not conceive what he said in his heart? since it is the same to say in the heart, and to conceive.

But, if really, nay, since really, he both conceived, because he said in his heart; and did not say in his heart, because he could not conceive; there is more than one way in which a thing is said in the heart or conceived. For, in one sense, an object is conceived, when the word signifying it is conceived; and in another, when the very entity, which the object is, is understood.

In the former sense, then, God can be conceived not to exist; but in the latter, not at all. For no one who understands what fire and water are can conceive fire to be water, in accordance with the nature of the facts themselves, although this is possible according to the words. So, then, no one who understands what God is can conceive that God does not exist; although he says these words in his heart, either without any, or with some foreign, signification. For, God is that than which a greater cannot be conceived. And he who thoroughly understands this, assuredly understands that this being so truly exists, that not even in concept can it be non-existent. Therefore, he who understands that God so exists, cannot conceive that he does not exist.

I thank thee, gracious Lord, I thank thee; because what I formerly believed by thy bounty, I now so understand by thine illumination, that if I were unwilling to believe that thou dost exist, I should not be able not to understand this to be true.

CHAPTER V

God is whatever it is better to be than not to be; and he, as the only self-existent being, creates all things from nothing.

What art thou, then, Lord God, than whom nothing greater can be conceived? But what art thou, except that which, as the highest of all beings, alone exists through itself, and creates all other things from nothing? For, whatever is not this is less than a thing which can be conceived of. But this cannot be conceived of thee. What good, therefore, does the supreme Good lack, through which every good is? Therefore, thou art just, truthful, blessed, and whatever it is better to be than not to be. For it is better to be just than not just; better to be blessed than not blessed.

CHAPTER VI

How God is sensible (*sensibilis*) although he is not a body.—God is sensible, omnipotent, compassionate, passionless; for it is better to be these than not be. He who in any way knows, is not improperly said in some sort to feel.

But, although it is better for thee to be sensible, omnipotent, compassionate, passionless, than not to be these things; how art thou sensible, if thou art not a body; or omnipotent, if thou hast not all powers; or at once compassionate and passionless. For, if only corporeal things are sensible, since the senses encompass a body and are in a body, how art thou sensible, although thou art not a body, but a supreme Spirit, who is superior to body. But, if feeling is only cognition, or for the sake of cognition,—for he who feels obtains knowledge in accordance with the proper functions of his senses; as through sight, of colors;

through taste, of flavors,—whatever in any way cognises is not inappropriately said, in some sort, to feel.

Therefore, O Lord, although thou art not a body, yet thou art truly sensible in the highest degree in respect of this, that thou dost cognise all things in the highest degree; and not as an animal cognises, through a corporeal sense.

❖ ❖ ❖

From *St. Anselm: Basic Writings*. Translated by S. N. Deane. Second edition. Copyright 1962 by © Open Court Publishing Co. Used by permission of Open Court Publishing Co.

✦✦✦✦✦✦✦✦✦✦✦✦✦✦✦✦✦✦✦✦✦✦

ST. THOMAS AQUINAS

Born in Italy, Thomas Aquinas (1225–1274) spent his career in Paris, Cologne, and Naples. He is surely one of the greatest thinkers of all time. Among his many enduring achievements, one of the most prominent is his revision and thorough integration of Aristotle into Christian theology. The goal of this marriage was to create a discipline by which God's revelation, which is unique and beyond human reason, can be discussed and taught reasonably and systematically — in short, to create a divine science. Holding that some truths are beyond reason and accessible only to faith, Thomas believed that they could nevertheless serve as first principles of discussion. There are divine truths, however, that can be understood by the intellect. Among these is that God is first cause and pure act, which Thomas seeks to demonstrate in the first of our selections. In the second selection, in encountering the problem of how we can at all speak of such a transcendent being to whom none of our categories fully and accurately apply, Thomas develops his "doctrine of analogy." This doctrine is particularly crucial to his project, as no science, past or present, can be undertaken with completely ambiguous and equivocal terms. At the same time it is also a *caveat* to recognize that none of our discussion fully comprehends God.

The Existence of God
(*Summa Theologica* Part I, Question II)

Question II
THE EXISTENCE OF GOD

First Article
WHETHER THE EXISTENCE OF GOD IS SELF-EVIDENT?

We proceed thus to the First Article:—

Objection 1. It seems that the existence of God is self-evident. For those things are said to be self-evident to us the knowledge of which exists naturally in us, as we can see in regard to first principles. But as Damascene says, *the knowledge of God is naturally implanted in all.* Therefore the existence of God is self-evident.

Obj. 2. Further, those things are said to be self-evident which are known as soon as the terms are known, which the Philosopher says is true of the first principles of demonstration. Thus, when the nature of a whole and of a part is known, it is at once recognized that every whole is greater than its part. But as soon as the signification of the name *God* is understood, it is at once seen that God exists. For by this name is signified that thing than which nothing greater can be conceived. But that which exists actually and mentally is greater than that which exists only mentally. Therefore, since as soon as the name *God* is understood it exists mentally, it also follows that it exists actually. Therefore the proposition *God exists* is self-evident.

Obj. 3. Further, the existence of truth is self-evident. For whoever denies the existence of truth grants that truth does not exist: and, if truth does not exist then the proposition *Truth does not exist* is true: and if there is anything true, there must be truth. But God is truth itself: *I am the way, the truth, and the life* (*Jo.* xiv. 6). Therefore *God exists* is self-evident.

On the contrary, No one can mentally admit the opposite of what is self-evident, as the Philosopher states concerning the first principles of demonstration. But the opposite of the proposition *God is* can be mentally admitted: *The fool said in his heart, There is no God* (*Ps.* lii. 1). Therefore, that God exists is not self-evident.

I answer that, A thing can be self-evident in either of two ways: on the one hand, self-evident in itself, though not to us; on the other, self-evident in itself, and to us. A proposition is self-evident because the predicate is included in the essence of the subject: *e.g., Man is an animal,* for animal is contained in the essence of man. If, therefore, the essence of the predicate and subject be known to all, the proposition will be self-evident to all; as is clear with regard to the first principles of demonstration, the terms of which are certain common notions that no one is ignorant of, such as being and non-being, whole and part, and the like. If, however, there are some to whom the essence of the predicate and subject is unknown, the proposition will be self-evident in itself, but not to those who do not know the meaning of the predicate and subject of the proposition. Therefore, it happens, as Boethius says, that there are some notions of the mind which are common and self-evident only to the learned, as that incorporeal substances are not in space. Therefore I say that this proposition, *God exists,* of itself is self-evident, for the predicate is the same as the subject, because God is His own existence as will be hereafter shown. Now because we do not know the essence of God, the proposition is not self-evident to us, but needs to be demonstrated by things that are more known to us, though less known in their nature — namely, by His effects.

Reply Obj. 1. To know that God exists in a general and confused way is implanted in us by nature, inasmuch as God is man's beatitude. For man naturally desires happiness, and what is naturally desired by man is naturally known by him. This, however, is not to know absolutely that God exists; just as to know that someone is approaching is not the same as to know that Peter is approaching, even though it is Peter who is approaching; for there are many who imagine that man's perfect good, which is happiness, consists in riches, and others in pleasures, and others in something else.

Reply Obj. 2. Perhaps not everyone who hears this name *God* understands it to signify something than which nothing greater can be thought, seeing that some have believed God to be a body. Yet, granted that everyone understands that by this name *God* is signified something than which nothing greater can be thought, nevertheless, it does not therefore follow that he understands that what the name signifies exists actually, but only that it exists mentally. Nor can it be argued that it actually exists, unless it be admitted that there actually exists something than which nothing greater can be thought; and this precisely is not admitted by those who hold that God does not exist.

Reply Obj. 3. The existence of truth in general is self-evident, but the existence of a Primal Truth is not self-evident to us.

Second Article
WHETHER IT CAN BE DEMONSTRATED THAT GOD EXISTS?

We proceed thus to the Second Article: —

Objection 1. It seems that the existence of God cannot be demonstrated. For it is an article of faith that God exists. But what is of faith cannot be demonstrated, because a demonstration produces scientific knowledge, whereas faith is of the unseen, as is clear from the Apostle (*Heb.* xi. 1). Therefore it cannot be demonstrated that God exists.

Obj. 2. Further, essence is the middle term of demonstration. But we cannot know in what God's essence consists, but solely in what it does not consist, as Damascene says. Therefore we cannot demonstrate that God exists.

Obj. 3. Further, if the existence of God were demonstrated, this could only be from His effects. But His effects are not proportioned to Him, since He is infinite and His effects are finite, and between the finite and infinite there is no proportion. Therefore, since a cause cannot be demonstrated by an effect not proportioned to it, it seems that the existence of God cannot be demonstrated.

On the contrary, The Apostle says: *The invisible things of Him are clearly seen, being understood by the things that are made* (*Rom.* i. 20). But this would not be unless the existence of God could be demonstrated through the things that are made; for the first thing we must know of anything is, whether it exists.

I answer that, Demonstration can be made in two ways: One is through the cause, and is called *propter quid,* and this is to argue from what is prior absolutely. The other is through the effect, and is called a demonstration *quia;* this is to argue from what is prior relatively only to us. When an effect is better known to us than its cause, from the effect we proceed to the knowledge of the cause. And from every effect the existence of its proper cause can be demonstrated, so long as its effects are better known to us; because, since every effect depends upon its cause, if the effect exists, the cause must pre-exist. Hence the existence of God, in so far as it is not self-evident to us, can be demonstrated from those of His effects which are known to us.

Reply Obj. 1. The existence of God and other like truths about God, which can be known by natural reason, are not articles of faith, but are preambles to the articles; for faith presupposes natural knowledge, even as grace presupposes nature and perfection the perfectible. Nevertheless, there is nothing to prevent a man, who cannot grasp a proof, from accepting, as a matter of faith, something which in itself is capable of being scientifically known and demonstrated.

Reply Obj. 2. When the existence of a cause is demonstrated from an effect, this effect takes the place of the definition of the cause in proving the cause's existence. This is especially the case in regard to God, because, in order to prove the existence of anything, it is necessary to accept as a middle term the meaning of the name, and not its essence, for the question of its essence follows on the question of its existence. Now the names given to God are derived from His effects, as will be later shown. Consequently, in demonstrating the existence of God from His effects, we may take for the middle term the meaning of the name *God.*

Reply Obj. 3. From effects not proportioned to the cause no perfect knowledge of that cause can be obtained. Yet from every effect the existence of the cause can be clearly demonstrated, and so we can demonstrate the existence of God from His effects; though from them we cannot know God perfectly as He is in His essence.

Third Article
WHETHER GOD EXISTS?

We proceed thus to the Third Article:—

Objection 1. It seems that God does not exist; because if one of two contraries be infinite, the other would be altogether destroyed. But the name *God* means that He is infinite goodness. If, therefore, God existed, there would be no evil discoverable; but there is evil in the world. Therefore God does not exist.

Obj. 2. Further, it is superfluous to suppose that what can be accounted for by a few principles has been produced by many. But it seems that everything we see in the world can be accounted for by other principles, supposing God did not exist. For all natural things can be reduced to one principle, which is nature; and all voluntary things can be reduced to one principle, which is human reason, or will. Therefore there is no need to suppose God's existence.

On the contrary, It is said in the person of God: *I am Who am (Exod.* iii. 14).

I answer that, The existence of God can be proved in five ways.

The first and more manifest way is the argument from motion. It is certain, and evident to our senses, that in the world some things are in motion. Now whatever is moved is moved by another, for nothing can be moved except it is in potentiality to that towards which it is moved; whereas a thing moves inasmuch as it is in act. For motion is nothing else than the reduction of something from potentiality to actuality. But nothing can be reduced from potentiality to actuality, except by something in a state of actuality. Thus that which is actually hot, as fire, makes wood, which is potentially hot, to be actually hot, and thereby moves and changes it. Now it is not possible that the same thing should be at once in actuality and potentiality in the same respect, but only in different respects. For what is actually hot cannot simultaneously be potentially hot; but it is simultaneously potentially cold. It is therefore impossible that in the same respect and in the same way a thing should be both mover and moved, *i.e.,* that it should move itself. Therefore, whatever is moved must be moved by another. If that by which it is moved be itself moved, then this also must needs be moved by another, and that by another again. But this cannot go on to infinity, because then there would be no first mover, and, consequently, no other mover, seeing that subsequent movers move only inasmuch as they are moved by the first mover; as the staff moves only because it is moved by the hand. Therefore it is necessary to arrive at a first mover, moved by no other; and this everyone understands to be God.

The second way is from the nature of efficient cause. In the world of sensible things we find there is an order of efficient causes. There is no case known (neither is it, indeed, possible) in which a thing is found to be the efficient cause of itself; for so it would be prior to itself, which is impossible. Now in efficient causes it is not possible to go on to infinity, because in all efficient causes following in order, the first is the cause of the intermediate cause, and the intermediate is the cause of the ultimate cause, whether the intermediate cause be several, or one only. Now to take away the cause is to take away the effect.

Therefore, if there be no first cause among efficient causes, there will be no ultimate, nor any intermediate, cause. But if in efficient causes it is possible to go on to infinity, there will be no first efficient cause, neither will there be an ultimate effect, nor any intermediate efficient causes; all of which is plainly false. Therefore it is necessary to admit a first efficient cause, to which everyone gives the name of God.

The third way is taken from possibility and necessity, and runs thus. We find in nature things that are possible to be and not to be, since they are found to be generated, and to be corrupted, and consequently, it is possible for them to be and not to be. But it is impossible for these always to exist, for that which can not-be at some time is not. Therefore, if everything can not-be, then at one time there was nothing in existence. Now if this were true, even now there would be nothing in existence, because that which does not exist begins to exist only through something already existing. Therefore, if at one time nothing was in existence, it would have been impossible for anything to have begun to exist; and thus even now nothing would be in existence—which is absurd. Therefore, not all beings are merely possible, but there must exist something the existence of which is necessary. But every necessary thing either has its necessity caused by another, or not. Now it is impossible to go on to infinity in necessary things which have their necessity caused by another, as has been already proved in regard to efficient causes. Therefore we cannot but admit the existence of some being having of itself its own necessity, and not receiving it from another, but rather causing in others their necessity. This all men speak of as God.

The fourth way is taken from the gradation to be found in things. Among beings there are some more and some less good, true, noble, and the like. But *more* and *less* are predicated of different things according as they resemble in their different ways something which is the maximum, as a thing is said to be hotter according as it more nearly resembles that which is hottest; so that there is something which is truest, something best, something noblest, and, consequently, something which is most being, for those things that are greatest in truth are greatest in being, as it is written in *Metaph.* ii. Now the maximum in any genus is the cause of all in that genus, as fire, which is the maximum of heat, is the cause of all hot things, as is said in the same book. Therefore there must also be something which is to all beings the cause of their being, goodness, and every other perfection; and this we call God.

The fifth way is taken from the governance of the world. We see that things which lack knowledge, such as natural bodies, act for an end, and this is evident from their acting always, or nearly always, in the same way, so as to obtain the best result. Hence it is plain that they achieve their end, not fortuitously, but designedly. Now whatever lacks knowledge cannot move towards an end, unless it be directed by some being endowed with knowledge and intelligence; as the arrow is directed by the archer. Therefore some intelligent being exists by whom all natural things are directed to their end; and this being we call God.

Reply Obj. 1. As Augustine says: *Since God is the highest good, He would not allow any evil to exist in His works, unless His omnipotence and goodness were such as to bring good even out of evil.* This is part of the infinite goodness of God, that He should allow evil to exist, and out of it produce good.

Reply Obj. 2. Since nature works for a determinate end under the direction of a higher agent, whatever is done by nature must be traced back to God as to its first cause. So likewise whatever is done voluntarily must be traced back to some higher cause other than human reason and will, since these can change and fail; for all things that are changeable and capable of defect must be traced back to an immovable and self-necessary first principle, as has been shown.

✦ ✦ ✦

From *The Basic Writings of St. Thomas Aquinas.* Translated by Anton Pegis. Used by permission of the Estate of Anton C. Pegis.

The Doctrine of Analogy
(*Summa Contra Gentiles* Book I, Chapters 28–34)

CHAPTER 28

ON THE DIVINE PERFECTION

[1] Although the things that exist and live are more perfect than the things that merely exist, nevertheless, God, Who is not other than His

being, is a universally perfect being. And I call *universally perfect* that to which the excellence of no genus is lacking.

[2]   Every excellence in any given thing belongs to it according to its being. For man would have no excellence as a result of his wisdom unless through it he *were* wise. So, too, with the other excellences. Hence, the mode of a thing's excellence is according to the mode of its being. For a thing is said to be more or less excellent according as its being is limited to a certain greater or lesser mode of excellence. Therefore, if there is something to which the whole power of being belongs, it can lack no excellence that is proper to some thing. But for a thing that is its own being it is proper to be according to the whole power of being. For example, if there were a separately existing whiteness, it could not lack any of the power of whiteness. For a given white thing lacks something of the power of whiteness through a defect in the receiver of the whiteness, which receives it according to its mode and perhaps not according to the whole power of whiteness. God, therefore, Who is His being, as we have proved above, has being according to the whole power of being itself. Hence, He cannot lack any excellence that belongs to any given thing.

[3]   But just as every excellence and perfection is found in a thing according as that thing *is,* so every defect is found in it according as in some way it *is not.* Now, just as God has being wholly, so non-being is wholly absent from Him. For as a thing has being, in that way is it removed from non-being. Hence, all defect is absent from God. He is, therefore, universally perfect.

[4]   Those things that merely exist are not imperfect because of an imperfection in absolute being. For they do not possess being according to its whole power; rather, they participate in it through a certain particular and most imperfect mode.

[5]   Furthermore, everything that is imperfect must be preceded by something perfect. Thus, the seed is from the animal or the plant. The first being must, therefore, be most perfect. But we have shown that God is the first being. He is, therefore, most perfect.

[6]   Again, each thing is perfect according as it is in act, and imperfect according as it is in potency and lacking act. Hence, that which is in

no way in potency, but is pure act, must be most perfect. Such, however, is God. God is, therefore, most perfect.

[7]   Nothing, moreover, acts except as it is in act. Hence, action follows the mode of act in the agent. It is therefore impossible that an effect brought forth by an action be of a more excellent act than is the act of the agent. On the other hand, it is possible that the act of the effect be less perfect than the act of the efficient cause, since an action can become weakened through the effect in which it terminates. Now, in the genus of the efficient cause there is a reduction to one cause, called God, as is evident from what we have said; and from this cause, as we shall show later on, all things come. Hence, it is necessary that whatever is found in act in any thing whatever must be found in God in a more eminent way than in that thing itself. But the converse is not true. God, therefore, is most perfect.

[8]   In every genus, furthermore, there is something that is most perfect for that genus, acting as a measure for all other things in the genus. For each thing is shown to be more or less perfect according as it approaches more or less to the measure of its genus. Thus, *white* is said to be the measure among all colors, and the *virtuous man* among all men. Now, the measure of all beings cannot be other than God, Who is His own being. No perfection, consequently, that is appropriate to this or that thing is lacking to Him; otherwise, He would not be the common measure of all things.

[9]   This is why, when Moses asked to see the divine countenance or glory, he received this reply from the Lord: "I will show thee all good," as it is written in Exodus (33:18, 19); by which the Lord gave Moses to understand that the fullness of all goodness was in Him. Dionysius likewise says: "God does not exist in a certain way; He possesses, and this before all others, all being within Himself absolutely and limitlessly."

[10]   We must note, however, that *perfection* cannot be attributed to God appropriately if we consider the signification of the name according to its origin; for it does not seem that what is not made [*factum*] can be called perfect [*perfectum*]. But everything that comes to be is brought forth from potency to act and from non-being to being when it has been made. That is why it is rightly said to be perfect, as being

completely made, at that moment when the potency is wholly reduced to act, so that it retains no non-being but has a completed being. By a certain extension of the name, consequently, *perfect* is said not only of that which by way of becoming reaches a completed act, but also of that which, without any making whatever, is in complete act. It is thus that, following the words of Matthew (5:48), we say that God is perfect: "Be ye perfect as also your heavenly Father is perfect."

CHAPTER 29

ON THE LIKENESS OF CREATURES TO GOD

[1]   In the light of what we have said, we are able to consider how a likeness to God is and is not possible in things.

[2]   Effects that fall short of their causes do not agree with them in name and nature. Yet, some likeness must be found between them, since it belongs to the nature of action that an agent produce its like, since each thing acts according as it is in act. The form of an effect, therefore, is certainly found in some measure in a transcending cause, but according to another mode and another way. For this reason the cause is called an *equivocal* cause. Thus, the sun causes heat among these sublunary bodies by acting according as it is in act. Hence, the heat generated by the sun must bear some likeness to the active power of the sun, through which heat is caused in this sublunary world; and because of this heat the sun is said to be hot, even though not in one and the same way. And so the sun is said to be somewhat like those things in which it produces its effects as an efficient cause. Yet the sun is also unlike all these things in so far as such effects do not possess heat and the like in the same way as they are found in the sun. So, too, God gave things all their perfections and thereby is both like and unlike all of them.

[3]   Hence it is that Sacred Scripture recalls the likeness between God and creatures, as when it is said in Genesis (1:26): "Let us make man to our image and likeness." At times the likeness is denied, as in the text of Isaiah (40:18): "To whom then have you likened God, and what

image will you make for Him?" or in the Psalm (82:1): "O God, who shall be like to Thee?"

[4] Dionysius is in agreement with this argument when he says: "The same things are both like and unlike God. They are like according as they imitate as much as they can Him Who is not perfectly imitable; they are unlike according as effects are lesser than their causes."

[5] In the light of this likeness, nevertheless, it is more fitting to say that a creature is like God rather than the converse. For that is called *like* something which possesses a quality or form of that thing. Since, then, that which is found in God perfectly is found in other things according to a certain diminished participation, the basis on which the likeness is observed belongs to God absolutely, but not to the creature. Thus, the creature has what belongs to God and, consequently, is rightly said to be like God. But we cannot in the same way say that God has what belongs to the creature. Neither, then, can we appropriately say that God is like a creature, just as we do not say that man is like his image, although the image is rightly said to be like him.

[6] All the less proper, moreover, is the expression that God is likened to a creature. For likening expresses a motion towards likeness and thus belongs to the being that receives from another that which makes it like. But a creature receives from God that which makes it like Him. The converse, however, does not hold. God, then, is not likened to a creature; rather, the converse is true.

CHAPTER 30

THE NAMES THAT CAN BE PREDICATED OF GOD

[1] From what we have said we can further consider what it is possible to say or not to say of God, what is said of Him alone, and also what is said of Him and other things together.

[2] Since it is possible to find in God every perfection of creatures, but in another and more eminent way, whatever names unqualifiedly designate a perfection without defect are predicated of God and of other things: for example, goodness, wisdom, being, and the like. But when

any name expresses such perfections along with a mode that is proper to a creature, it can be said of God only according to likeness and metaphor. According to metaphor, what belongs to one thing is transferred to another, as when we say that a man is a *stone* because of the hardness of his intellect. Such names are used to designate the species of a created thing, for example, *man* and *stone;* for to each species belongs its own mode of perfection and being. The same is true of whatever names designate the properties of things, which are caused by the proper principles of their species. Hence, they can be said of God only metaphorically. But the names that express such perfections along with the mode of supereminence with which they belong to God are said of God alone. Such names are the *highest good, the first being,* and the like.

[3]   I have said that some of the aforementioned names signify a perfection without defect. This is true with reference to that which the name was imposed to signify; for as to the mode of signification, every name is defective. For by means of a name we express things in the way in which the intellect conceives them. For our intellect, taking the origin of its knowledge from the senses, does not transcend the mode which is found in sensible things, in which the form and the subject of the form are not identical owing to the composition of form and matter. Now, a simple form is indeed found among such things, but one that is imperfect because it is not subsisting; on the other hand, though a subsisting subject of a form is found among sensible things, it is not simple but rather concreted. Whatever our intellect signifies as subsisting, therefore, it signifies in concretion; but what it signifies as simple, it signifies, not as *that which is,* but as *that by which something is.* As a result, with reference to the mode of signification there is in every name that we use an imperfection, which does not befit God, even though the thing signified in some eminent way does befit God. This is clear in the name *goodness* and *good.* For *goodness* has signification as something not subsisting, while *good* has signification as something concreted. And so with reference to the mode of signification no name is fittingly applied to God; this is done only with reference to that which the name has been imposed to signify. Such names, therefore, as Dionysius teaches, can be both affirmed and denied of God.

They can be affirmed because of the meaning of the name; they can be denied because of the mode of signification.

[4] Now, the mode of supereminence in which the above-mentioned perfections are found in God can be signified by names used by us only through negation, as when we say that God is *eternal* or *infinite,* or also through a relation of God to other things, as when He is called the *first cause* or the *highest good.* For we cannot grasp what God is, but only what He is not and how other things are related to Him, as is clear from what we said above.

CHAPTER 31

THAT THE DIVINE PERFECTION
AND THE PLURALITY OF DIVINE NAMES
ARE NOT OPPOSED TO THE DIVINE SIMPLICITY

[1] From what has been said it can likewise be seen that the divine perfection and the plurality of names said of God are not opposed to His simplicity.

[2] We have said that all the perfections found in other things are attributed to God in the same way as effects are found in their equivocal causes. These effects are in their causes virtually, as heat is in the sun. For, unless the power of the sun belonged to some extent to the genus of heat, the sun acting through this power would not generate anything like itself. The sun, then, is said to be hot through this power not only because it produces heat, but also because the power through which it does this has some likeness to heat. But through the same power through which it produces heat, the sun produces also many other effects among sublunary bodies — for example, dryness. And thus heat and dryness, which in fire are diverse qualities, belong to the sun through one and the same power. So, too, the perfections of all things, which belong to the rest of things through diverse forms, must be attributed to God through one and the same power in Him. This power is nothing other than His essence, since, as we have proved, there can be no accident in God. Thus, therefore, God is called *wise* not only in so far as He produces wisdom, but also because, in so far as we

are wise, we imitate to some extent the power by which He makes us wise. On the other hand, God is not called a *stone,* even though He has made stones, because in the name *stone* there is understood a determinate mode of being according to which a stone is distinguished from God. But the stone imitates God as its cause in being and goodness, and other such characteristics, as do also the rest of creatures.

[3] A similar situation obtains among the knowing and operative powers of man. For by its single power the intellect knows all the things that the sensitive part of the soul grasps through a diversity of powers — and many other things as well. So, too, the higher an intellect is, the more it can know more things through one likeness, while a lesser intellect manages to know many things only through many likenesses. So, too, a ruling power extends to all those things to which diverse powers under it are ordered. In this way, therefore, through His one simple being God possesses every kind of perfection that all other things come to possess, but in a much more diminished way, through diverse principles.

[4] From this we see the necessity of giving to God many names. For, since we cannot know Him naturally except by arriving at Him from His effects, the names by which we signify His perfection must be diverse, just as the perfections belonging to things are found to be diverse. Were we able to understand the divine essence itself as it is and give to it the name that belongs to it, we would express it by only one name. This is promised to those who will see God through His essence: "In that day there shall be one Lord, and His name shall be one" (Zach. 14:9).

CHAPTER 32

THAT NOTHING IS PREDICATED UNIVOCALLY OF GOD AND OTHER THINGS

[1] It is thereby evident that nothing can be predicated univocally of God and other things.

[2] An effect that does not receive a form specifically the same as that through which the agent acts cannot receive according to a univocal

predication the name arising from that form. Thus, the heat generated by the sun and the sun itself are not called univocally *hot*. Now, the forms of the things God has made do not measure up to a specific likeness of the divine power; for the things that God has made receive in a divided and particular way that which in Him is found in a simple and universal way. It is evident, then, that nothing can be said univocally of God and other things.

[3] If, furthermore, an effect should measure up to the species of its cause, it will not receive the univocal predication of the name unless it receives the same specific form according to the same mode of being. For the house that is in the art of the maker is not univocally the same house that is in matter, for the form of the house does not have the same being in the two locations. Now, even though the rest of things were to receive a form that is absolutely the same as it is in God, yet they do not receive it according to the same mode of being. For, as is clear from what we have said, there is nothing in God that is not the divine being itself, which is not the case with other things. Nothing, therefore, can be predicated of God and other things univocally.

[4] Moreover, whatever is predicated of many things univocally is either a genus, a species, a difference, an accident, or a property. But, as we have shown, nothing is predicated of God as a genus or a difference; and thus neither is anything predicated as a definition, nor likewise as a species, which is constituted of genus and difference. Nor, as we have shown, can there be any accident in God, and therefore nothing is predicated of Him either as an accident or a property, since property belongs to the genus of accidents. It remains, then, that nothing is predicated univocally of God and other things.

[5] Again, what is predicated of many things univocally is simpler than both of them, at least in concept. Now, there can be nothing simpler than God either in reality or in concept. Nothing, therefore, is predicated univocally of God and other things.

[6] Everything, likewise, that is predicated univocally of many things belongs through participation to each of the things of which it is predicated; for the species is said to participate in the genus and the individual in the species. But nothing is said of God by participation, since whatever is participated is determined to the mode of that which

is participated and is thus possessed in a partial way and not according to every mode of perfection. Nothing, therefore, can be predicated univocally of God and other things.

[7]   Then, too, what is predicated of some things according to priority and posteriority is certainly not predicated univocally. For the prior is included in the definition of the posterior, as *substance* is included in the definition of accident according as an accident is a being. If, then, being were said univocally of substance and accident, substance would have to be included in the definition of being in so far as being is predicated of substance. But this is clearly impossible. Now nothing is predicated of God and creatures as though they were in the same order, but, rather, according to priority and posteriority. For all things are predicated of God essentially. For God is called being as being entity itself, and He is called good as being goodness itself. But in other beings predications are made by participation, as Socrates is said to be a man, not because he is humanity itself, but because he possesses humanity. It is impossible, therefore, that anything be predicated univocally of God and other things.

CHAPTER 33

THAT NOT ALL NAMES ARE SAID OF GOD
AND CREATURES IN A PURELY EQUIVOCAL WAY

[1]   From what we have said it likewise appears that not everything predicated of God and other things is said in a purely equivocal way, in the manner of equivocals by chance.

[2]   For in equivocals by chance there is no order or reference of one to another, but it is entirely accidental that one name is applied to diverse things: the application of the name to one of them does not signify that it has an order to the other. But this is not the situation with names said of God and creatures, since we note in the community of such names the order of cause and effect, as is clear from what we have said. It is not, therefore, in the manner of pure equivocation that something is predicated of God and other things.

[3]   Furthermore, where there is pure equivocation, there is no likeness in things themselves; there is only the unity of a name. But, as is clear

from what we have said, there is a certain mode of likeness of things to God. It remains, then, that names are not said of God in a purely equivocal way.

[4] Moreover, when one name is predicated of several things in a purely equivocal way, we cannot from one of them be led to the knowledge of another; for the knowledge of things does not depend on words, but on the meaning of names. Now, from what we find in other things, we do arrive at a knowledge of divine things, as is evident from what we have said. Such names, then, are not said of God and other things in a purely equivocal way.

[5] Again, equivocation in a name impedes the process of reasoning. If, then, nothing was said of God and creatures except in a purely equivocal way, no reasoning proceeding from creatures to God could take place. But, the contrary is evident from all those who have spoken about God.

[6] It is also a fact that a name is predicated of some being uselessly unless through that name we understand something of the being. But, if names are said of God and creatures in a purely equivocal way, we understand nothing of God through those names; for the meanings of those names are known to us solely to the extent that they are said of creatures. In vain, therefore, would it be said or proved of God that He is a being, good, or the like.

[7] Should it be replied that through such names we know only what God is not, namely, that God is called *living* because He does not belong to the genus of lifeless things, and so with the other names, it will at least have to be the case that *living* said of God and creatures agrees in the denial of the lifeless. Thus, it will not be said in a purely equivocal way.

CHAPTER 34

THAT NAMES SAID OF GOD AND CREATURES ARE SAID ANALOGICALLY

[1] From what we have said, therefore, it remains that the names said of God and creatures are predicated neither univocally nor equivocally

but analogically, that is, according to an order or reference to something one.

[2]   This can take place in two ways. In one way, according as many things have reference to something one. Thus, with reference to one *health* we say that an animal is healthy as the subject of health, medicine is healthy as its cause, food as its preserver, urine as its sign.

[3]   In another way, the analogy can obtain according as the order or reference of two things is not to something else but to one of them. Thus, *being* is said of substance and accident according as an accident has reference to a substance, and not according as substance and accident are referred to a third thing.

[4]   Now, the names said of God and things are not said analogically according to the first mode of analogy, since we should then have to posit something prior to God, but according to the second mode.

[5]   In this second mode of analogical predication the order according to the name and according to reality is sometimes found to be the same and sometimes not. For the order of the name follows the order of knowledge, because it is the sign of an intelligible conception. When, therefore, that which is prior in reality is found likewise to be prior in knowledge, the same thing is found to be prior both according to the meaning of the name and according to the nature of the thing. Thus, substance is prior to accident both in nature, in so far as substance is the cause of accident, and in knowledge, in so far as substance is included in the definition of accident. Hence, *being* is said of substance by priority over accident both according to the nature of the thing and according to the meaning of the name. But when that which is prior in nature is subsequent in our knowledge, then there is not the same order in analogicals according to reality and according to the meaning of the name. Thus, the power to heal, which is found in all health-giving things, is by nature prior to the health that is in the animal, as a cause is prior to an effect; but because we know this healing power through an effect, we likewise name it from its effect. Hence it is that the *health-giving* is prior in reality, but animal is by priority called *healthy* according to the meaning of the name.

[6] Thus, therefore, because we come to a knowledge of God from other things, the reality in the names said of God and other things belongs

by priority in God according to His mode of being, but the meaning of the name belongs to God by posteriority. And so He is said to be named from His effects.

RENÉ DESCARTES

René Descartes (1596–1650) is considered to be the father of modern philosophy. Deep Platonic influences, such as a belief in innate ideas, the rejection of sensible appearances as a source of genuine knowledge, a belief in mathematics as the language of nature, and a virtual identification of the self with our reason, permeate his work. Yet his treatment of these themes was so revolutionary that his views largely set the agenda for subsequent philosophic inquiry in the early modern period.

In this selection from the *Meditations on First Philosophy* Descartes seeks foundations for all inquiry (with the exceptions of ethics and theology). Paradoxically, he believed that it was by the practice of methodical doubt that we can discover absolutely certain foundations for knowledge.

Among Descartes' intellectual achievements was the development of a conception of nature as a vast machine, operating by mechanical causes, and capable of being fully understood by the human mind. This conception of nature was a source of the deistic view of God's creative and providential activity, which is often conflated with a Christian view in present-day philosophy of religion.

Certainty of Self and God
(Meditations I–III)

MEDITATIONS ON THE FIRST PHILOSOPHY
IN WHICH THE EXISTENCE OF GOD
AND THE DISTINCTION BETWEEN MIND AND BODY
ARE DEMONSTRATED.

Meditation I.
Of the things which may be brought within the sphere
of the doubtful.

It is now some years since I detected how many were the false beliefs that I had from my earliest youth admitted as true, and how doubtful was everything I had since constructed on this basis; and from that time I was convinced that I must once for all seriously undertake to rid myself of all the opinions which I had formerly accepted, and commence to build anew from the foundation, if I wanted to establish any firm and permanent structure in the sciences. But as this enterprise appeared to be a very great one, I waited until I had attained an age so mature that I could not hope that at any later date I should be better fitted to execute my design. This reason caused me to delay so long that I should feel that I was doing wrong were I to occupy in deliberation the time that yet remains to me for action. To-day, then, since very opportunely for the plan I have in view I have delivered my mind from every care [and am happily agitated by no passions] and since I have procured for myself an assured leisure in a peaceable retirement, I shall at last seriously and freely address myself to the general upheaval of all my former opinions.

Now for this object it is not necessary that I should show that all of these are false — I shall perhaps never arrive at this end. But inasmuch as reason already persuades me that I ought no less carefully to withhold my assent from matters which are not entirely certain and indubitable than from those which appear to me manifestly to be false, if I am able to find in each one some reason to doubt, this will suffice to justify my rejecting the whole. And for that end it will not be requisite that I should examine each in particular, which would be an endless undertaking; for owing to the fact that the destruction of the foundations of necessity brings with it the downfall of the rest of the edifice, I shall only in the first place attack those principles upon which all my former opinions rested.

All that up to the present time I have accepted as most true and certain I have learned either from the senses or through the senses; but it is sometimes proved to me that these senses are deceptive, and it is wiser not to trust entirely to any thing by which we have once been deceived.

But it may be that although the senses sometimes deceive us concerning things which are hardly perceptible, or very far away, there are yet many others to be met with as to which we cannot reasonably have any doubt, although we recognise them by their means. For example, there is the fact that I am here, seated by the fire, attired in a dressing gown, having this paper in my hands and other similar matters. And how could I deny that these hands and this body are mine, were it not perhaps that I compare myself to certain persons, devoid of sense, whose cerebella are so troubled and clouded by the violent vapours of black bile, that they constantly assure us that they think they are kings when they are really quite poor, or that they are clothed in purple when they are really without covering, or who imagine that they have an earthenware head or are nothing but pumpkins or are made of glass. But they are mad, and I should not be any the less insane were I to follow examples so extravagant.

At the same time I must remember that I am a man, and that consequently I am in the habit of sleeping, and in my dreams representing to myself the same things or sometimes even less probable things, than do those who are insane in their waking moments. How often has it happened to me that in the night I dreamt that I found myself in this particular place, that I was dressed and seated near the fire, whilst in reality I was lying undressed in bed! At this moment it does indeed seem to me that it is with eyes awake that I am looking at this paper; that this head which I move is not asleep, that it is deliberately and of set purpose that I extend my hand and perceive it; what happens in sleep does not appear so clear nor so distinct as does all this. But in thinking over this I remind myself that on many occasions I have in sleep been deceived by similar illusions, and in dwelling carefully on this reflection I see so manifestly that there are no certain indications by which we may clearly distinguish wakefulness from sleep that

I am lost in astonishment. And my astonishment is such that it is almost capable of persuading me that I now dream.

Now let us assume that we are asleep and that all these particulars, e.g. that we open our eyes, shake our head, extend our hands, and so on, are but false delusions; and let us reflect that possibly neither our hands nor our whole body are such as they appear to us to be. At the same time we must at least confess that the things which are represented to us in sleep are like painted representations which can only have been formed as the counterparts of something real and true, and that in this way those general things at least, i.e. eyes, a head, hands, and a whole body, are not imaginary things, but things really existent. For, as a matter of fact, painters, even when they study with the greatest skill to represent sirens and satyrs by forms the most strange and extraordinary, cannot give them natures which are entirely new, but merely make a certain medley of the members of different animals; or if their imagination is extravagant enough to invent something so novel that nothing similar has ever before been seen, and that then their work represents a thing purely fictitious and absolutely false, it is certain all the same that the colours of which this is composed are necessarily real. And for the same reason, although these general things, to wit, [a body], eyes, a head, hands, and such like, may be imaginary, we are bound at the same time to confess that there are at least some other objects yet more simple and more universal, which are real and true; and of these just in the same way as with certain real colours, all these images of things which dwell in our thoughts, whether true and real or false and fantastic, are formed.

To such a class of things pertains corporeal nature in general, and its extension, the figure of extended things, their quantity or magnitude and number, as also the place in which they are, the time which measures their duration, and so on.

That is possibly why our reasoning is not unjust when we conclude from this that Physics, Astronomy, Medicine and all other sciences which have as their end the consideration of composite things, are very dubious and uncertain; but that Arithmetic, Geometry and other sciences of that kind which only treat of things that are very simple and very general, without taking great trouble to ascertain whether they are actually existent or not, contain some measure of certainty and an element of the indubitable. For whether I am awake or asleep, two and three together always form five, and the square can never have more than four sides, and it does not seem possible that truths so clear and apparent can be suspected of any falsity [or uncertainty].

Nevertheless I have long had fixed in my mind the belief that an all-powerful God existed by whom I have been created such as I am. But how do I know that He has not brought it to pass that there is no earth, no heaven, no extended body, no magnitude, no place, and that nevertheless [I possess the perceptions of all these things and that] they seem to me to exist just exactly as I now see them? And, besides, as I sometimes imagine that others deceive themselves in the things which they think they know best, how do I know that I am not deceived every time that I add two and three, or count the sides of a square, or judge of things yet simpler, if anything simpler can be imagined? But possibly God has not desired that I should be thus deceived, for He is said to be supremely good. If, however, it is contrary to His goodness to have made me such that I constantly deceive myself, it would also appear to be contrary to His goodness to permit me to be sometimes deceived, and nevertheless I cannot doubt that He does permit this.

There may indeed be those who would prefer to deny the existence of a God so powerful, rather than believe that all other things are uncertain. But let us not oppose them for the present, and grant that all that is here said of a God is a fable; nevertheless in whatever way they suppose that I have arrived at the state of being that I have reached — whether they attribute it to fate or to accident, or make out that it is by a continual succession of antecedents, or by some other method — since to err and deceive oneself is a defect, it is clear that the greater will be the probability of my being so imperfect as to deceive myself ever, as is the Author to whom they assign my origin the less powerful. To these reasons I have certainly nothing to reply, but at the end I feel constrained to confess that there is nothing in all that I formerly believed to be true, of which I cannot in some measure doubt, and that not merely through want of thought or through levity, but for reasons which are very powerful and maturely considered; so that henceforth I ought not the less carefully to refrain from giving credence to these opinions than to that which is manifestly false, if I desire to arrive at any certainty [in the sciences].

But it is not sufficient to have made these remarks, we must also be careful to keep them in mind. For these ancient and commonly held

opinions still revert frequently to my mind, long and familiar custom
having given them the right to occupy my mind against my inclination
and rendered them almost masters of my belief; nor will I ever lose
the habit of deferring to them or of placing my confidence in them,
so long as I consider them as they really are, i.e. opinions in some
measure doubtful, as I have just shown, and at the same time highly
probable, so that there is much more reason to believe in than to deny
them. That is why I consider that I shall not be acting amiss, if, taking
of set purpose a contrary belief, I allow myself to be deceived, and for
a certain time pretend that all these opinions are entirely false and
imaginary, until at last, having thus balanced my former prejudices with
my latter [so that they cannot divert my opinions more to one side than
to the other], my judgment will no longer be dominated by bad usage
or turned away from the right knowledge of the truth. For I am assured
that there can be neither peril nor error in this course, and that I cannot at present yield too much to distrust, since I am not considering
the question of action, but only of knowledge.

I shall then suppose, not that God who is supremely good and the
fountain of truth, but some evil genius not less powerful than deceit-
ful, has employed his whole energies in deceiving me; I shall consider
that the heavens, the earth, colours, figures, sound, and all other
external things are nought but the illusions and dreams of which this
genius has availed himself in order to lay traps for my credulity; I shall
consider myself as having no hands, no eyes, no flesh, no blood, nor
any senses, yet falsely believing myself to possess all these things; I shall
remain obstinately attached to this idea, and if by this means it is not
in my power to arrive at the knowledge of any truth, I may at least
do what is in my power [i.e. suspend my judgment], and with firm
purpose avoid giving credence to any false thing, or being imposed upon
by this arch deceiver, however powerful and deceptive he may be. But
this task is a laborious one, and insensibly a certain lassitude leads me
into the course of my ordinary life. And just as a captive who in sleep
enjoys an imaginary liberty, when he begins to suspect that his liberty
is but a dream, fears to awaken, and conspires with these agreeable
illusions that the deception may be prolonged, so insensibly of my own
accord I fall back into my former opinions, and I dread awakening from
this slumber, lest the laborious wakefulness which would follow the
tranquillity of this repose should have to be spent not in daylight, but

in the excessive darkness of the difficulties which have just been discussed.

Meditation II.
*Of the Nature of the Human Mind;
and that it is more easily known than the Body.*

The Meditation of yesterday filled my mind with so many doubts that it is no longer in my power to forget them. And yet I do not see in what manner I can resolve them; and, just as if I had all of a sudden fallen into very deep water, I am so disconcerted that I can neither make certain of setting my feet on the bottom, nor can I swim and so support myself on the surface. I shall nevertheless make an effort and follow anew the same path as that on which I yesterday entered, i.e. I shall proceed by setting aside all that in which the least doubt could be supposed to exist, just as if I had discovered that it was absolutely false; and I shall ever follow in this road until I have met with something which is certain, or at least, if I can do nothing else, until I have learned for certain that there is nothing in the world that is certain. Archimedes, in order that he might draw the terrestrial globe out of its place, and transport it elsewhere, demanded only that one point should be fixed and immoveable; in the same way I shall have the right to conceive high hopes if I am happy enough to discover one thing only which is certain and indubitable.

I suppose, then, that all the things that I see are false; I persuade myself that nothing has ever existed of all that my fallacious memory represents to me. I consider that I possess no senses; I imagine that body, figure, extension, movement and place are but the fictions of my mind. What, then, can be esteemed as true? Perhaps nothing at all, unless that there is nothing in the world that is certain.

But how can I know there is not something different from those things that I have just considered, of which one cannot have the slightest doubt? Is there not some God, or some other being by whatever name we call it, who puts these reflections into my mind? That is not necessary, for is it not possible that I am capable of producing them myself? I myself, am I not at least something? But I have already denied that I had senses and body. Yet I hesitate, for what follows from that? Am I so dependent on body and senses that I cannot exist without these?

117

But I was persuaded that there was nothing in all the world, that there was no heaven, no earth, that there were no minds, nor any bodies: was I not then likewise persuaded that I did not exist? Not at all; of a surety I myself did exist since I persuaded myself of something [or merely because I thought of something]. But there is some deceiver or other, very powerful and very cunning, who ever employs his ingenuity in deceiving me. Then without doubt I exist also if he deceives me, and let him deceive me as much as he will, he can never cause me to be nothing so long as I think that I am something. So that after having reflected well and carefully examined all things, we must come to the definite conclusion that this proposition: I am, I exist, is necessarily true each time that I pronounce it, or that I mentally conceive it.

But I do not yet know clearly enough what I am, I who am certain that I am; and hence I must be careful to see that I do not imprudently take some other object in place of myself, and thus that I do not go astray in respect of this knowledge that I hold to be the most certain and most evident of all that I have formerly learned. That is why I shall now consider anew what I believed myself to be before I embarked upon these last reflections; and of my former opinions I shall withdraw all that might even in a small degree be invalidated by the reasons which I have just brought forward, in order that there may be nothing at all left beyond what is absolutely certain and indubitable.

What then did I formerly believe myself to be? Undoubtedly I believed myself to be a man. But what is a man? Shall I say a reasonable animal? Certainly not; for then I should have to inquire what an animal is, and what is reasonable; and thus from a single question I should insensibly fall into an infinitude of others more difficult; and I should not wish to waste the little time and leisure remaining to me in trying to unravel subtleties like these. But I shall rather stop here to consider the thoughts which of themselves spring up in my mind, and which were not inspired by anything beyond my own nature alone when I applied myself to the consideration of my being. In the first place, then, I considered myself as having a face, hands, arms, and all that system of members composed of bones and flesh as seen in a corpse which I designated by the name of body. In addition to this I considered that I was nourished, that I walked, that I felt, and that I thought, and I referred all these actions to the soul: but I did not stop to consider what the soul was, or if I did stop, I imagined that it was something extremely rare and subtle like a wind, a flame, or an ether, which was spread throughout my grosser parts. As to body I had no manner of doubt about its nature, but thought I had a very clear knowledge of it; and if I had desired to explain it according to the notions that I had then formed of it, I should have described it thus: By the body I understand all that which can be defined by a certain figure: something which can be confined in a certain place, and which can fill a given space in such a way that every other body will be excluded from it; which can be perceived either by touch, or by sight, or by hearing, or by taste, or by smell: which can be moved in many ways not, in truth, by itself, but by something which is foreign to it, by which it is touched [and from which it receives impressions]: for to have the power of self-movement, as also of feeling or of thinking, I did not consider to appertain to the nature of body: on the contrary, I was rather astonished to find that faculties similar to them existed in some bodies.

But what am I, now that I suppose that there is a certain genius which is extremely powerful, and, if I may say so, malicious, who employs all his powers in deceiving me? Can I affirm that I possess the least of all those things which I have just said pertain to the nature of body? I pause to consider, I revolve all these things in my mind, and I find none of which I can say that it pertains to me. It would be tedious to stop to enumerate them. Let us pass to the attributes of soul and see if there is any one which is in me? What of nutrition or walking [the first mentioned]? But if it is so that I have no body it is also true that I can neither walk nor take nourishment. Another attribute is sensation. But one cannot feel without body, and besides I have thought I perceived many things during sleep that I recognised in my waking moments as not having been experienced at all. What of thinking? I find here that thought is an attribute that belongs to me; it alone cannot be separated from me. I am, I exist, that is certain. But how often? Just when I think; for it might possibly be the case if I ceased entirely to think, that I should likewise cease altogether to exist. I do not now admit anything which is not necessarily true: to speak accurately I am not more than a thing which thinks, that is to say a mind or a soul, or an understanding, or a reason, which are terms whose significance was formerly unknown to me. I am, however, a real thing and really exist; but what thing? I have answered: a thing which thinks.

And what more? I shall exercise my imagination [in order to see if I am not something more]. I am not a collection of members which we call the human body: I am not a subtle air distributed through these members, I am not a wind, a fire, a vapour, a breath, nor anything at all which I can imagine or conceive; because I have assumed that all these were nothing. Without changing that supposition I find that I only leave myself certain of the fact that I am somewhat. But perhaps it is true that these same things which I supposed were non-existent because they are unknown to me, are really not different from the self which I know. I am not sure about this, I shall not dispute about it now; I can only give judgment on things that are known to me. I know that I exist, and I inquire what I am, I whom I know to exist. But it is very certain that the knowledge of my existence taken in its precise significance does not depend on things whose existence is not yet known to me; consequently it does not depend on those which I can feign in imagination. And indeed the very term *feign* in imagination proves to me my error, for I really do this if I image myself a something, since to imagine is nothing else than to contemplate the figure or image of a corporeal thing. But I already know for certain that I am, and that it may be that all these images and, speaking generally, all things that relate to the nature of body are nothing but dreams [and chimeras]. For this reason I see clearly that I have as little reason to say, 'I shall stimulate my imagination in order to know more distinctly what I am,' than if I were to say, 'I am now awake, and I perceive somewhat that is real and true: but because I do not yet perceive it distinctly enough, I shall go to sleep of express purpose, so that my dreams may represent the perception with greatest truth and evidence.' And, thus, I know for certain that nothing of all that I can understand by means of my imagination belongs to this knowledge which I have of myself, and that it is necessary to recall the mind from this mode of thought with the utmost diligence in order that it may be able to know its own nature with perfect distinctness.

But what then am I? A thing which thinks. What is a thing which thinks? It is a thing which doubts, understands, [conceives], affirms, denies, wills, refuses, which also imagines and feels.

Certainly it is no small matter if all these things pertain to my nature. But why should they not so pertain? Am I not that being who now doubts nearly everything, who nevertheless understands certain things, who affirms that one only is true, who denies all the others, who desires to know more, is averse from being deceived, who imagines many things, sometimes indeed despite his will, and who perceives many likewise, as by the intervention of the bodily organs? Is there nothing in all this which is as true as it is certain that I exist, even though I should always sleep and though he who has given me being employed all his ingenuity in deceiving me? Is there likewise any one of these attributes which can be distinguished from my thought, or which might be said to be separated from myself? For it is so evident of itself that it is I who doubts, who understands, and who desires, that there is no reason here to add anything to explain it. And I have certainly the power of imagining likewise; for although it may happen (as I formerly supposed) that none of the things which I imagine are true, nevertheless this power of imagining does not cease to be really in use, and it forms part of my thought. Finally, I am the same who feels, that is to say, who perceives certain things, as by the organs of sense, since in truth I see light, I hear noise, I feel heat. But it will be said that these phenomena are false and that I am dreaming. Let it be so; still it is at least quite certain that it seems to me that I see light, that I hear noise and that I feel heat. That cannot be false; properly speaking it is what is in me called feeling; and used in this precise sense that is no other thing than thinking.

From this time I begin to know what I am with a little more clearness and distinction than before; but nevertheless it still seems to me, and I cannot prevent myself from thinking, that corporeal things, whose images are framed by thought, which are tested by the senses, are much more distinctly known than that obscure part of me which does not come under the imagination. Although really it is very strange to say that I know and understand more distinctly these things whose existence seems to me dubious, which are unknown to me, and which do not belong to me, than others of the truth of which I am convinced, which are known to me and which pertain to my real nature, in a word, than myself. But I see clearly how the case stands: my mind loves to wander, and cannot yet suffer itself to be retained within the just limits of truth. Very good, let us once more give it the freest rein, so that, when afterwards we seize the proper occasion for pulling up, it may the more easily be regulated and controlled.

Let us begin by considering the commonest matters, those which we believe to be the most distinctly comprehended, to wit, the bodies which we touch and see; not indeed bodies in general, for these general ideas are usually a little more confused, but let us consider one body in particular. Let us take, for example, this piece of wax: it has been taken quite freshly from the hive, and it has not yet lost the sweetness of the honey which it contains; it still retains somewhat of the odour of the flowers from which it has been culled; its colour, its figure, its size are apparent; it is hard, cold, easily handled, and if you strike it with the finger, it will emit a sound. Finally all the things which are requisite to cause us distinctly to recognise a body, are met with in it. But notice that while I speak and approach the fire what remained of the taste is exhaled, the smell evaporates, the colour alters, the figure is destroyed, the size increases, it becomes liquid, it heats, scarcely can one handle it, and when one strikes it, no sound is emitted. Does the same wax remain after this change? We must confess that it remains; none would judge otherwise. What then did I know so distinctly in this piece of wax? It could certainly be nothing of all that the senses brought to my notice, since all these things which fall under taste, smell, sight, touch, and hearing, are found to be changed, and yet the same wax remains.

Perhaps it was what I now think, viz. that this wax was not that sweetness of honey, nor that agreeable scent of flowers, nor that particular whiteness, nor that figure, nor that sound, but simply a body which a little while before appeared to me as perceptible under these forms, and which is now perceptible under others. But what, precisely, is it that I imagine when I form such conceptions? Let us attentively consider this, and, abstracting from all that does not belong to the wax, let us see what remains. Certainly nothing remains excepting a certain extended thing which is flexible and movable. But what is the meaning of flexible and movable? Is it not that I imagine that this piece of wax being round is capable of becoming square and of passing from a square to a triangular figure? No, certainly it is not that, since I imagine it admits of an infinitude of similar changes, and I nevertheless do not know how to compass the infinitude by my imagination, and consequently this conception which I have of the wax is not brought about by the faculty of imagination. What now is this extension? Is it not also unknown? For it becomes greater when the wax is melted, greater when it is boiled, and greater still when the heat increases; and I should not conceive [clearly] according to truth what wax is, if I did not think that even this piece that we are considering is capable of receiving more variations in extension than I have ever imagined. We must then grant that I could not even understand through the imagination what this piece of wax is, and that it is my mind alone which perceives it. I say this piece of wax in particular, for as to wax in general it is yet clearer. But what is this piece of wax which cannot be understood excepting by the [understanding or] mind? It is certainly the same that I see, touch, imagine, and finally it is the same which I have always believed it to be from the beginning. But what must particularly be observed is that its perception is neither an act of vision, nor of touch, nor of imagination, and has never been such although it may have appeared formerly to be so, but only an intuition of the mind, which may be imperfect and confused as it was formerly, or clear and distinct as it is at present, according as my attention is more or less directed to the elements which are found in it, and of which it is composed.

Yet in the meantime I am greatly astonished when I consider [the great feebleness of mind] and its proneness to fall [insensibly] into error; for although without giving expression to my thoughts I consider all this in my own mind, words often impede me and I am almost deceived by the terms of ordinary language. For we say that we see the same wax, if it is present, and not that we simply judge that it is the same from its having the same colour and figure. From this I should conclude that I knew the wax by means of vision and not simply by the intuition of the mind; unless by chance I remember that, when looking from a window and saying I see men who pass in the street, I really do not see them, but infer that what I see is men, just as I say that I see wax. And yet what do I see from the window but hats and coats which may cover automatic machines? Yet I judge these to be men. And similarly solely by the faculty of judgment which rests in my mind, I comprehend that which I believed I saw with my eyes.

A man who makes it his aim to raise his knowledge above the common should be ashamed to derive the occasion for doubting from the forms of speech invented by the vulgar; I prefer to pass on and consider whether I had a more evident and perfect conception of what the wax was when I first perceived it, and when I believed I knew it by means of the external senses or at least by the common sense, as it is called, that is to say by the imaginative faculty, or whether my present conception is clearer now that I have most carefully examined what it is, and in what way it can be known. It would certainly be absurd to doubt as to this. For what was there in this first perception which was distinct? What was there which might not as well have been perceived by any of the animals? But when I distinguish the wax from its external forms, and when, just as if I had taken from it its vestments, I consider it quite naked, it is certain that although some error may still be found in my judgment, I can nevertheless not perceive it thus without a human mind.

But finally what shall I say of this mind, that is, of myself, for up to this point I do not admit in myself anything but mind? What then, I who seem to perceive this piece of wax so distinctly, do I not know myself, not only with much more truth and certainty, but also with much more distinctness and clearness? For if I judge that the wax is or exists from the fact that I see it, it certainly follows much more clearly that I am or that I exist myself from the fact that I see it. For it may be that what I see is not really wax, it may also be that I do not possess eyes with which to see anything; but it cannot be that when I see, or (for I no longer take account of the distinction) when I think I see, that I myself who think am nought. So if I judge that the wax exists from the fact that I touch it, the same thing will follow, to wit, that I am; and if I judge that my imagination, or some other cause, whatever it is, persuades me that the wax exists, I shall still conclude the same. And what I have here remarked of wax may be applied to all other things which are external to me [and which are met with outside of me]. And further, if the [notion or] perception of wax has seemed to me clearer and more distinct, not only after the sight or the touch, but also after many other causes have rendered it quite manifest to me, with how much more [evidence] and distinctness must it be said that I now know myself, since all the reasons which contribute to the knowledge of wax, or any other body whatever, are yet better proofs of the nature of my mind! And there are so many other things in the mind itself which may contribute to the elucidation of its nature, that those which depend on body such as these just mentioned, hardly merit being taken into account.

But finally here I am, having insensibly reverted to the point I desired, for, since it is now manifest to me that even bodies are not properly speaking known by the senses or by the faculty of imagination, but by the understanding only, and since they are not known from the fact that they are seen or touched, but only because they are understood, I see clearly that there is nothing which is easier for me to know than my mind. But because it is difficult to rid oneself so promptly of an opinion to which one was accustomed for so long, it will be well that I should halt a little at this point, so that by the length of my meditation I may more deeply imprint on my memory this new knowledge.

Meditation III.
Of God: that He exists.

I shall now close my eyes, I shall stop my ears, I shall call away all my senses, I shall efface even from my thoughts all the images of corporeal things, or at least (for that is hardly possible) I shall esteem them as vain and false; and thus holding converse only with myself and considering my own nature, I shall try little by little to reach a better knowledge of and a more familiar acquaintanceship with myself. I am a thing that thinks, that is to say, that doubts, affirms, denies, that knows a few things, that is ignorant of many [that loves, that hates], that wills, that desires, that also imagines and perceives; for as I remarked before, although the things which I perceive and imagine are perhaps nothing at all apart from me and in themselves, I am nevertheless assured that these modes of thought that I call perceptions and imaginations, inasmuch only as they are modes of thought, certainly reside [and are met with] in me.

And in the little that I have just said, I think I have summed up all that I really know, or at least all that hitherto I was aware that I knew. In order to try to extend my knowledge further, I shall now look around more carefully and see whether I cannot still discover in myself some other things which I have not hitherto perceived. I am certain that I am a thing which thinks; but do I not then likewise know what is requisite to render me certain of a truth? Certainly in this first knowledge there is nothing that assures me of its truth, excepting the clear and distinct perception of that which I state, which would not indeed suffice to assure me that what I say is true, if it could ever happen that a thing which I conceived so clearly and distinctly could be false; and accordingly it seems to me that already I can establish as a general rule that all things which I perceive very clearly and very distinctly are true.

At the same time I have before received and admitted many things to be very certain and manifest, which yet I afterwards recognised as being dubious. What then were these things? They were the earth, sky, stars and all other objects which I apprehended by means of the senses. But what did I clearly [and distinctly] perceive in them? Nothing more than that the ideas or thoughts of these things were presented to my mind. And not even now do I deny that these ideas are met with in me. But there was yet another thing which I affirmed, and which, owing to the habit which I had formed of believing it, I thought I perceived very clearly, although in truth I did not perceive it at all, to wit, that there were objects outside of me from which these ideas proceeded, and to which they were entirely similar. And it was in this that I erred, or, if perchance my judgment was correct, this was not due to any knowledge arising from my perception.

But when I took anything very simple and easy in the sphere of arithmetic or geometry into consideration, e.g. that two and three together made five, and other things of the sort, were not these present to my mind so clearly as to enable me to affirm that they were true? Certainly if I judged that since such matters could be doubted, this would not have been so for any other reason than that it came into my mind that perhaps a God might have endowed me with such a nature that I may have been deceived even concerning things which seemed to me most manifest. But every time that this preconceived opinion of the sovereign power of a God presents itself to my thought, I am constrained to confess that it is easy to Him, if He wishes it, to cause me to err, even in matters in which I believe myself to have the best evidence. And, on the other hand, always when I direct my attention to things which I believe myself to perceive very clearly, I am so persuaded of their truth that I let myself break out into words such as these: Let who will deceive me, He can never cause me to be nothing while I think that I am, or some day cause it to be true to say that I have never been, it being true now to say that I am, or that two and three make more or less than five, or any such thing in which I see a manifest contradiction. And, certainly, since I have no reason to believe that there is a God who is a deceiver, and as I have not yet satisfied myself that there is a God at all, the reason for doubt which depends on this opinion alone is very slight, and so to speak metaphysical. But in order to be able altogether to remove it, I must inquire whether there is a God as soon as the occasion presents itself; and if I find that there is a God, I must also inquire whether He may be a deceiver; for without a knowledge of these two truths I do not see that I can ever be certain of anything.

And in order that I may have an opportunity of inquiring into this in an orderly way [without interrupting the order of meditation which I have proposed to myself, and which is little by little to pass from the notions which I find first of all in my mind to those which I shall later on discover in it] it is requisite that I should here divide my thoughts into certain kinds, and that I should consider in which of these kinds there is, properly speaking, truth or error to be found. Of my thoughts some are, so to speak, images of the things, and to these alone is the title 'idea' properly applied; examples are my thought of a man or of a chimera, of heaven, of an angel, or [even] of God. But other thoughts possess other forms as well. For example in willing, fearing, approving, denying, though I always perceive something as the subject of the action of my mind, yet by this action I always add something else to the idea which I have of that thing; and of the thoughts of this kind some are called volitions or affections, and others judgments.

Now as to what concerns ideas, if we consider them only in themselves and do not relate them to anything else beyond themselves, they cannot properly speaking be false; for whether I imagine a goat or a chimera, it is not less true that I imagine the one than the other. We must not fear likewise that falsity can enter into will and into affections, for although I may desire evil things, or even things that never existed, it is not the less true that I desire them. Thus there remains no more than the judgments which we make, in which I must take the greatest care not to deceive myself. But the principal error and the commonest which we may meet with in them, consists in my judging that the ideas which are in me are similar or conformable to the things which are outside me; for without doubt if I considered the ideas only as certain modes of my thoughts, without trying to relate them to anything beyond, they could scarcely give me material for error.

But among these ideas, some appear to me to be innate, some adventitious, and others to be formed [or invented] by myself; for, as I have the power of understanding what is called a thing, or a truth, or a thought, it appears to me that I hold this power from no other source than my own nature. But if I now hear some sound, if I see the sun, or feel heat, I have hitherto judged that these sensations proceeded from certain things that exist outside of me; and finally it appears to me that sirens, hippogryphs, and the like, are formed out of my own mind. But again I may possibly persuade myself that all these ideas are of the nature of those which I term adventitious, or else that they are all innate, or all fictitious: for I have not yet clearly discovered their true origin.

And my principal task in this place is to consider, in respect to those ideas which appear to me to proceed from certain objects that are outside me, what are the reasons which cause me to think them similar to these objects. It seems indeed in the first place that I am taught this lesson by nature; and, secondly, I experience in myself that these ideas do not depend on my will nor therefore on myself—for they often present themselves to my mind in spite of my will. Just now, for instance, whether I will or whether I do not will, I feel heat, and thus I persuade myself that this feeling, or at least this idea of heat, is produced in me by something which is different from me, i.e. by the heat of the fire near which I sit. And nothing seems to me more obvious than to judge that this object imprints its likeness rather than anything else upon me.

Now I must discover whether these proofs are sufficiently strong and convincing. When I say that I am so instructed by nature, I merely mean a certain spontaneous inclination which impels me to believe in this connection, and not a natural light which makes me recognise that it is true. But these two things are very different; for I cannot doubt that which the natural light causes me to believe to be true, as, for example, it has shown me that I am from the fact that I doubt, or other facts of the same kind. And I possess no other faculty whereby to distinguish truth from falsehood, which can teach me that what this light shows me to be true is not really true, and no other faculty that is equally trustworthy. But as far as [apparently] natural impulses are concerned, I have frequently remarked, when I had to make active choice between virtue and vice, that they often enough led me to the part that was worse; and this is why I do not see any reason for following them in what regards truth and error.

And as to the other reason, which is that these ideas must proceed from objects outside me, since they do not depend on my will, I do not find it any the more convincing. For just as these impulses of which I have spoken are found in me, notwithstanding that they do not always concur with my will, so perhaps there is in me some faculty fitted to produce these ideas without the assistance of any external things, even though it is not yet known by me; just as, apparently, they have hitherto always been found in me during sleep without the aid of any external objects.

And finally, though they did proceed from objects different from myself, it is not a necessary consequence that they should resemble these. On the contrary, I have noticed that in many cases there was a great difference between the object and its idea. I find, for example, two completely diverse ideas of the sun in my mind; the one derives its origin from the senses, and should be placed in the category of adventitious ideas; according to this idea the sun seems to be extremely small; but the other is derived from astronomical reasonings, i.e. is elicited from certain notions that are innate in me, or else it is formed by me in some other manner; in accordance with it the sun appears to be several times greater than the earth. These two ideas cannot, indeed, both resemble the same sun, and reason makes me believe that the one which seems to have originated directly from the sun itself, is the one which is most dissimilar to it.

All this causes me to believe that until the present time it has not been by a judgment that was certain [or premeditated], but only by a sort of blind impulse that I believed that things existed outside of, and different from me, which, by the organs of my senses, or by some other method whatever it might be, conveyed these ideas or images to me [and imprinted on me their similitudes].

But there is yet another method of inquiring whether any of the objects of which I have ideas within me exist outside of me. If ideas are only taken as certain modes of thought, I recognise amongst them no difference or inequality, and all appear to proceed from me in the same manner; but when we consider them as images, one representing one thing and the other another, it is clear that they are very different one from the other. There is no doubt that those which represent to me substances are something more and contain so to speak more objective reality within them [that is to say, by representation participate in a higher degree of being or perfection] than those that simply represent modes or accidents; and that idea again by which I understand a supreme God, eternal, infinite, [immutable], omniscient, omnipotent, and Creator of all things which are outside of Himself, has certainly more objective reality in itself than those ideas by which finite substances are represented.

Now it is manifest by the natural light that there must at least be as much reality in the efficient and total cause as in its effect. For, pray, whence can the effect derive its reality, if not from its cause? And in what way can this cause communicate this reality to it, unless it possessed it in itself? And from this it follows, not only that something cannot proceed from nothing, but likewise that what is more perfect—that is to say, which has more reality within itself—cannot proceed from the less perfect. And this is not only evidently true of those effects which possess actual or formal reality, but also of the ideas in which we consider merely what is termed objective reality. To take an example, the stone which has not yet existed not only cannot now commence to be unless it has been produced by something which possesses within itself, either formally or eminently, all that enters into the composition of the stone [i.e. it must possess the same things or other more excellent things than those which exist in the stone] and heat can only be produced in a subject in which it did not previously exist by a cause that is of an order [degree or kind] at least as perfect as heat, and so in all other cases. But further, the idea of heat, or of a stone, cannot exist in me unless it has been placed within me by some cause which possesses within it at least as much reality as that which I conceive to exist in the heat or the stone. For although this cause does not transmit anything of its actual or formal reality to my idea, we must not for that reason imagine that it is necessarily a less real cause; we must remember that [since every idea is a work of the mind] its nature is such that it demands of itself no other formal reality than that which it borrows from my thought, of which it is only a mode [i.e. a manner or way of thinking]. But in order that an idea should contain some one certain objective reality rather than another, it must without doubt derive it from some cause in which there is at least as much formal reality as this idea contains of objective reality. For if we imagine that something is found in an idea which is not found in the cause, it must then have been derived from nought; but however imperfect may be this mode of being by which a thing is objectively [or by representation] in the understanding by its idea, we cannot certainly say that this mode of being is nothing, nor, consequently, that the idea derives its origin from nothing.

Nor must I imagine that, since the reality that I consider in these ideas is only objective, it is not essential that this reality should be formally in the causes of my ideas, but that it is sufficient that it should be found objectively. For just as this mode of objective existence pertains to ideas by their proper nature, so does the mode of formal existence pertain to the causes of those ideas (this is at least true of the first and principal) by the nature peculiar to them. And although it may be the case that one idea gives birth to another idea, that cannot continue to be so indefinitely; for in the end we must reach an idea whose cause shall be so to speak an archetype, in which the whole reality [or perfection] which is so to speak objectively [or by representation] in these ideas is contained formally [and really]. Thus the light of nature causes me to know clearly that the ideas in me are like [pictures or] images which can, in truth, easily fall short of the perfection of the objects from which they have been derived, but which can never contain anything greater or more perfect.

And the longer and the more carefully that I investigate these matters, the more clearly and distinctly do I recognise their truth. But what am I to conclude from it all in the end? It is this, that if the objective reality of any one of my ideas is of such a nature as clearly to make me recognise that it is not in me either formally or eminently, and that consequently I cannot myself be the cause of it, it follows of necessity that I am not alone in the world, but that there is another being which exists, or which is the cause of this idea. On the other hand, had no such an idea existed in me, I should have had no sufficient argument to convince me of the existence of any being beyond myself; for I have made very careful investigation everywhere and up to the present time have been able to find no other ground.

But of my ideas, beyond that which represents me to myself, as to which there can here be no difficulty, there is another which represents a God, and there are others representing corporeal and inanimate things, others angels, others animals, and others again which represent to me men similar to myself.

As regards the ideas which represent to me other men or animals, or angels, I can however easily conceive that they might be formed by an admixture of the other ideas which I have of myself, of corporeal things, and of God, even although there were apart from me neither men nor animals, nor angels, in all the world.

And in regard to the ideas of corporeal objects, I do not recognise in them anything so great or so excellent that they might not have possibly proceeded from myself; for if I consider them more closely, and examine them individually, as I yesterday examined the idea of wax, I find that there is very little in them which I perceive clearly and distinctly. Magnitude or extension in length, breadth, or depth, I do so perceive; also figure which results from a termination of this extension, the situation which bodies of different figure preserve in relation to one another, and movement or change of situation; to which we may also add substance, duration and number. As to other things such as light, colours, sounds, scents, tastes, heat, cold and the other tactile qualities, they are thought by me with so much obscurity and confusion that I do not even know if they are true or false, i.e. whether the ideas which I form of these qualities are actually the ideas of real objects or not [or whether they only represent chimeras which cannot exist in fact]. For although I have before remarked that it is only in judgments that falsity, properly speaking, or formal falsity, can be met with, a certain material falsity may nevertheless be found in ideas, i.e. when these ideas represent what is nothing as though it were something. For example, the ideas which I have of cold and heat are so far from clear and distinct that by their means I cannot tell whether cold is merely a privation of heat, or heat a privation of cold, or whether both are real qualities, or are not such. And inasmuch as [since ideas resemble images] there cannot be any ideas which do not appear to represent some things, if it is correct to say that cold is merely a privation of heat, the idea which represents it to me as something real and positive will not be improperly termed false, and the same holds good of other similar ideas.

To these it is certainly not necessary that I should attribute any author other than myself. For if they are false, i.e. if they represent things which do not exist, the light of nature shows me that they issue from nought, that is to say, that they are only in me in so far as something is lacking to the perfection of my nature. But if they are true, nevertheless because they exhibit so little reality to me that I cannot even clearly distinguish the thing represented from non-being, I do not see any reason why they should not be produced by myself.

As to the clear and distinct idea which I have of corporeal things, some of them seem as though I might have derived them from the idea which I possess of myself, as those which I have of substance, duration, number, and such like. For [even] when I think that a stone is a substance, or at least a thing capable of existing of itself, and that I am a substance also, although I conceive that I am a thing that thinks and not one that is extended, and that the stone on the other hand is an extended thing which does not think, and that thus there is a notable difference between the two conceptions — they seem, nevertheless, to agree in this, that both represent substances. In the same way, when I perceive that I now exist and further recollect that I have in former times existed, and when I remember that I have various thoughts of which I can recognise the number, I acquire ideas of duration and number which I can afterwards transfer to any object that I please. But as to all the other qualities of which the ideas of corporeal things are composed, to wit, extension, figure, situation and motion, it is true that they are not formally in me, since I am only a thing that thinks; but because they are merely certain modes of substance [and so to speak the vestments under which corporeal substance appears to us] and because I myself am also a substance, it would seem that they might be contained in me eminently.

Hence there remains alone the idea of God, concerning which we must consider whether it is not something that is capable of proceeding from me myself. By the name God I understand a substance that is infinite [eternal, immutable], independent, all-knowing, all-powerful, and by which I myself and everything else, if anything else does exist, have been created. Now all these characteristics are such that the more diligently I attend to them, the less do they appear capable of proceeding from me alone; hence, from what has been already said, we must conclude that God necessarily exists.

For although the idea of substance is within me owing to the fact that I am substance, nevertheless I should not have the idea of an infinite substance — since I am finite — if it had not proceeded from some substance which was veritably infinite.

Nor should I imagine that I do not perceive the infinite by a true idea, but only by the negation of the finite, just as I perceive repose and darkness by the negation of movement and of light; for, on the contrary, I see that there is manifestly more reality in infinite substance than in finite, and therefore that in some way I have in me the notion of the infinite earlier than the finite — to wit, the notion of God before

133

that of myself. For how would it be possible that I should know that I doubt and desire, that is to say, that something is lacking to me, and that I am not quite perfect, unless I had within me some idea of a Being more perfect than myself, in comparison with which I should recognise the deficiencies of my nature?

And we cannot say that this idea of God is perhaps materially false and that consequently I can derive it from nought [i.e. that possibly it exists in me because I am imperfect], as I have just said is the case with ideas of heat, cold and other such things; for, on the contrary, as this idea is very clear and distinct and contains within it more objective reality than any other, there can be none which is of itself more true, nor any in which there can be less suspicion of falsehood. The idea, I say, of this Being who is absolutely perfect and infinite, is entirely true; for although, perhaps, we can imagine that such a Being does not exist, we cannot nevertheless imagine that His idea represents nothing real to me, as I have said of the idea of cold. This idea is also very clear and distinct; since all that I conceive clearly and distinctly of the real and the true, and of what conveys some perfection, is in its entirety contained in this idea. And this does not cease to be true although I do not comprehend the infinite, or though in God there is an infinitude of things which I cannot comprehend, nor possibly even reach in any way by thought; for it is of the nature of the infinite that my nature, which is finite and limited, should not comprehend it; and it is sufficient that I should understand this, and that I should judge that all things which I clearly perceive and in which I know that there is some perfection, and possibly likewise an infinitude of properties of which I am ignorant, are in God formally or eminently, so that the idea which I have of Him may become the most true, most clear, and most distinct of all the ideas that are in my mind.

But possibly I am something more than I suppose myself to be, and perhaps all those perfections which I attribute to God are in some way potentially in me, although they do not yet disclose themselves, or issue in action. As a matter of fact I am already sensible that my knowledge increases [and perfects itself] little by little, and I see nothing which can prevent it from increasing more and more into infinitude; nor do I see, after it has thus been increased [or perfected], anything to prevent my being able to acquire by its means all the other perfections of the Divine nature; nor finally why the power I have of acquiring these perfections, if it really exists in me, shall not suffice to produce the ideas of them.

At the same time I recognise that this cannot be. For, in the first place, although it were true that every day my knowledge acquired new degrees of perfection, and that there were in my nature many things potentially which are not yet there actually, nevertheless these excellences do not pertain to [or make the smallest approach to] the idea which I have of God in whom there is nothing merely potential [but in whom all is present really and actually]; for it is an infallible token of imperfection in my knowledge that it increases little by little. And further, although my knowledge grows more and more, nevertheless I do not for that reason believe that it can ever be actually infinite, since it can never reach a point so high that it will be unable to attain to any greater increase. But I understand God to be actually infinite, so that He can add nothing to His supreme perfection. And finally I perceive that the objective being of an idea cannot be produced by a being that exists potentially only, which properly speaking is nothing, but only by a being which is formal or actual.

To speak the truth, I see nothing in all that I have just said which by the light of nature is not manifest to anyone who desires to think attentively on the subject; but when I slightly relax my attention, my mind, finding its vision somewhat obscured and so to speak blinded by the images of sensible objects, I do not easily recollect the reason why the idea that I possess of a being more perfect than I, must necessarily have been placed in me by a being which is really more perfect; and this is why I wish here to go on to inquire whether I, who have this idea, can exist if no such being exists.

And I ask, from whom do I then derive my existence? Perhaps from myself or from my parents, or from some other source less perfect than God; for we can imagine nothing more perfect than God, or even as perfect as He is.

But [were I independent of every other and] were I myself the author of my being, I should doubt nothing and I should desire nothing, and finally no perfection would be lacking to me; for I should have bestowed on myself every perfection of which I possessed any idea and should thus be God. And it must not be imagined that those things that are lacking to me are perhaps more difficult of attainment than those which I already possess; for, on the contrary, it is quite evident that it was a matter of much greater difficulty to bring to pass that I, that is to say, a thing or a substance that thinks, should emerge out of nothing, than it would be to attain to the knowledge of many things of which I am ignorant, and which are only the accidents of this thinking substance. But it is clear that if I had of myself possessed this greater perfection of which I have just spoken [that is to say, if I had been the author of my own existence], I should not at least have denied myself the things which are the more easy to acquire [to wit, many branches of knowledge of which my nature is destitute]; nor should I have deprived myself of any of the things contained in the idea which I form of God, because there are none of them which seem to me specially difficult to acquire: and if there were any that were more difficult to acquire, they would certainly appear to me to be such (supposing I myself were the origin of the other things which I possess) since I should discover in them that my powers were limited.

But though I assume that perhaps I have always existed just as I am at present, neither can I escape the force of this reasoning, and imagine that the conclusion to be drawn from this is, that I need not seek for any author of my existence. For all the course of my life may be divided into an infinite number of parts, none of which is in any way dependent on the other; and thus from the fact that I was in existence a short time ago it does not follow that I must be in existence now, unless some cause at this instant, so to speak, produces me anew, that is to say, conserves me. It is as a matter of fact perfectly clear and evident to all those who consider with attention the nature of time, that, in order to be conserved in each moment in which it endures, a substance has need of the same power and action as would be necessary to produce and create it anew, supposing it did not yet exist, so that the light of nature shows us clearly that the distinction between creation and conservation is solely a distinction of the reason.

All that I thus require here is that I should interrogate myself, if I wish to know whether I possess a power which is capable of bringing it to pass that I who now am shall still be in the future; for since I am nothing but a thinking thing, or at least since thus far it is only this portion of myself which is precisely in question at present, if such a power did reside in me, I should certainly be conscious of it. But I am conscious of nothing of the kind, and by this I know clearly that I depend on some being different from myself.

Possibly, however, this being on which I depend is not that which I call God, and I am created either by my parents or by some other cause less perfect than God. This cannot be, because, as I have just said, it is perfectly evident that there must be at least as much reality in the cause as in the effect; and thus since I am a thinking thing, and possess an idea of God within me, whatever in the end be the cause assigned to my existence, it must be allowed that it is likewise a thinking thing and that it possesses in itself the idea of all the perfections which I attribute to God. We may again inquire whether this cause derives its origin from itself or from some other thing. For if from itself, it follows by the reasons before brought forward, that this cause must itself be God; for since it possesses the virtue of self-existence, it must also without doubt have the power of actually possessing all the perfections of which it has the idea, that is, all those which I conceive as existing in God. But if it derives its existence from some other cause than itself, we shall again ask, for the same reason, whether this second cause exists by itself or through another, until from one step to another, we finally arrive at an ultimate cause, which will be God.

And it is perfectly manifest that in this there can be no regression into infinity, since what is in question is not so much the cause which formerly created me, as that which conserves me at the present time.

Nor can we suppose that several causes may have concurred in my production, and that from one I have received the idea of one of the perfections which I attribute to God, and from another the idea of some other, so that all these perfections indeed exist somewhere in the universe, but not as complete in one unity which is God. On the contrary, the unity, the simplicity or the inseparability of all things which are in God is one of the principal perfections which I conceive to be in Him. And certainly the idea of this unity of all Divine perfections cannot have been placed in me by any cause from which I have not likewise received the ideas of all the other perfections; for this cause could not make me able to comprehend them as joined together in an inseparable unity without having at the same time caused me in some measure to know what they are [and in some way to recognise each one of them].

Finally, so far as my parents [from whom it appears I have sprung] are concerned, although all that I have ever been able to believe of them were true, that does not make it follow that it is they who conserve me, nor are they even the authors of my being in any sense, in so far as I am a thinking being; since what they did was merely to implant certain dispositions in that matter in which the self—i.e. the mind, which alone I at present identify with myself—is by me deemed to exist. And thus there can be no difficulty in their regard, but we must of necessity conclude from the fact alone that I exist, or that the idea of a Being supremely perfect—that is of God—is in me, that the proof of God's existence is grounded on the highest evidence.

It only remains to me to examine into the manner in which I have acquired this idea from God; for I have not received it through the senses, and it is never presented to me unexpectedly, as is usual with the ideas of sensible things when these things present themselves, or seem to present themselves, to the external organs of my senses; nor is it likewise a fiction of my mind, for it is not in my power to take from or to add anything to it; and consequently the only alternative is that it is innate in me, just as the idea of myself is innate in me.

And one certainly ought not to find it strange that God, in creating me, placed this idea within me to be like the mark of the workman imprinted on his work; and it is likewise not essential that the mark shall be something different from the work itself. For from the sole fact that God created me it is most probable that in some way he has placed his image and similitude upon me, and that I perceive this similitude (in which the idea of God is contained) by means of the same faculty by which I perceive myself—that is to say, when I reflect on myself I not only know that I am something [imperfect], incomplete and dependent on another, which incessantly aspires after something which is better and greater than myself, but I also know that He on whom I depend possesses in Himself all the great things towards which I aspire [and the ideas of which I find within myself], and that not indefinitely or potentially alone, but really, actually and infinitely; and that thus He is God. And the whole strength of the argument which I have here made use of to prove the existence of God consists in this, that I recognise that it is not possible that my nature should be what it is, and indeed that I should have in myself the idea of a God, if God did not veritably exist—a God, I say, whose idea is in me, i.e. who possesses all those supreme perfections of which our mind may indeed have some idea but without understanding them all, who is liable to no errors or defect [and who has none of all those marks which denote imperfection]. From this it is manifest that He cannot be a deceiver, since the light of nature teaches us that fraud and deception necessarily proceed from some defect.

But before I examine this matter with more care, and pass on to the consideration of other truths which may be derived from it, it seems to me right to pause for a while in order to contemplate God Himself, to ponder at leisure His marvellous attributes, to consider, and admire, and adore, the beauty of this light so resplendent, at least as far as the strength of my mind, which is in some measure dazzled by the sight, will allow me to do so. For just as faith teaches us that the supreme felicity of the other life consists only in this contemplation of the Divine Majesty, so we continue to learn by experience that a similar meditation, though incomparably less perfect, causes us to enjoy the greatest satisfaction of which we are capable in this life.

From *The Philosophical Works of Descartes, Volume I.* Translated by E. Haldane and G. Ross. Cambridge: Cambridge University Press, 1911. Used by permission of Cambridge University Press.

JOHN LOCKE

John Locke (1632–1704) created empiricism, a new approach in epistemology, by his denial of innate ideas and principles. The selection from his celebrated *Essay concerning Human Understanding* is an example of what he called the "plain historical method." Locke sought to trace all ideas or concepts back to their origin in experience. He did not limit experience to sense experience, but included introspective awareness of the mind as it performed various mental operations as part of what he meant by experience, a qualification often not noticed by his immediate followers.

Although Descartes, as a rationalist, is frequently contrasted to Locke, an empiricist, Locke endorsed Descartes' view of knowledge and certainty. We have knowledge only when something is self-evident (we intuit its truth and it is immune to doubt), or when by discursive reasoning we proceed from what is self-evident, step by self-evident step, to a conclusion. For Locke such knowledge was far more rare than Descartes believed, but Locke agreed with Descartes concerning the nature of knowledge.

Locke, however, stressed that though knowledge was often not possible we could achieve probability on the basis of experience — and indeed great probability on many important matters. Locke thus was able to meet the skepticism that resulted as a reaction to our inability to achieve knowledge that met Descartes' very high, not to say impossible, standards. For Locke, probability was a sufficient basis for the conduct of science, and thoroughly adequate for practical life.

Ideas
(*Essay concerning Human Understanding,* Book II, Chapters I–III)

BOOK II

Chapter I
Of Ideas in General and Their Original

1. *Idea is the object of thinking.* — Every man being conscious to himself that he thinks, and that which his mind is applied about whilst thinking being the ideas that are there, it is past doubt that men have in their minds several ideas, such as are those expressed by the words, 'whiteness, hardness, sweetness, thinking, motion, man, elephant, army, drunkenness', and others. It is in the first place then to be enquired, How he comes by them? I know it is a received doctrine, that men have native ideas and original characters stamped upon their minds in their very first being. This opinion I have at large examined already; and, I suppose, what I have said in the foregoing Book will be much more easily admitted, when I have shown whence the understanding may get all the ideas it has, and by what ways and degrees they may come into the mind; for which I shall appeal to every one's own observation and experience.

2. *All ideas come from sensation or reflection.* — Let us then suppose the mind to be, as we say, white paper, void of all characters, without any ideas; how comes it to be furnished? Whence comes it by that vast store, which the busy and boundless fancy of man has painted on it with an almost endless variety? Whence has it all the materials of reason and knowledge? To this I answer, in one word, from EXPERIENCE; in that all our knowledge is founded, and from that it ultimately derives itself. Our observation, employed either about external sensible objects, or about the internal operations of our minds, perceived and reflected on by ourselves, is that which supplies our understandings with all the materials of thinking. These two are the fountains of knowledge, from whence all the ideas we have, or can naturally have, do spring.

3. *The objects of sensation one source of ideas.* — First, our senses, conversant about particular sensible objects, do convey into the mind

several distinct perceptions of things, according to those various ways wherein those objects do affect them; and thus we come by those *ideas* we have of yellow, white, heat, cold, soft, hard, bitter, sweet, and all those which we call sensible qualities; which when I say the senses convey into the mind, I mean, they from external objects convey into the mind what produces there those perceptions. This great source of most of the ideas we have, depending wholly upon our senses, and derived by them to the understanding, I call, SENSATION.

4. *The operations of our minds the other source of them.* — Secondly, the other fountain, from which experience furnisheth the understanding with ideas, is the perception of the operations of our own minds within us, as it is employed about the ideas it has got; which operations, when the soul comes to reflect on and consider, do furnish the understanding with another set of ideas which could not be had from things without: and such are perception, thinking, doubting, believing, reasoning, knowing, willing, and all the different actings of our own minds; which we being conscious of, and observing in ourselves, do from these receive into our understanding as distinct ideas, as we do from bodies affecting our senses. This source of ideas every man has wholly in himself: and though it be not sense, as having nothing to do with external objects, yet it is very like it, and might properly enough be called internal sense. But as I call the other Sensation, so I call this REFLECTION, the ideas it affords being such only as the mind gets by reflecting on its own operations within itself. By Reflection, then, in the following part of this discourse, I would be understood to mean that notice which the mind takes of its own operations, and the manner of them, by reason whereof there come to be ideas of these operations in the understanding. These two, I say, viz., external material things as the objects of Sensation, and the operations of our own minds within as the objects of Reflection, are, to me, the only originals from whence all our ideas take their beginnings. The term *operations* here, I use in a large sense, as comprehending not barely the actions of the mind about its ideas, but some sort of passions arising sometimes from them, such as is the satisfaction or uneasiness arising from any thought.

5. *All our ideas are of the one or the other of these.* — The understanding seems to me not to have the least glimmering of any ideas which it doth not receive from one of these two. *External objects* furnish

the mind with the ideas of sensible qualities, which are all those different perceptions they produce in us; and *the mind* furnishes the understanding with ideas of its own operations. These, when we have taken a full survey of them, and their several modes, combinations, and relations, we shall find to contain all our whole stock of ideas; and that we have nothing in our minds which did not come in one of these two ways. Let any one examine his own thoughts, and thoroughly search into his understanding, and then let him tell me, whether all the original ideas he has there, are any other than of the objects of his senses, or of the operations of his mind considered as objects of his reflection; and how great a mass of knowledge soever he imagines to be lodged there, he will, upon taking a strict view, see that he has not any idea in his mind but what one of these two have imprinted, though perhaps with infinite variety compounded and enlarged by the understanding, as we shall see hereafter.

6. *Observable in children.* — He that attentively considers the state of a child at his first coming into the world, will have little reason to think him stored with plenty of ideas that are to be the matter of his future knowledge. It is by degrees he comes to be furnished with them: and though the ideas of obvious and familiar qualities imprint themselves before the memory begins to keep a register of time and order, yet it is often so late before some unusual qualities come in the way, that there are few men that cannot recollect the beginning of their acquaintance with them: and if it were worth while, no doubt a child might be so ordered as to have but a very few even of the ordinary ideas till he were grown up to a man. But all that are born into the world being surrounded with bodies that perpetually and diversely affect them, variety of ideas, whether care be taken about it or no, are imprinted on the minds of children. Light and colours are busy and at hand everywhere when the eye is but open; sounds and some tangible qualities fail not to solicit their proper senses, and force an entrance to the mind; but yet I think it will be granted easily, that if a child were kept in a place where he never saw any other but black and white till he were a man, he would have no more ideas of scarlet or green, than he that from his childhood never tasted an oyster or a pine-apple has of those particular relishes.

7. *Men are differently furnished with these according to the different objects they converse with.*—Men then come to be furnished with fewer or more simple ideas from without, according as the objects they converse with afford greater or less variety; and from the operations of their minds within, according as they more or less reflect on them. For, though he that contemplates the operations of his mind cannot but have plain and clear ideas of them; yet, unless he turn his thoughts that way, and considers them *attentively,* he will no more have clear and distinct ideas of all the operations of his mind, and all that may be observed therein, than he will have all the particular ideas of any landscape, or of the parts and motions of a clock, who will not turn his eyes to it, and with attention heed all the parts of it. The picture or clock may be so placed, that they may come in his way every day; but yet he will have but a confused idea of all the parts they are made up of, till he applies himself with attention to consider them each in particular.

8. *Ideas of reflection later, because they need attention.*—And hence we see the reason why it is pretty late before most children get ideas of the operations of their own minds; and some have not any very clear or perfect ideas of the greatest part of them all their lives. Because, though they pass there continually, yet, like floating visions, they make not deep impressions enough to leave in the mind clear, distinct, lasting ideas, till the understanding turns inwards upon itself, reflects on its own operations, and makes them the object of its own contemplation. Children, when they come first into it, are surrounded with a world of new things, which, by a constant solicitation of their senses, draw the mind constantly to them, forward to take notice of new, and apt to be delighted with the variety of changing objects. Thus the first years are usually employed and diverted in looking abroad. Men's business in them is to acquaint themselves with what is to be found without; and so, growing up in a constant attention to outward sensations, seldom make any considerable reflection on what passes within them till they come to be of riper years; and some scarce ever at all.

9. *The soul begins to have ideas when it begins to perceive.*—To ask, at what *time* a man has first any ideas, is to ask when he begins to perceive; having ideas, and perception, being the same thing. I know it is an opinion, that the soul always thinks; and that it has the actual

perception of ideas in itself constantly, as long as it exists; and that actual thinking is as inseparable from the soul, as actual extension is from the body: which if true, to enquire after the beginning of a man's ideas is the same as to enquire after the beginning of his soul. For by this account, soul and its ideas, as body and its extension, will begin to exist both at the same time.

10. *The soul thinks not always; for this wants proofs.* — But whether the soul be supposed to exist antecedent to, or coeval with, or some time after the first rudiments or organization, or the beginnings of life in the body, I leave to be disputed by those who have better thought of that matter. I confess myself to have one of those dull souls that doth not perceive itself always to contemplate ideas; nor can conceive it any more necessary for the soul always to think, than for the body always to move: the perception of ideas being, as I conceive, to the soul, what motion is to the body, not its essence, but one of its operations. And, therefore, though thinking be supposed never so much the proper action of the soul, yet it is not necessary to suppose that it should be always thinking, always in action. That, perhaps, is the privilege of the infinite Author and Preserver of all things, 'who never slumbers nor sleeps'; but is not competent to any finite being, at least not to the soul of man. We know certainly by experience, that we sometimes think; and thence draw this infallible consequence — that there is something in us that has a power to think: but whether that substance perpetually thinks, or no, we can be no farther assured than experience informs us. For to say, that actual thinking is essential to the soul and inseparable from it, is to beg what is in question, and not to prove it by reason; which is necessary to be done, if it be not a self-evident proposition. But whether this, that 'the soul always thinks', be a self-evident proposition, that everybody assents to at first hearing, I appeal to mankind. [It is doubted whether I thought all last night, or no; the question being about a matter of fact, it is begging it to bring as a proof for it an hypothesis which is the very thing in dispute; which way of proving amounts to this, — that I must necessarily think all last night because another supposes I always think, though I myself cannot perceive that I always do so. But men in love with their opinions may not only suppose what is in question, but allege wrong matter of fact. How else could any one make it an inference of mine, that a thing is not, because

145

we are not sensible of it in our sleep? I do not say there is no soul in a man because he is not sensible of it in his sleep; but I do say, he cannot think at any time, waking or sleeping, without being sensible of it. Our being sensible of it is not necessary to anything but to our thoughts; and to them it is, and to them it will always be, necessary, till we can think without being conscious of it.]

13. Thus, methinks, every drowsy nod shakes their doctrine who teach that the soul is always thinking. Those, at least, who do at any time sleep without dreaming can never be convinced that their thoughts are sometimes for four hours busy without their knowing of it, and if they are taken in the very act, waked in the middle of that sleeping contemplation, can give no manner of account of it.

14. *That men dream without remembering it, in vain urged.* — It will perhaps be said, that the soul thinks even in the soundest sleep, but the memory retains it not. That the soul in a sleeping man should be this moment busy a-thinking, and the next moment in a waking man not remember, nor be able to recollect one jot of all those thoughts, is very hard to be conceived, and would need some better proof than bare assertion to make it be believed. For who can without any more ado but being barely told so, imagine that the greatest part of men do, during all their lives, for several hours every day think of something which, if they were asked even in the middle of these thoughts, they could remember nothing at all of?

17. *If I think when I know it not, nobody else can know it.* — Those who so confidently tell us that the soul always actually thinks, I would they would also tell us what those ideas are that are in the soul of a child before or just at the union with the body, before it hath received any by sensation. The dreams of sleeping men are, as I take it, all made up of the waking man's ideas, though for the most part oddly put together. It is strange, if the soul has ideas of its own that it derived not from sensation or reflection (as it must have, if it thought before it received any impressions from the body), that it should never in its private thinking (so private that the man himself perceives it not) retain any of them the very moment it wakes out of them, and then make the man glad with new discoveries. It is strange the soul should never once, in a man's whole life, recall over any of its pure native thoughts,

and those ideas it had before it borrowed anything from the body; never bring into the waking man's view any other ideas but what have a tang of the cask, and manifestly derive their original from that union.

18. *How knows any one that the soul always thinks? For if it be not a self-evident proposition it needs proof.* — I would be glad also to learn from these men, who so confidently pronounce that the human soul, or, which is all one, that a man always thinks, how they come to know it. [19.] Consciousness is the perception of what passes in a man's own mind. Can another man perceive that I am conscious of anything, when I perceive it not myself? No man's knowledge here can go beyond his experience. Wake a man out of a sound sleep, and ask him what he was that moment thinking on. If he himself be conscious of nothing he then thought on, he must be a notable diviner of thoughts that can assure him that he was thinking: may he not with more reason assure him he was not asleep? This is something beyond philosophy; and it cannot be less than revelation, that discovers to another, thoughts in my mind, when I can find none there myself: and they must needs have a penetrating sight who can certainly see that I think, when I cannot perceive it myself, and when I declare that I do not; and yet can see that dogs or elephants do not think, when they give all the demonstration of it imaginable, except only telling us that they do so. But it is but defining the soul to be a substance that always thinks, and the business is done. If such definition be of any authority, I know not what it can serve for, but to make many men suspect that they have no souls at all, since they find a good part of their lives pass away without thinking. For no definitions that I know, no suppositions of any sect, are of force enough to destroy constant experience; and perhaps it is the affectation of knowing beyond what we perceive that makes so much useless dispute and noise in the world.

20. *No ideas but from sensation or reflection evident, if we observe children.* — I see no reason therefore to believe that the soul thinks before the senses have furnished it with ideas to think on; and as those are increased and retained, so it comes by exercise to improve its faculty of thinking in the several parts of it; as well as afterwards, by compounding those ideas and reflecting on its own operations, it increases its stock, as well as facility in remembering, imagining, reasoning, and other modes of thinking. [23.] If it shall be demanded, then, *when a*

man begins to have any ideas? I think the true answer is, when he first has any sensation. For since there appear not to be any ideas in the mind before the senses have conveyed any in, I conceive that ideas in the understanding are coeval with sensation; which is such an impression or motion made in some part of the body as produces some perception in the understanding. [It is about these impressions made on our senses by outward objects, that the mind seems first to employ itself in such operations as we call perception, remembering, consideration, reasoning, &c.]

24. *The original of all our knowledge.* — In time the mind comes to reflect on its own operations about the ideas got by sensation, and thereby stores itself with a new set of ideas which I call ideas of reflection. These — the impressions that are made on our senses by outward objects, that are extrinsical to the mind, and its own operations, proceeding from powers intrinsical and proper to itself, which, when reflected on by itself, become also objects of its contemplation — are, as I have said, the original of all knowledge. Thus the first capacity of human intellect is, that the mind is fitted to receive the impressions made on it, either through the senses by outward objects, or by its own operations when it reflects on them. This is the first step a man makes towards the discovery of anything, and the groundwork whereon to build all those notions which ever he shall have naturally in this world. All those sublime thoughts which tower above the clouds, and reach as high as heaven itself, take their rise and footing here: in all that great extent wherein the mind wanders in those remote speculations it may seem to be elevated with, it stirs not one jot beyond those ideas which *sense* or *reflection* have offered for its contemplation.

25. *In the reception of simple ideas, the understanding is most of all passive.* — In this part the understanding is merely passive; and whether or no it will have these beginnings and, as it were, materials of knowledge, is not in its own power. For the objects of our senses do many of them obtrude their particular ideas upon our minds, whether we will or no; and the operations of our minds will not let us be without at least some obscure notions of them. No man can be wholly ignorant of what he does when he thinks. These simple ideas, when offered to the mind, the understanding can no more refuse to have, nor alter when they are imprinted, nor blot them out and make

new ones itself, than a mirror can refuse, alter, or obliterate the images or ideas, which the objects set before it do therein produce. As the bodies that surround us do diversely affect our organs, the mind is forced to receive the impressions, and cannot avoid the perception of those ideas that are annexed to them.

Chapter II
Of Simple Ideas

1. *Uncompounded appearances.*—The better to understand the nature, manner, and extent of our knowledge, one thing is carefully to be observed concerning the ideas we have; and that is, that some of them are *simple,* and some *complex.*

Though the qualities that affect our senses are, in the things them-selves, so united and blended that there is no separation, no distance between them; yet it is plain the ideas they produce in the mind enter by the senses simple and unmixed. For though the sight and touch often take in from the same object at the same time different ideas; as a man sees at once motion and colour, the hand feels softness and warmth in the same piece of wax; yet the simple ideas thus united in the same subject are as perfectly distinct as those that come in by different senses. The coldness and hardness which a man feels in a piece of ice being as distinct ideas in the mind as the smell and whiteness of a lily, or as the taste of sugar and smell of a rose: and there is nothing can be plainer to a man than the clear and distinct perception he has of those simple ideas; which, being each in itself uncompounded, contains in it nothing but one uniform appearance or conception in the mind, and is not distinguishable into different ideas.

2. *The mind can neither make nor destroy them.*—These simple ideas, the materials of all our knowledge, are suggested and furnished to the mind only by those two ways above mentioned, viz., sensation and reflection. When the understanding is once stored with these simple ideas, it has the power to repeat, compare, and unite them, even to an almost infinite variety, and so can make at pleasure new complex ideas. But it is not in the power of the most exalted wit or enlarged understanding, by any quickness or variety of thought, to invent or frame one new simple idea in the mind, not taken in by the ways before

mentioned; nor can any force of the understanding destroy those that are there. The dominion of man in this little world of his own understanding, being much-what the same as it is in the great world of visible things, wherein his power, however managed by art and skill, reaches no farther than to compound and divide the materials that are made to his hand, but can do nothing towards the making the least particle of new matter, or destroying one atom of what is already in being. The same inability will every one find in himself, who shall go about to fashion in his understanding any simple idea not received in by his senses from external objects, or by reflection from the operations of his own mind about them. I would have any one try to fancy any taste which had never affected his palate, or frame the idea of a scent he had never smelt; and when he can do this, I will also conclude, that a blind man hath ideas of colours, and a deaf man true distinct notions of sounds.

3. This is the reason why, though we cannot believe it impossible to God to make a creature with other organs, and more ways to convey into the understanding the notice of corporeal things than those five, as they are usually counted, which he has given to man: yet I think it is *not possible* for any one *to imagine* any other qualities in bodies, howsoever constituted, whereby they can be taken notice of, besides sounds, tastes, smells, visible and tangible qualities. And had mankind been made with but four senses, the qualities then which are the object of the fifth sense, had been as far from our notice, imagination, and conception, as now any belonging to a sixth, seventh, or eighth sense, can possibly be: which, whether yet some other creatures, in some other parts of this vast and stupendous universe, may not have, will be a great presumption to deny. He that will not set himself proudly at the top of all things, but will consider the immensity of this fabric, and the great variety that is to be found in this little and inconsiderable part of it which he has to do with, may be apt to think, that in other mansions of it there may be other and different intelligible beings, of whose faculties he has as little knowledge or apprehension, as a worm shut up in one drawer of a cabinet hath of the senses or understanding of a man; such variety and excellency being suitable to the wisdom and power of the Maker. I have here followed the common opinion of man's having but five senses, though perhaps there may be justly counted more; but either supposition serves equally to my present purpose.

Chapter III
Of Ideas of One Sense

1. *Division of simple ideas.*—The better to conceive the ideas we receive from sensation, it may not be amiss for us to consider them in reference to the different ways whereby they make their approaches to our minds, and make themselves perceivable by us.

First, then, There are some which come into our minds *by one sense* only.

Secondly. There are others that convey themselves into the mind *by more senses than one.*

Thirdly. Others that are had from *reflection* only.

Fourthly. There are some that make themselves way, and are suggested to the mind *by all the ways of sensation and reflection.*

We shall consider them apart under these several heads.

First, There are some ideas which have admittance only through one sense, which is peculiarly adapted to receive them. Thus light and colours, as white, red, yellow, blue, with their several degrees or shades and mixtures, as green, scarlet, purple sea-green, and the rest, come in only by the eyes; all kinds of noises, sounds, and tones, only by the ears; the several tastes and smells, by the nose and palate. And if these organs, or the nerves which are the conduits to convey them from without to their audience in the brain, the mind's presence-room (as I may so call it), are, any of them, so disordered as not to perform their functions, they have no postern to be admitted by, no other way to bring themselves into view, and be perceived by the understanding.

The most considerable of those belonging to the touch are heat, and cold, and solidity; all the rest, consisting almost wholly in the sensible configuration, as smooth and rough; or else, more or less firm adhesion of the parts, as hard and soft, tough and brittle, are obvious enough.

2. *Few simple ideas have names.*—I think it will be needless to enumerate all the particular simple ideas belonging to each sense. Nor indeed is it possible if we would, there being a great many more of them belonging to most of the senses than we have names for. The variety of smells, which are as many almost, if not more than species of bodies in the world, do most of them want names. Sweet and stinking commonly serve our turn for these ideas, which in effect is little more than

to call them pleasing or displeasing; though the smell of a rose and violet, both sweet, are certainly very distinct ideas. Nor are the different tastes that by our palates we receive ideas of, much better provided with names. Sweet, bitter, sour, harsh, and salt, are almost all the epithets we have to denominate that numberless variety of relishes which are to be found distinct, not only in almost every sort of creatures, but in the different parts of the same plant, fruit, or animal. The same may be said of colours and sounds. I shall therefore, in the account of simple ideas I am here giving, content myself to set down only such as are most material to our present purpose, or are in themselves less apt to be taken notice of, though they are very frequently the ingredients of our complex ideas; amongst which, I think, I may well account solidity, which therefore I shall treat of in the next chapter.

DAVID HUME

David Hume (1711–1776) called into question both Cartesian rationalism and Lockean empiricism in his attempt to trace our knowledge back to its sources. He found that neither reason nor experience provided a basis for certainty or probability. He found himself forced to rely on instinct and habit for our belief in the continuing existence of material substances, the self, and the causal operations of nature. In addition, Hume raised serious questions about the viability of natural religion, or deism, and about the reasonableness of revealed religion, or Christianity.

The selection from *An Enquiry Concerning Human Understanding* deals with revealed religion. Hume does not deny the possibility of miracles, but argues that we should never believe reports of miracles. It is always more likely that the reports are untrue than that the events that are contrary to the ordinary course of nature have occurred. It is important to remember that Hume was far better known in his day as the author of a multivolume work on the history of England than as a philosopher. Because Hume was used to sifting documents to reconstruct and reinterpret the past, his arguments concerning the use of historical argument to establish the truth of Christianity are of particular interest.

Of Miracles
(An Enquiry Concerning Human Understanding, Section X, Parts I–II)

MIRACLES

Part I

There is, in Dr. Tillotson's writings, an argument against the *real presence*, which is as concise, and elegant, and strong as any argument can possibly be supposed against a doctrine so little worthy of a serious refutation. It is acknowledged on all hands, says that learned prelate, that the authority, either of the scripture or of tradition, is founded merely in the testimony of the apostles, who were eye-witnesses to those miracles of our Saviour, by which he proved his divine mission. Our evidence, then, for the truth of the *Christian* religion is less than the evidence for the truth of our senses; because, even in the first authors of our religion, it was no greater; and it is evident it must diminish in passing from them to their disciples; nor can anyone rest such confidence in their testimony, as in the immediate object of his senses. But a weaker evidence can never destroy a stronger; and therefore, were the doctrine of the real presence ever so clearly revealed in scripture, it were directly contrary to the rules of just reasoning to give our assent to it. It contradicts sense, though both the scripture and tradition, on which it is supposed to be built, carry not such evidence with them as sense; when they are considered merely as external evidences, and are not brought home to everyone's breast, by the immediate operation of the Holy Spirit.

Nothing is so convenient as a decisive argument of this kind, which must at least *silence* the most arrogant bigotry and superstition, and free us from their impertinent solicitations. I flatter myself, that I have discovered an argument of a like nature, which, if just, will, with the wise and learned, be an everlasting check to all kinds of superstitious delusion, and consequently, will be useful as long as the world endures. For so long, I presume, will the accounts of miracles and prodigies be found in all history, sacred and profane.

Though experience be our only guide in reasoning concerning matters of fact; it must be acknowledged, that this guide is not altogether infallible, but in some cases is apt to lead us into errors. One, who in our climate, should expect better weather in any week of June than in one of December, would reason justly, and conformably to experience; but it is certain that he may happen, in the event, to find himself mistaken. However, we may observe, that, in such a case, he would have no cause to complain of experience; because it commonly informs us beforehand of the uncertainty, by that contrariety of events, which we may learn from a diligent observation. All effects follow not with like certainty from their supposed causes. Some events are found, in all countries and all ages, to have been constantly conjoined together: Others are found to have been more variable, and sometimes to disappoint our expectations; so that, in our reasonings concerning matter of fact, there are all imaginable degrees of assurance, from the highest certainty to the lowest species of moral evidence.

A wise man, therefore, proportions his belief to the evidence. In such conclusions as are founded on an infallible experience, he expects the event with the last degree of assurance, and regards his past experience as a full *proof* of the future existence of that event. In other cases, he proceeds with more caution: he weighs the opposite experiments: he considers which side is supported by the greater number of experiments: to that side he inclines, with doubt and hesitation; and when at last he fixes his judgement, the evidence exceeds not what we properly call probability. All probability, then, supposes an opposition of experiments and observations, where the one side is found to overbalance the other, and to produce a degree of evidence, proportioned to the superiority. A hundred instances or experiments on one side, and fifty on another, afford a doubtful expectation of any event; though a hundred uniform experiments, with only one that is contradictory, reasonably beget a pretty strong degree of assurance. In all cases, we must balance the opposite experiments, where they are opposite, and deduct the smaller number from the greater, in order to know the exact force of the superior evidence.

To apply these principles to a particular instance; we may observe, that there is no species of reasoning more common, more useful, and even necessary to human life, than that which is derived from the testimony of men, and the reports of eye-witnesses and spectators. This species of reasoning, perhaps, one may deny to be founded on the relation of cause and effect. I shall not dispute about a word. It will be sufficient to observe that our assurance in any argument of this kind is derived from no other principle than our observation of the veracity of human testimony, and of the usual conformity of facts to the reports of witnesses. It being a general maxim that no objects have any discoverable connexion together, and all the inferences, which we can draw from one to another, are founded merely on our experience of their constant and regular conjunction; it is evident, that we ought not to make an exception to this maxim in favour of human testimony, whose connection with any event seems, in itself, as little necessary as any other. Were not the memory tenacious to a certain degree; had not men commonly an inclination to truth and a principle of probity; were they not sensible to shame, when detected in a falsehood: were not these, I say, discovered by *experience* to be qualities inherent in human nature, we should never repose the least confidence in human testimony. A man delirious, or noted for falsehood and villainy, has no manner of authority with us.

And as the evidence, derived from witnesses and human testimony, is founded on past experience, so it varies with the experience, and is regarded either as a *proof* or a *probability,* according as the conjunction between any particular kind of report and any kind of object has been found to be constant or variable. There are a number of circumstances to be taken into consideration in all judgements of this kind; and the ultimate standard, by which we determine all disputes that may arise concerning them, is always derived from experience and observation. Where this experience is not entirely uniform on any side, it is attended with an unavoidable contrariety in our judgements, and with the same opposition and mutual destruction of argument as in every other kind of evidence. We frequently hesitate concerning the reports of others. We balance the opposite circumstances, which cause any doubt or uncertainty; and when we discover a superiority on any side, we incline to it; but still with a diminution of assurance, in proportion to the force of its antagonist.

This contrariety of evidence, in the present case, may be derived from several different causes from the opposition of contrary testimony; from the character or number of the witnesses; from the manner of their delivering their testimony; or from the union of all these circumstances.

We entertain a suspicion concerning any matter of fact, when the witnesses contradict each other; when they are but few, or of a doubtful character; when they have an interest in what they affirm; when they deliver their testimony with hesitation, or on the contrary, with too violent asseverations. There are many other particulars of the same kind, which may diminish or destroy the force of any argument, derived from human testimony.

Suppose, for instance, that the fact, which the testimony endeavours to establish, partakes of the extraordinary and the marvellous; in that case, the evidence, resulting from the testimony, admits of a diminution, greater or less, in proportion as the fact is more or less unusual. The reason why we place any credit in witnesses and historians, is not derived from any *connexion,* which we perceive *a priori,* between testimony and reality, but because we are accustomed to find a conformity between them. But when the fact attested is such a one as has seldom fallen under our observation, here is a contest of two opposite experiences; of which the one destroys the other, as far as its force goes, and the superior can only operate on the mind by the force, which remains. The very same principle of experience, which gives us a certain degree of assurance in the testimony of witnesses, gives us also, in this case, another degree of assurance against the fact, which they endeavour to establish; from which contradiction there necessarily arises a counterpoise, and mutual destruction of belief and authority.

"I should not believe such a story were it told me by Cato" was a proverbial saying in Rome, even during the lifetime of that philosophical patriot. The incredibility of a fact, it was allowed, might invalidate so great an authority.

The Indian prince, who refused to believe the first relations concerning the effects of frost, reasoned justly; and it naturally required very strong testimony to engage his assent to facts that arose from a state of nature, with which he was unacquainted, and which bore so little analogy to those events, of which he had had constant and uniform experience. Though they were not contrary to his experience, they were not conformable to it.[1]

---

[1]No Indian, it is evident, could have experience that water did not freeze in cold climates. This is placing nature in a situation quite unknown to him; and it is impossible for him to tell *a priori* what will result from it. It is making a new experiment, the consequence

But in order to increase the probability against the testimony of witnesses, let us suppose that the fact, which they affirm, instead of being only marvellous, is really miraculous; and suppose also, that the testimony considered apart and in itself, amounts to an entire proof; in that case, there is proof against proof, of which the strongest must prevail, but still with a diminution of its force, in proportion to that of its antagonist.

A miracle is a violation of the laws of nature; and as a firm and unalterable experience has established these laws, the proof against a miracle, from the very nature of the fact, is as entire as any argument from experience can possibly be imagined. Why is it more than probable that all men must die; that lead cannot, of itself, remain suspended in the air; that fire consumes wood, and is extinguished by water; unless it be that these events are found agreeable to the laws of nature, and there is required a violation of these laws, or in other words, a miracle to prevent them? Nothing is esteemed a miracle, if it ever happen in the common course of nature. It is no miracle that a man, seemingly in good health, should die on a sudden: because such a kind of death, though more unusual than any other, has yet been frequently observed to happen. But it is a miracle that a dead man should come to life; because that has never been observed in any age or country. There must, therefore, be a uniform experience against every miraculous event, otherwise the event would not merit that appellation. And as a uniform experience amounts to a proof, there is here a direct and full *proof,* from the nature of the fact, against the existence of any miracle; nor

---

of which is always uncertain. One may sometimes conjecture from analogy what will follow; but still this is but conjecture. And it must be confessed, that, in the present case of freezing, the event follows contrary to the rules of analogy, and is such as a rational Indian would not look for. The operations of cold upon water are not gradual, according to the degrees of cold; but whenever it comes to the freezing point, the water passes in a moment, from the utmost liquidity to perfect hardness. Such an event, therefore, may be denominated *extraordinary,* and requires a pretty strong testimony, to render it credible to people in a warm climate: But still it is not *miraculous,* nor contrary to uniform experience of the course of nature in cases where all the circumstances are the same. The inhabitants of Sumatra have always seen water fluid in their own climate, and the freezing of their rivers ought to be deemed a prodigy: But they never saw water in Muscovy during the winter; and therefore they cannot reasonably be positive what would there be the consequence.

can such a proof be destroyed, or the miracle rendered credible, but by an opposite proof, which is superior.[2]

The plain consequence is (and it is a general maxim worthy of our attention) "that no testimony is sufficient to establish a miracle, unless the testimony be of such a kind that its falsehood would be more miraculous than the fact which it endeavours to establish; and even in that case there is a mutual destruction of arguments, and the superior only gives us an assurance suitable to that degree of force, which remains, after deducting the inferior." When anyone tells me that he saw a dead man restored to life, I immediately consider with myself whether it be more probable that this person should either deceive or be deceived, or that the fact, which he relates, should really have happened. I weigh the one miracle against the other; and according to the superiority which I discover, I pronounce my decision, and always reject the greater miracle. If the falsehood of his testimony would be more miraculous than the event which he relates; then, and not till then, can he pretend to command my belief or opinion.

Part II

In the foregoing reasoning we have supposed that the testimony, upon which a miracle is founded, may possibly amount to an entire proof,

---

[2]Sometimes an event may not, *in itself, seem* to be contrary to the laws of nature, and yet, if it were real, it might, be reason of some circumstances, be denominated a miracle; because, in *fact*, it is contrary to these laws. Thus if a person, claiming a divine authority, should command a sick person to be well, a healthful man to fall down dead, the clouds to pour rain, the winds to blow, in short, should order many natural events, which immediately follow upon his command; these might justly be esteemed miracles, because they are really, in this case, contrary to the laws of nature. For if any suspicion remain that the event and command concurred by accident, there is no miracle and no transgression of the laws of nature. If this suspicion be removed, there is evidently a miracle, and a transgression of these laws; because nothing can be more contrary to nature than that the voice or command of a man should have such an influence. A miracle may be accurately defined, *a transgression of a law of nature by a particular volition of the Deity, or by the interposition of some invisible agent.* A miracle may either be discoverable by men or not. This alters not its nature and essence. The raising of a house or ship into the air is a visible miracle. The raising of a feather, when the wind wants ever so little of a force requisite for that purpose, is as real a miracle, though not so sensible with regard to us.

and that the falsehood of that testimony would be a real prodigy. But it is easy to show that we have been a great deal too liberal in our concession, and that there never was a miraculous event established on so full an evidence.

For *first,* there is not to be found, in all history, any miracle attested by a sufficient number of men, of such unquestioned good sense, education, and learning, as to secure us against all delusion in themselves; of such undoubted integrity, as to place them beyond all suspicion of any design to deceive others; of such credit and reputation in the eyes of mankind, as to have a great deal to lose in case of their being detected in any falsehood; and at the same time, attesting facts performed in such a public manner and in so celebrated a part of the world, as to render the detection unavoidable. All which circumstances are requisite to give us a full assurance in the testimony of men.

Secondly. We may observe in human nature a principle which, if strictly examined, will be found to diminish extremely the assurance, which we might, from human testimony, have, in any kind of prodigy. The maxim, by which we commonly conduct ourselves in our reasonings, is that the objects of which we have no experience resemble those of which we have; that what we have found to be most usual is always most probable; and that where there is an opposition of arguments, we ought to give the preference to such as are founded on the greatest number of past observations. But though, in proceeding by this rule, we readily reject any fact which is unusual and incredible in an ordinary degree; yet in advancing farther, the mind observes not always the same rule; but when anything is affirmed utterly absurd and miraculous, it rather the more readily admits of such a fact, upon account of that very circumstance, which ought to destroy all its authority. The passion of *surprise* and *wonder,* arising from miracles, being an agreeable emotion, gives a sensible tendency towards the belief of those events, from which it is derived. And this goes so far, that even those who cannot enjoy this pleasure immediately, nor can believe those miraculous events, of which they are informed, yet love to partake of the satisfaction at second-hand or by rebound, and place a pride and delight in exciting the admiration of others.

With what greediness are the miraculous accounts of travellers received, their descriptions of sea and land monsters, their relations of wonderful adventures, strange men, and uncouth manners? But if the spirit of religion join itself to the love of wonder, there is an end of common sense; and human testimony, in these circumstances, loses all pretensions to authority. A religionist may be an enthusiast, and imagine he sees what has no reality: he may know his narrative to be false, and yet persevere in it, with the best intentions in the world, for the sake of promoting so holy a cause: or even where this delusion has not place, vanity, excited by so strong a temptation, operates on him more powerfully than on the rest of mankind in any other circumstances; and self-interest with equal force. His auditors may not have, and commonly have not, sufficient judgement to canvass his evidence: what judgement they have, they renounce by principle, in these sublime and mysterious subjects: or if they were ever so willing to employ it, passion and a heated imagination disturb the regularity of its operations. Their credulity increases his impudence: and his impudence overpowers their credulity.

Eloquence, when at its highest pitch, leaves little room for reason or reflection; but addressing itself entirely to the fancy or the affections, captivates the willing hearers, and subdues their understanding. Happily, this pitch it seldom attains. But what a Tully or a Demosthenes could scarcely effect over a Roman or Athenian audience, every *Capuchin,* every itinerant or stationary teacher can perform over the generality of mankind, and in a higher degree, by touching such gross and vulgar passions.

The many instances of forged miracles, and prophecies, and supernatural events, which, in all ages, have either been detected by contrary evidence, or which detect themselves by their absurdity, prove sufficiently the strong propensity of mankind to the extraordinary and the marvellous, and ought reasonably to beget a suspicion against all relations of this kind. This is our natural way of thinking, even with regard to the most common and most credible events. For instance: There is no kind of report which rises so easily, and spreads so quickly, especially in country places and provincial towns, as those concerning marriages; insomuch that two young persons of equal condition never see each other twice, but the whole neighborhood immediately join them together. The pleasure of telling a piece of news so interesting, of propagating it, and of being the first reporters of it, spreads the intelligence. And this is so well known, that no man of sense gives attention to these reports, till he find them confirmed by some greater evidence. Do not the same passions, and others still stronger, incline the generality of mankind to believe and report, with the greatest vehemence and assurance, all religious miracles?

Thirdly. It forms a strong presumption against all supernatural and miraculous relations, that they are observed chiefly to abound among ignorant and barbarous nations; or if a civilized people has ever given admission to any of them, that people will be found to have received them from ignorant and barbarous ancestors, who transmitted them with that inviolable sanction and authority, which always attend received opinions. When we peruse the first histories of all nations, we are apt to imagine ourselves transported into some new world; where the whole frame of nature is disjointed, and every element performs its operations in a different manner from what it does at present. Battles, revolutions, pestilence, famine, and death are never the effect of those natural causes which we experience. Prodigies, omens, oracles, judgements, quite obscure the few natural events that are intermingled with them. But as the former grow thinner every page, in proportion as we advance nearer the enlightened ages, we soon learn that there is nothing mysterious or supernatural in the case, but that all proceeds from the usual propensity of mankind towards the marvellous, and that, though this inclination may at intervals receive a check from sense and learning, it can never be thoroughly extirpated from human nature.

"It is strange," a judicious reader is apt to say, upon the perusal of these wonderful historians, "that such prodigious events never happen in our days." But it is nothing strange, I hope, that men should lie in all ages. You must surely have seen instances enough of that frailty. You have yourself heard many such marvellous relations started, which, being treated with scorn by all the wise and judicious, have at last been abandoned even by the vulgar. Be assured that those renowned lies, which have spread and flourished to such a monstrous height, arose from like beginnings but being sown in a more proper soil, shot up at last into prodigies almost equal to those which they relate.

It was a wise policy in that false prophet, Alexander, who though now forgotten, was once so famous, to lay the first scene of his impostures in Paphlagonia, where, as Lucian tells us, the people were extremely ignorant and stupid, and ready to swallow even the grossest delusion. People at a distance, who are weak enough to think the matter at all worth inquiry, have no opportunity of receiving better information. The stories come magnified to them by a hundred circumstances. Fools are industrious in propagating the imposture; while the wise and learned are contented, in general, to deride its absurdity, without informing themselves of the particular facts, by which it may be distinctly refuted. And thus the impostor above mentioned was enabled to proceed, from his ignorant Paphlagonians, to the enlisting of votaries, even among the Grecian philosophers, and men of the most eminent rank and distinction in Rome: nay, could engage the attention of that sage emperor Marcus Aurelius; so far as to make him trust the success of a military expedition to his delusive prophecies.

The advantages are so great, of starting an imposture among an ignorant people, that, even though the delusion should be too gross to impose on the generality of them (*which, though seldom, is sometimes the case*) it has a much better chance for succeeding in remote countries than if the first scene had been laid in a city renowned for arts and knowledge. The most ignorant and barbarous of these barbarians carry the report abroad. None of their countrymen have a large correspondence, or sufficient credit and authority to contradict and beat down the delusion. Men's inclination to the marvellous has full opportunity to display itself. And thus a story, which is universally exploded in the place where it was first started, shall pass for certain at a thousand miles distance. But had Alexander fixed his residence at Athens, the philosophers of that renowned mart of learning had immediately spread, throughout the whole Roman empire, their sense of the matter; which, being supported by so great authority, and displayed by all the force of reason and eloquence, had entirely opened the eyes of mankind. It is true; Lucian, passing by chance through Paphlagonia, had an opportunity of performing this good office. But, though much to be wished, it does not always happen that every Alexander meets with a Lucian, ready to expose and detect his impostures.

I may add as a *fourth* reason, which diminishes the authority of prodigies, that there is no testimony for any, even those which have not been expressly detected, that is not opposed by an infinite number of witnesses; so that not only the miracle destroys the credit of testimony, but the testimony destroys itself. To make this the better understood, let us consider that, in matters of religion, whatever is different is contrary; and that it is impossible the religions of ancient Rome, of Turkey, of Siam, and of China should, all of them, be established on any solid foundation. Every miracle, therefore, pretended to have been wrought in any of these religions (and all of them abound in miracles), as its direct scope is to establish the particular system to which it is attributed; so has it the same force, though more indirectly, to overthrow every other system. In destroying a rival system, it likewise destroys the credit of those miracles, on which that system was established; so that all the prodigies of different religions are to be regarded as contrary facts, and the evidences of these prodigies, whether weak or strong, as opposite to each other. According to this method of reasoning, when we believe any miracle of Mahomet or his successors, we have for our warrant the testimony of a few barbarous Arabians: and on the other hand, we are to regard the authority of Titus Livius, Plutarch, Tacitus, and, in short, of all the authors and witnesses, Grecian, Chinese, and Roman Catholic, who have related any miracle in their particular religion; I say, we are to regard their testimony in the same light as if they had mentioned that Mahometan miracle, and had in express terms contradicted it, with the same certainty as they have for the miracle they relate. This argument may appear over subtle and refined; but is not in reality different from the reasoning of a judge, who supposes that the credit of two witnesses, maintaining a crime against anyone, is destroyed by the testimony of two others, who affirm him to have been two hundred leagues distant, at the same instant when the crime is said to have been committed.

One of the best attested miracles in all profane history, is that which Tacitus reports of Vespasian, who cured a blind man in Alexandria, by means of his spittle, and a lame man by the mere touch of his foot; in obedience to a vision of the god Serapis, who had enjoined them to have recourse to the emperor, for these miraculous cures. The story may be seen in that fine historian; where every circumstance seems to add weight to the testimony, and might be displayed at large with all the force of argument and eloquence, if anyone were now concerned to enforce the evidence of that exploded and idolatrous superstition. The gravity, solidity, age, and probity of so great an emperor, who, through the whole course of his life, conversed in a familiar manner with his friends and courtiers, and never affected those extraordinary airs of divinity assumed by Alexander and Demetrius. The historian, a contemporary writer, noted for candour and veracity, and withal, the greatest and most penetrating genius, perhaps, of all antiquity; and

164

so free from any tendency to credulity, that he even lies under the contrary imputation, of atheism and profaneness: the persons, from whose authority he related the miracle, of established character for judgement and veracity, as we may well presume; eye-witnesses of the fact, and confirming their testimony, after the Flavian family was despoiled of the empire, and could no longer give any reward, as the price of a lie. *Utrumque, qui interfuere, nunc quoque memorant, postquam nullum mendacio pretium.* [Now those who were present remember afterwards, when there is no reward for lying.] To which if we add the public nature of the facts, as related, it will appear that no evidence can well be supposed stronger for so gross and so palpable a falsehood.

There is also a memorable story related by Cardinal de Retz, which may well deserve our consideration. When that intriguing politician fled into Spain, to avoid the persecution of his enemies, he passed through Saragossa, the capital of Arragon, where he was shown, in the cathedral, a man, who had served seven years as a doorkeeper, and was well known to everybody in town, that had ever paid his devotions at that church. He had been seen, for so long a time, wanting a leg; but recovered that limb by the rubbing of holy oil upon the stump; and the cardinal assures us that he saw him with two legs. This miracle was vouched by all the canons of the church; and the whole company in town were appealed to for a confirmation of the fact; whom the cardinal found, by their zealous devotion, to be thorough believers of the miracle. Here the relater was also contemporary to the supposed prodigy, of an incredulous and libertine character, as well as of great genius; the miracle of so *singular* a nature as could scarcely admit of a counterfeit, and the witnesses very numerous, and all of them, in a manner, spectators of the fact, to which they gave their testimony. And what adds mightily to the force of the evidence, and may double our surprise on this occasion, is that the cardinal himself, who relates the story, seems not to give any credit to it, and consequently cannot be suspected of any concurrence in the holy fraud. He considered justly that it was not requisite, in order to reject a fact of this nature, to be able accurately to disprove the testimony, and to trace its falsehood, through all the circumstances of knavery and credulity which produced it. He knew that, as this was commonly altogether impossible at any small distance of time and place, so was it extremely difficult, even where one was immediately present, by reason of the bigotry, ignorance, cunning, and roguery of a great part of mankind. He therefore concluded, like a just reasoner, that such an evidence carried falsehood upon the very face of it, and that a miracle, supported by any human testimony, was more properly a subject of derision than of argument.

There surely never was a greater number of miracles ascribed to one person than those which were lately said to have been wrought in France upon the tomb of Abbé Paris, the famous Jansenist, with whose sanctity the people were so long deluded. The curing of the sick, giving hearing to the deaf, and sight to the blind, were everywhere talked of as the usual effects of that holy sepulchre. But what is more extraordinary; many of the miracles were immediately proved upon the spot, before judges of unquestioned integrity, attested by witnesses of credit and distinction, in a learned age, and on the most eminent theatre that is now in the world. Nor is this all: a relation of them was published and dispersed everywhere; nor were the *Jesuits,* though a learned body, supported by the çivil magistrate, and determined enemies to those opinions, in whose favour the miracles were said to have been wrought, ever able distinctly to refute or detect them. Where shall we find such a number of circumstances, agreeing to the corroboration of one fact? And what have we to oppose to such a cloud of witnesses, but the absolute impossibility or miraculous nature of the events which they relate? And this surely, in the eyes of all reasonable people, will alone be regarded as a sufficient refutation.

Is the consequence just, because some human testimony has the utmost force and authority in some cases, when it relates the battle of Philippi or Pharsalia for instance; that therefore all kinds of testimony must, in all cases, have equal force and authority? Suppose that the Caesarean and Pompeian factions had, each of them, claimed the victory in these battles, and that the historians of each party had uniformly ascribed the advantage to their own side; how could mankind, at this distance, have been able to determine between them? The contrariety is equally strong between the miracles related by Herodotus or Plutarch, and those delivered by Mariana, Bede, or any monkish historian.

The wise lend a very academic faith to every report which favours the passion of the reporter; whether it magnifies his country, his family, or himself, or in any other way strikes in with his natural inclinations and propensities. But what greater temptation than to appear a missionary, a prophet, an ambassador from heaven? Who would not encounter many dangers and difficulties, in order to attain so sublime a character? Or if, by the help of vanity and a heated imagination, a man has first made a convert of himself, and entered seriously into the delusion; who ever scruples to make use of pious frauds, in support of so holy and meritorious a cause?

The smallest spark may here kindle into the greatest flame, because the materials are always prepared for it. The *avidum genus auricularum,* the gazing populace, receive greedily, without examination, whatever sooths superstition, and promotes wonder.

How many stories of this nature have, in all ages, been detected and exploded in their infancy? How many more have been celebrated for a time, and have afterwards sunk into neglect and oblivion? Where such reports, therefore, fly about, the solution of the phenomenon is obvious; and we judge in conformity to regular experience and observation, when we account for it by the known and natural principles of credulity and delusion. And shall we, rather than have a recourse to so natural a solution, allow of a miraculous violation of the most established laws of nature?

I need not mention the difficulty of detecting a falsehood in any private or even public history, at the place, where it is said to happen; much more when the scene is removed to ever so small a distance. Even a court of judicature, with all the authority, accuracy, and judgement, which they can employ, find themselves often at a loss to distinguish between truth and falsehood in the most recent actions. But the matter never comes to any issue, if trusted to the common method of altercations and debate and flying rumours; especially when men's passions have taken part on either side.

In the infancy of new religions, the wise and learned commonly esteem the matter too inconsiderable to deserve their attention or regard. And when afterwards they would willingly detect the cheat, in order to undeceive the deluded multitude, the season is now past, and the records and witnesses, which might clear up the matter, have perished beyond recovery.

No means of detection remain, but those which must be drawn from the very testimony itself of the reporters: and these, though always sufficient with the judicious and knowing, are commonly too fine to fall under the comprehension of the vulgar.

Upon the whole, then, it appears that no testimony for any kind of miracle has ever amounted to a probability, much less to a proof; and that, even supposing it amounted to a proof, it would be opposed by another proof; derived from the very nature of the fact, which it would endeavour to establish. It is experience only which gives authority to human testimony; and it is the same experience which assures us of the laws of nature. When, therefore, these two kinds of experience are contrary, we have nothing to do but subtract the one from the other, and embrace an opinion, either on one side or the other, with that assurance which arises from the remainder. But according to the principle here explained, this subtraction, with regard to all popular religions, amounts to an entire annihilation; and therefore we may establish it as a maxim that no human testimony can have such force as to prove a miracle, and make it a just foundation for any such system of religion.

I beg the limitations here made may be remarked, when I say that a miracle can never be proved, so as to be the foundation of a system of religion. For I own that otherwise there may possibly be miracles, or violations of the usual course of nature, of such a kind as to admit of proof from human testimony; though, perhaps, it will be impossible to find any such in all the records of history. Thus, suppose all authors, in all languages, agree that, from the first of January 1600, there was a total darkness over the whole earth for eight days: suppose that the tradition of this extraordinary event is still strong and lively among the people: that all travellers, who return from foreign countries, bring us accounts of the same tradition, without the least variation or contradiction: it is evident that our present philosophers, instead of doubting the fact, ought to receive it as certain, and ought to search for the causes whence it might be derived. The decay, corruption, and dissolution of nature is an event rendered probable by so many analogies, that any phenomenon, which seems to have a tendency towards that catastrophe, comes within the reach of human testimony, if that testimony be very extensive and uniform.

But suppose that all the historians who treat of England should agree that, on the first of January 1600, Queen Elizabeth died; that both before and after her death she was seen by her physicians and the whole court, as is usual with persons of her rank; that her successor was acknowledged and proclaimed by the parliament; and that, after being interred a month, she again appeared, resumed the throne, and governed

England for three years: I must confess that I should be surprised at the concurrence of so many odd circumstances, but should not have the least inclination to believe so miraculous an event. I should not doubt of her pretended death, and of those other public circumstances that followed it: I should only assert it to have been pretended, and that it neither was, nor possibly could be real. You would in vain object to me the difficulty, and almost impossibility of deceiving the world in an affair of such consequence; the wisdom and solid judgement of that renowned queen; with the little or no advantage which she could reap from so poor an artifice. All this might astonish me; but I would still reply that the knavery and folly of men are such common phenomena, that I should rather believe the most extraordinary events to arise from their concurrence than admit of so signal a violation of the laws of nature.

But should this miracle be ascribed to any new system of religion; men, in all ages, have been so much imposed on by ridiculous stories of that kind, that this very circumstance would be a full proof of a cheat, and sufficient, with all men of sense, not only to make them reject the fact, but even reject it without further examination. Though the Being to whom the miracle is ascribed, be, in this case, Almighty, it does not, upon that account, become a whit more probable; since it is impossible for us to know the attributes or actions of such a Being, otherwise than from the experience which we have of His productions, in the usual course of nature. This still reduces us to past observation, and obliges us to compare the instances of the violation of truth in the testimony of men, with those of the violation of the laws of nature by miracles, in order to judge which of them is most likely and probable. As the violations of truth are more common in the testimony concerning religious miracles than in that concerning any other matter of fact; this must diminish very much the authority of the former testimony, and make us form a general resolution, never to lend any attention to it, with whatever specious pretence it may be covered.

Lord Bacon seems to have embraced the same principles of reasoning. "We ought," says he, "to make a collection or particular history of all monsters and prodigious births or productions, and in a word of everything new, rare, and extraordinary in nature. But this must be done with the most severe scrutiny, lest we depart from truth. Above all, every relation must be considered as suspicious, which depends in any degree upon religion, as the prodigies of Livy: and no less so, everything that is to be found in the writers of natural magic or alchimy, or such authors, who seem, all of them, to have an unconquerable appetite for falsehood and fable."[3]

I am the better pleased with the method of reasoning here delivered, as I think it may serve to confound those dangerous friends or disguised enemies to the *Christian religion,* who have undertaken to defend it by the principles of human reason. Our most holy religion is founded on *faith,* not on reason; and it is a sure method of exposing it to put it to such a trial as it is, by no means, fitted to endure. To make this more evident, let us examine those miracles related in scripture; and not to lose ourselves in too wide a field, let us confine ourselves to such as we find in the *Pentateuch,* which we shall examine, according to the principles of these pretended Christians, not as the word or testimony of God Himself, but as the production of a mere human writer and historian. Here then we are first to consider a book, presented to us by a barbarous and ignorant people, written in an age when they were still more barbarous, and in all probability long after the facts which it relates, corroborated by no concurring testimony, and resembling those fabulous accounts, which every nation gives of its origin. Upon reading this book, we find it full of prodigies and miracles. It gives an account of a state of the world and of human nature entirely different from the present: of our fall from that state: of the age of man, extended to near a thousand years: of the destruction of the world by a deluge: of the arbitrary choice of one people, as the favourites of heaven; and that people the countrymen of the author: of their deliverance from bondage by prodigies the most astonishing imaginable: I desire anyone to lay his hand upon his heart, and after a serious consideration declare whether he thinks that the falsehood of such a book, supported by such a testimony, would be more extraordinary and miraculous than all the miracles it relates; which is, however, necessary to make it be received, according to the measures of probability above established.

What we have said of miracles may be applied, without any variation, to prophecies; and indeed, all prophecies are real miracles, and as such only, can be admitted as proofs of any revelation. If it did not exceed the capacity of human nature to foretell future events, it would

---

[3]*Novum Organum,* Bk. II, Aphorism 19.

be absurd to employ any prophecy as an argument for a divine mission or authority from heaven. So that, upon the whole, we may conclude, that the *Christian religion* not only was at first attended with miracles, but even at this day cannot be believed by any reasonable person without one. Mere reason is insufficient to convince us of its veracity: and whoever is moved by *faith* to assent to it is conscious of a continued miracle in his own person, which subverts all the principles of his understanding and gives him a determination to believe what is most contrary to custom and experience.

IMMANUEL KANT

Immanuel Kant (1724–1804), because he was thoroughly schooled in the German rationalism of Christian Wolff, believed that knowledge was and had to be necessary and universal. He was convinced that Euclidean geometry and Newtonian mechanics were true and that nature's laws are fixed. When he read a summary of Hume's analysis of causality, he was forced to agree that there were no observable necessary connections between our sense impressions. This challenge led him to abandon his inherited rationalism and to reconceive completely his understanding of how knowledge was possible in mathematics, physics, and metaphysics. He found that he could retain his convictions about the necessity and universality of mathematics and physics only at the cost of turning all knowledge into a construct of human sensibility and reason. Our knowledge is genuine but is a knowledge of appearances, not of reality as it is in itself. Theology was denied the status of knowledge. Within Kant's system this was an advantage, since it meant that theology was not dealing with the constructs of the human faculty of knowing, that is, with appearances, as were mathematics and physics. Kant claimed that by limiting knowledge to appearances, he was making room for faith.

Pure Reason and the Question of God
(Selections from *Critique of Pure Reason*)

PREFACE

Whenever the cognitive efforts of reason come to a standstill or must frequently backtrack and embark on a new course, we may be convinced that they have not yet found the secure road of a science.

Dealing with nothing but the formal rules of all thought, logic has not taken any backward step since Aristotle and seems to be complete as a science. What assured this success was abstraction from all objects and their differences and concentration on the mere form of the understanding.

If reason is to manifest itself in sciences properly and objectively so called, something in them must be cognized a priori. There are two ways in which a cognition of reason may refer to its object: either by merely *determining* the object and its concept or by also *making it actual.* The first is the *theoretical,* the second the *practical* cognition of reason. Of these the pure part, in which reason determines its object completely a priori, must be presented first by itself without confounding it with what comes from other sources.

Mathematics and physics are the two theoretical cognitions of reason which are to determine their objects a priori, the former as an entirely pure science, the latter at least partially so, but also according to cognitive sources other than reason.

From the times of the ancient Greeks, *mathematics* has been advancing on the course of a secure science after someone, in a revolutionary turn of thought, had found that in order to demonstrate the properties of the isosceles triangle he must neither pore over what he saw in its figure nor investigate its mere concept. It struck him that he must not, as it were, collect the properties of the triangle in a copying way but produce them through what he himself, according to concepts, thought into the figure and exhibited by construction a priori. He found that in order to gain any secure knowledge a priori, he must ascribe to the matter only what necessarily follows, in accordance with his concept, from his own input into it.

Not until Bacon came forward with his ingenious proposals did *natural science* enter on the high-road of a science in a rapid intellectual revolution through the discoveries of Galilei, Toricelli, and Stahl. They comprehended that reason has insight only into what it produces according to its own design. Holding in one hand principles of its judgments according to which alone conforming appearances can have the validity of laws, and in the other hand the experiment designed after those principles, reason must approach nature to be taught by it indeed, though not in the capacity of a pupil but of an appointed judge who makes witnesses answer the questions he puts to them.

Metaphysics, an entirely isolated speculative cognition of reason, which rises above the instruction of experience, has been less fortunate. No doubt, its activities so far have been a mere groping among mere concepts.

One should think that the examples of mathematics and natural science, which have reached their present status through one-time revolutions, are noteworthy enough to try a similarly revised mode of thought for metaphysics and to imitate them herein as much as the analogy of cognitions of reason permits. Heretofore one assumed that all our cognition must conform to the objects. Any attempt, however, to expand our cognition of them a priori through concepts foundered on this presupposition. Let us therefore see, for once, whether in tasks of metaphysics we may not make better progress by assuming that the objects must conform to our cognition. This already agrees better with the possibility of their cognition a priori, a cognition that shall establish something about objects before they are given to us. The situation is here the same as with the first thought of Copernicus. After it did not go too well with an explanation of celestial movements when he assumed that the whole starry sky turned round the spectator, he tried, whether it might not go better if he made the spectator turn and left the stars alone.

In metaphysics one may try a similar procedure. If the object of the senses must conform to qualities of our faculty of intuiting, and if the concepts by which intuitions are determined conform to rules of the understanding expressed in concepts a priori, the possibility of cognition a priori is readily conceivable. With regard to objects that cannot be given in any experience but are merely thought by reason, and indeed necessarily so, the attempts to think them (for it must be possible to think them) will provide a magnificent touchstone of the changed method of thought, namely, that we cognize a priori of things only what we have put into them ourselves.

This attempt succeeds according to expectation. It promises the secure progress of a science in the first part of metaphysics, where we are dealing with concepts a priori the corresponding objects of which can be given in experience. This deduction of our faculty of cognition a priori, however, has a result that seems very detrimental to the second part of metaphysics, as it does not enable us to advance beyond the limit of possible experience, which is the very purpose of this science.

But herein consists the experiment of a counter-check of the truth of our first appreciation of reason's cognition a priori, namely, that it covers appearances only, leaving the matter in itself untouched as actual by itself but unknown to us. For what necessarily drives us to go beyond the limit of experience and of all appearances is *the unconditioned* which reason necessarily and rightly demands in the things in themselves for all that is conditioned, thereby completing the series of conditions. If the unconditioned can be thought without contradiction in this way only: that it belongs to things not as we know them (they are given to us) but as we do not know them (as matters in themselves), then our original assumption, which we adopted by way of a trial only, turns out to be justified. I am proposing this revised mode of thought here in the Preface as a hypothesis only, although in the treatise itself it is proved apodictically out of the quality of our presentations of space and time and the elemental concepts of the understanding. If speculative reason, however, is denied any advance in the field of the supersensible, we nevertheless remain free to try whether practical cognition may not provide data to determine reason's transcendent concept of the unconditioned.

The present critique of pure speculative reason attempts to alter the old procedure of metaphysics by revolutionizing it after the example of geometers and physicists. It is a tractate on method, not a system of the science itself. But it delineates the whole of metaphysics in respect of both its boundaries and its inner organization. Reason being a separate self-contained unity, metaphysics has the good fortune, once it is led by critique onto a secure scientific course, of being able to encompass the entire field of its cognition and deposit its work for posterity as a never to be augmented capital stock of principles, including advice on the restrictions of their use.

One will ask: Is this science not merely negative, as it does not permit us to transcend the boundaries of experience? Its advantage is positive as soon as we become aware that the unbridled use of speculative reason actually restricts reason's use by crowding out its practical use. Protecting the latter is a positive and very important benefit. To deny this would be as much as saying that the police render no positive service when they enable citizens to attend to their affairs unimpeded by violence. In confining reason's speculative cognition to objects of experience it is to be noted, however, that we must remain free, if not to *cognize,* yet to think the same objects also as things in themselves. For otherwise the absurd proposition would follow that appearance is without anything that appears. To *cognize* an object requires that I can prove its possibility, either according to the testimony of experience from its actuality or a priori through reason. On the other hand, I may think whatever I please, provided I do not contradict myself, that is, my concept is a possible thought.

Without the distinction between things as objects of experience [appearances] and things in themselves, I could not say that the will is free and at the same time subject to natural necessity, that is, not free. Although I cannot cognize freedom as the property of a being, because I would have to cognize it as determined in its existence and yet as not determined, I can nevertheless think freedom, that is, my presentation of it at least contains no contradiction. If moral science introduces original principles of reason as data a priori that would be outright impossible without the presupposition of freedom, morality maintains its place as long as freedom does not contradict its own concept and is no obstacle to admitting nature's mechanism.

The same positive advantage of critical principles holds good for the concepts of God and the simple nature of the soul. I cannot even *assume* God, freedom, and immortality for the sake of the necessary practical use of reason, unless I deprive speculative reason of its presumptuous insights. I thus had to suspend knowledge in order to make room for belief.

A system of metaphysics drawn up according to standards of the *Critique of Pure Reason* is no trifling bequest, as it endows us with the means of putting an end, once and for all, to any objection against morality and religion in Socratic fashion, namely by the clearest proof of the opponent's nescience. As there will always be some kind of metaphysics and, with it, a natural dialectic of pure reason, it is the first and most important task of philosophy to deprive it of its damaging influence by sealing off the source of errors.

Any loss herein concerns only the monopoly of the schools and their arrogant claims, not in the least, however, the interest of men. Something is left, though, also for the legitimate claims of speculative philosophers. They remain the sole depositaries of a science, the critique of reason, which can never become popular but benefits the public without it being aware of it. The scandal of quarreling metaphysicians can be prevented only by a thorough investigation of the rights of speculative reason, and critique alone cuts off the roots of materialism, fatalism, atheism, unbelief, bigotry, superstition, lastly also of [speculative] idealism and skepticism (which are primarily a danger to the schools).

The Critique is not opposed to the dogmatic procedure of reason in its pure cognition as a science—which must always be dogmatic, that is, strictly proving from secure principles a priori—but to dogmatism, to the presumption of a pure cognition out of concepts according to principles cultivated by reason without investigating the manner and rightfulness of their acquisition. Dogmatism thus is the dogmatic procedure of pure reason without preceding critique of its own faculty.

When carrying out the plan prescribed by the *Critique* in a future system of metaphysics, we must follow the strict method of Wolff, the greatest among all dogmatic philosophers. He showed how the secure course of a science is to be followed by setting up principles as laws, by distinct determination of concepts, by attempting rigorousness in proofs while avoiding jumps in conclusions. He would have been particularly gifted to raise metaphysics to the status of a science, had it occurred to him to clear the way for it by a critique of its organ, that is, pure reason itself. Those who reject Wolff's method and also the procedure of the *Critique of Pure Reason* can only aim at shaking off the fetters of science, turning work into play, certainty into opinion, and philosophy into philodoxy.

This second edition has provided an opportunity to remove, as much as possible, difficulties and obscurities in the work. In the propositions themselves and their grounds of proof, also in the form and completeness of the plan, I found nothing to alter. In matters of presentation, however, much is left to be done, and here I have tried improvements for this edition. Apart from adding a new refutation of psychological idealism and a strict proof of the objective reality of outer intuition . . . , my changes in presentation are meant to remedy misunderstandings of the Transcendental Aesthetic, especially of the concept of time, obscurity in the Deduction of the Pure Concepts of the Understanding, alleged lack of evidence in the proofs of the Cardinal Propositions of the Pure Understanding, and lastly misinterpretation of the Paralogisms of rational psychology. Certain cuts, if the book was not to become too voluminous by the insertion of new parts, should be off-set by better comprehensibility and need not be a loss, since the omitted parts can easily be looked up in the first edition.

In isolated passages every philosophic discourse is vulnerable, because it cannot appear as well armoured as a mathematical presentation. Even seeming contradictions may be picked from any writing that proceeds as free speech. They cast an unfavorable light on it in the eyes of those who rely on secondary judgment, but not with those who have mastered the idea of the whole and therefore can resolve them easily.

INTRODUCTION

I

Of the difference between pure and empirical cognition

In terms of time, no cognition in us precedes experience, and with experience all cognition begins. Although all cognition begins with experience, not all of it springs from experience. Experiential cognition itself could well be a composite of what we receive through impressions and what our own faculty of cognition, prompted by sensible impressions, yields out of itself. A cognition independent of experience and even of all impressions of the senses is called *a priori*. One distinguishes it from empirical cognitions, which have their sources *a posteriori,* that is in experience.

Of someone who undermined the foundation of his house one says: he could have known a priori that it would collapse. Completely a priori, however, he could not know this. That bodies are heavy and, without support, fall, had to become known to him first through experience.

By cognitions a priori we therefore do not understand cognitions that are independent of this or that experience but those which are completely independent of any experience.

Cognitions a priori that have no admixture of anything empirical are called pure. The proposition: Every change has its cause, is a proposition a priori, but not pure, because the concept of change can be drawn only from experience.

II

*We are in possession of certain cognitions a priori
and even common understanding is never without them*

Experience teaches us that something is of such and such a quality, but not that it could not be otherwise. If a proposition is at the same time (1) thought with its *necessity*, it is a judgment a priori; if moreover it is derived from none other but which itself is necessary, it is an a priori proposition without qualification.

Experience never gives its judgments true and strict, but only an assumed and comparative generality (through induction). If therefore a judgment is (2) thought in *strict generality* without the possibility of any exception, it is not derived from experience and is a proposition valid a priori without qualification.

Necessity and strict generality thus are, each by itself, secure marks of a cognition a priori and belong inseparably together. The propositions of mathematics can exemplify this; or, from the commonest use of the understanding, a proposition such as: All that is accidental has a cause.

Not only judgments, however, even certain concepts are showing their a-priori origin. If we drop from our empirical concept of an object — corporeal or non-corporeal — all properties gathered from experience: the one by which it is thought as a *substance* or as *inherent* in a substance can not be excluded from it (notwithstanding this concept of substance is more determinate than the concept of an object generatim).

III

*Philosophy requires a science determining the possibility,
the principles, and the scope of all cognitions a priori*

What is even more significant: some of our concepts a priori, such as God, freedom, immortality, leave the field of all possible experience and seem to extend the scope of our judgments beyond all limits of experience. The science aiming at a solution of these inevitable tasks of pure reason is metaphysics. It seems natural to ask, how can the understanding arrive at those cognitions a priori? What scope, validity, and value do they have? It is equally natural, however, that for a long time attempts to answer these questions should have been shelved and excuses offered to reassure us of the solidity of existing metaphysical edifices in order to protect them from dangerous scrutiny.

A great amount of reason's activity consists in the analysis of concepts which we already have. It produces many cognitions that are treated with the esteem of new insights, although they are nothing but clarifications of what already had been thought in our concept. Under the pretext of this procedure, which yields some actual cognition a priori, reason surreptitiously introduces assertions of a very different kind in making a-priori additions of completely new concepts to given ones, without anyone knowing or asking how reason arrives at them. We shall deal here right at the beginning with these two kinds of cognition.

IV

Of the difference between analytic
and synthetic judgments

In all judgments in which a relation between subject and predicate is thought (if we consider affirmative judgments only, for the application to negative judgments is easy), this relation is possible in a twofold way: either the predicate B belongs to the subject A as something that is (covertly) contained in the concept A; or B lies entirely outside A, although it is connected with it. In the first case I call the judgment *analytic,* in the second *synthetic.* In analytic judgments the connection of the predicate with the subject is thought through identity. Judgments in which the connection is thought without identity shall be called synthetic judgments. The former could also be called *explicative,* the latter *augmentative* judgments, because in those of the first kind the predicate adds nothing to the subject concept. Analytic judgments merely break up the subject concept into its conceptual components, which had already been thought in it (though in a disordered way). Augmentative judgments, on the other hand, add a predicate to the subject concept that had not been thought in it at all and could not have been extracted

180

from it by any analysis. If, for instance, I say: all bodies are extended, this is an analytic judgment. If, however, I say: all bodies are heavy, the predicate is something entirely different from what I think through the mere concept of a body generatim. The addition of such a predicate therefore yields a synthetic judgment.

All experiential judgments as such are synthetic. It is experience on which the possibility of the synthesis of the predicate "heavy" with the concept "body" is based. For both concepts—neither of which is contained in the other—belong to each other, though only contingently, as parts of a whole: of experience, which itself is a synthetic conjunction of intuitions.

This support is totally lacking in *a priori synthetic judgments.* Let us take the proposition: All that happens has its cause. In the concept of something that happens I think an existence preceded by a time, etc., and from this analytic judgments may be drawn. But the concept of a cause lies entirely outside that concept, indicating something different from that which happens. What is it that entitles me to predicate, of what happens generatim, something totally different, and to cognize the concept of cause, though not contained in it, as nevertheless belonging to it, and this even with necessity? What is here the unknown=X on which the understanding bases itself when it believes that it knows, outside the concept A, a foreign predicate B nevertheless to be connected with it?

In such fundamental synthetic (augmentative) propositions resides the whole ultimate purpose of our speculative cognition a priori.

V

*All theoretical sciences of reason
contain a priori synthetic judgements as principles*

1. *All mathematical judgments are synthetic.* Because it was found that the conclusions of mathematicians always proceed along the principle of contradiction, one became persuaded—quite erroneously—that also the basic propositions of mathematical conclusions are cognized out of the principle of contradiction. One may gain insight into a synthetic proposition by means of the principle of contradiction indeed, but only by presupposing another synthetic proposition from which it is concluded, never by itself.

All mathematical propositions are judgments a priori, because they carry necessity.

The proposition 7+5=12 is a synthetic proposition. The concept of twelve is by no means already thought by taking 7 and 5 together. In the concept of a sum of 7 and 5 I have only thought the concept of a unification of two numbers but not the sole number that comprises both. Intuition must be called in (for instance the points of Segner's arithmetic), and we must go beyond the conceptual content to obtain the answer. The arithmetical proposition is always synthetic, as becomes all the more noticeable in larger numbers.

The basic propositions of geometry are likewise synthetic. A few basic propositions in mathematics that are really analytic, e.g., a=a, (a+b) >a, serve only the chain of method (as do identical propositions).

2. *Natural science (physica) contains a priori synthetic judgments as principles,* for instance: in all changes of the corporeal world the quantity of matter remains unchanged; or: in all imparting of motion, action and reaction must be equal.

3. *Metaphysics is meant to contain synthetic cognitions a priori.* Metaphysics is not merely interested in analyzing concepts that we have formed a priori of things. What we want in metaphysics is an a-priori expansion of our cognition by the use of underlying propositions that add to the given concept something not contained in it and, in synthetic judgments a priori, even transcend experience, for instance in the proposition: The world must have a first beginning. At least from the viewpoint of its purpose, metaphysics consists of nothing but synthetic propositions a priori.

VI

General task of pure reason

Much is gained by bringing a multiplicity of investigations under the formula of one task. The task of pure reason is expressed in the question:

How are synthetic judgments a priori possible?

Metaphysics stands or falls with the solution of this problem. That it has remained in a state of uncertainty and contradictions must be ascribed solely to the fact that one did not contemplate this task and perhaps not even the distinction between analytic and synthetic judgments. David Hume came closest to seeing the problem but was far from conceiving it with sufficient definiteness and in its generality.

Comprised in the solution of the above task is the possibility of reason's use in establishing and executing all sciences that contain a theoretical cognition a priori of objects. It includes the answer to these questions:

How is pure mathematics possible?
How is pure natural science possible?

Of these sciences we may fittingly ask how they are possible, for that they must be possible is proved by their actuality.

As for metaphysics, everyone has a right to doubt its possibility because of its lamentable performance. But in a certain sense metaphysical cognition must also be considered to be given. Metaphysics is actual, not as a science, but as a natural disposition (*metaphysica naturalis*). For human reason, out of its own need, irrepressibly proceeds to questions that cannot be answered by any experiential use of reason. In all men, as soon as their reason rises to speculation, there has always been and always will be some metaphysics. Of this then it may also be asked:

How is metaphysics as a natural disposition possible?

Or: How do the questions posed by pure reason originate in the nature of general human reason?

In view of the inevitable contradictions engendered by such natural questions as, for instance, whether the world has a first beginning or is from eternity, it must be possible to reach certainty by a decision concerning the objects at issue or reason's ability (or inability) to judge them. Quite rightly then, the last question flowing from the above general task runs:

How is metaphysics as a science possible?

The critique of reason therefore leads at last to science, reason's dogmatic use without critique, however, to skepticism.

VII

Idea and division of a special science
under the name Critique of Pure Reason

From all this follows the idea of a special science that may be called critique of pure reason. For reason is the faculty which supplies the principles of cognition a priori. Pure reason contains the principles of cognizing something strictly a priori. An *organon* of pure reason would be a complex of those principles according to which all pure cognitions a priori may be acquired and actually produced. The complete application of such an organon would provide a system of pure reason. Since this is asking very much and since it is still undecided whether an expansion of our cognition, and in what cases, is here possible at all, we may regard a science passing judgment on pure reason, its sources, and its limits, as the *propaedeutic* to the system of pure reason. It would have to be called a *critique,* and not a doctrine, *of pure reason.*

I call all cognition *transcendental* that is occupied not so much with objects as with our manner of cognizing objects so far as it is meant to be possible a priori. A system of such concepts would be called *transcendental philosophy,* which again, to begin with, is too much. For such a science would have to comprise analytic and synthetic cognition a priori, whereas we need analysis only so far as it is indispensibly necessary to gain insight into the principles of synthesis a priori in their whole extent, which is our sole purpose here. This investigation is called *transcendental critique,* because it aims not at augmentation but at the correction of cognitions. It is to form the touchstone of the worth or worthlessness of all cognitions a priori. Such a critique therefore is a preparation, if possible, for an organon, or otherwise for a *canon* at least of pure reason according to which the complete system of its philosophy eventually may be presented analytically as well as synthetically, be it in expansion or mere limitation of its cognition.

The extent of such a system cannot be very large, because the object here is not the nature of things—which is inexhaustible—but the understanding which judges the nature of things, and this again only in respect of its cognition a priori. Still less should one expect here a critique of books and systems but only that of the pure faculty of reason itself.

To the critique of pure reason belongs everything that makes up transcendental philosophy, and this Critique is the complete idea of transcendental philosophy, but still not that science itself, because in analysis it goes only as far as is required for a complete estimation of synthetic cognition a priori.

The most important point in the division of such a science is that no concepts are admitted which contain anything empirical or that the cognition a priori be completely pure. The supreme principles of morality and its fundamental concepts therefore have no place in transcendental philosophy, in spite of their being cognitions a priori. They do not found their precepts on the concepts of pleasure and displeasure, it is true, but in drawing up the system of pure morality they nevertheless must include these empirical concepts in the concept of duty. Transcendental philosophy therefore is a philosophy of pure, merely speculative reason. For all that is practical, in so far as it contains motives, is related to feelings, which belong to empirical sources of cognition.

From the general viewpoint of a system, transcendental philosophy will comprise a *Doctrine of Elements* and a *Doctrine of Method.* There are two stems of human cognition springing perhaps from a common root: *sensibility* [*Sinnlichkeit*], and *understanding* [*Verstand*]. Through the former objects are *given to us,* by the latter they are *thought.* In so far as sensibility might contain presentations a priori forming the condition under which objects are given to us, it would belong to transcendental philosophy. A Transcendental Aesthetic would then form the first part of the science of elements, because the conditions under which alone objects of human cognition are given precede those under which they are thought.

TRANSCENDENTAL DOCTRINE OF ELEMENTS

Part I
Transcendental Aesthetic

§ 1

In whatever way and by whatever means a cognition may refer to objects, the immediate way of its referring to them, and the aim of all thought as a means, is *intuition* [*Anschauung*]. Intuition takes place only so far as the object is given to us, which requires, with human beings at least, that it affects the mind in a certain way. The capacity (receptivity) for obtaining presentations according as we are affected by objects is called *sensibility* [*Sinnlichkeit*]. By means of sensibility, therefore, objects are given to us, and it alone furnishes intuitions; these are *thought,* however, by the *understanding* [*Verstand*], and from it arise *concepts.* All thought, by means of certain characteristics, must refer directly or indirectly, lastly to intuitions, thus, with us, to sensibility, because in no other way can an object be given to us.

The effect of an object on the faculty of presentation as far as we are affected by it is *sensation* [*Empfindung*]. An intuition referring to the object through sensation is called empirical. The undetermined object of an empirical intuition is called *appearance* [*Erscheinung*].

What corresponds to sensation in the appearance I call its *matter;* that, however, which makes that the manifold of appearances can be ordered in certain relations, I call the *form* of appearance. Since that in which alone sensations can gain order and be placed in a certain form cannot itself be sensation, the matter of all appearance is given to us only a posteriori, its form, however, must lie ready, for all sensations, a priori in the mind and therefore lend itself to being considered apart from sensation.

I call presentations in which there is nothing that belongs to sensation pure (in the transcendental sense). The pure form of sensible intuitions accordingly will be found a priori in the mind, in which all the manifold of appearances is intuited in certain relations. This pure form of sensibility itself will also be called *pure intuition.* If I separate from the presentation of a body those components which are thought by the understanding, such as substance, force, divisibility, etc., and also those which belong to sensation, such as impenetrability, hardness, color, etc., something remains of this empirical intuition, namely, extension and shape [*Gestalt*]. These belong to pure intuition, which takes place a priori in the mind as a mere form of sensibility even without an actual object of the senses or sensation.

A science of all principles of sensibility a priori I call *transcendental aesthetic.* (It is advisable to retain the word "aesthetic" for this science, since a critique of taste, for which it is also used, cannot become a science.) A transcendental aesthetic will therefore form the first part of the Transcendental Doctrine of Elements, as distinguished from Transcendental Logic, the science of the principles of pure thought. We shall see that there are two pure forms of sensible intuition serving as principles of cognition a priori, namely, *space and time.*

First Section
Of Space

§ 2
Metaphysical exposition of this concept

By means of the outer sense (a property of our mind) we present to ourselves objects as external to us, and all of them in space. The inner sense, through which the mind views itself or its inner state, does not give an intuition of the soul itself as an object; but the intuition of its inner state is nevertheless possible only under a determinate form, so that everything internal is presented in relations of time. Time cannot be viewed externally, no more than space can be viewed as something in us. What then are space and time? Are they mere determinations or relations of things, such as would pertain, however, also to the things in themselves? Or are they determinations or relations that attach to the form of intuition only, thus to the subjective quality of our mind, without which they cannot be attributed to any thing?

We shall first give an exposition [*Erörterung*] of the concept of space. By exposition *(expositio)* I understand the distinct (though not complete) presentation of what belongs to a concept; metaphysical, however, is the exposition, if it contains what presents the concept as given a priori.

1. Space is *not an empirical concept* drawn from outer experiences. For in order to be able to refer certain sensations to something outside myself (to something in another locus of space) and likewise to present sensations as not only different but in different loci, the presentation of space must already be underlying. Accordingly, the presentation of space cannot be borrowed from the relations of outer appearance through experience. Rather, this outer experience itself becomes possible in the first place owing to the said presentation of space only.

187

2. Space is *a necessary presentation a priori* underlying all outer intuitions. One can never conceive of there being no space, although one can very well think that no objects are met with in it. Space therefore is considered the a-priori condition of the possibility of appearances and not a determination dependent on them.

3. Space is *not a discursive or,* as one says, *general concept* of relations of things, but pure intuition. For one can conceive of only one unitary space. If we speak of many spaces, we thereby understand parts only of one and the same space. The parts do not precede it as components; they can be thought only in it. Space is essentially one. The spatial manifold in it, thus also the general concept of spaces generatim, rests on delimitations only. Hence a non-empirical intuition a priori must underlie all concepts of space.

4. Space is conceived as an *infinite* given quantity. Now, every concept must be thought as a presentation contained in an infinite number of different possible presentations (as their common characteristic), thus containing these *under* itself. But no concept as such can be thought as containing an infinite number of presentations in itself. Yet, this is the way space is thought, for all parts of space to infinity are simultaneous. The original presentation of space therefore is *intuition* a priori and not *concept.*

§3
Transcendental exposition of the concept of space

By transcendental exposition, I understand the explanation of a concept as a principle from which insight may be gained into the possibility of other synthetic cognitions a priori. For this purpose it is required (1) that such cognitions actually flow from the given concept and (2) that these cognitions are possible only on the presupposition of a given manner of explanation of the concept.

Geometry determines the properties of space synthetically and yet a priori. Of what quality must the presentation of space be in order to make such a cognition possible? It must be intuition a priori. For from a mere concept no synthetic judgments can be drawn. As intuition, however, the presentation of space must be a priori, that is, pure non-empirical intuition, for the necessity (apodictic certainty) of geometrical propositions excludes empirical sources.

Conclusions from the above concepts

a) Space does not present a property of things in themselves or these in their relation to one another: space is not a determination that attaches to objects themselves and would remain if abstraction were made from all subjective conditions of intuition. For neither absolute nor relative determinations can be intuited prior to the existence of things to which they pertain, thus not a priori.

b) Space is nothing but the form of all appearances of outer senses, that is, the subjective condition of sensibility under which alone outer intuition is possible. Because the subject's receptivity of being affected by objects necessarily precedes all intuitions of these objects, it can be understood how the form of all appearances may be given prior to all actual perceptions, thus a priori in the mind, and how as pure intuition, in which all objects must be determined, it may contain principles of their relations prior to any experience.

As we cannot make the special conditions of sensibility conditions of the possibility of matters [*der Sachen*] but only conditions of their appearances, we may well say that space comprises all things that may appear externally to us, but not all things in themselves, whether intuited or not, or by whatever subject. If we add the restriction of a judgment to the subject concept, the judgment is valid unconditionally. The proposition: All things are beside one another in space, becomes universally valid when I say: All things, as outer appearances, are beside one another in space.

Accordingly, our exposition teaches the *reality* (objective validity) of space in respect of everything that may occur to us externally as an object, but at the same time the *ideality* of space in respect of things that reason ponders in themselves, that is, without regard to the quality of our sensibility. We therefore maintain the *empirical reality* of space (in respect of all possible experience), although we also maintain its *transcendental ideality,* meaning that space is nothing as soon as we drop the condition of the possibility of all experience and assume it as something underlying things in themselves.

Besides space there is no other subjective presentation related to

189

something *outer* that could be called a priori objective. For from no other such presentation can synthetic propositions a priori be derived as they can from the intuition of space (§ 3).

Second Section
Of Time

§ 4
Metaphysical exposition of this concept

1. Time is *not an empirical concept* drawn from any experience. For simultaneousness or succession themselves would not come into perception, if the presentation of time were not underlying a priori. Only if time is presupposed can one conceive of things being at one and the same time (simultaneous) or at different times (successive).

2. Time is *a necessary presentation* underlying all intuitions. One cannot, in respect of appearances generatim, suspend time itself, although one can very well take away the appearances out of time. Time therefore is given a priori. In it alone all actuality of appearances is possible. Time is the general condition of their possibility.

3. This necessity a priori is the basis of the possibility of apodictic propositions concerning the relations of time, or of axioms of time generatim: Time has only one dimension; different times are not simultaneous but successive (as different spaces are not successive but simultaneous). These basic propositions are valid as rules under which experiences generatim are possible, and they instruct us prior to experience, not through it.

4. Time is *not a discursive concept* but a pure form of sensible intuition. Different times are only parts of one and the same time. That presentation, however, which can be given only though a single object is intuition. Moreover, the proposition that different times cannot be simultaneous, could not be derived from a general concept. The proposition is synthetic and cannot originate in concepts alone.

5. The *infinity* of time means no more than that every determinate quantity of time is possible only through delimitations of one underlying time. The original presentation *time* must therefore be given as unlimited. When the parts themselves and every quantity of an object

can be imagined as determinate only through delimitation, the whole presentation cannot be given through concepts (for these contain partial presentations [*Teilvorstellungen*] only), but immediate intuition must be underlying them.

§ 5
Transcendental exposition of the concept of time

For this exposition I may refer to § 4, No. 3, where, in the interest of brevity, I have placed what is properly transcendental among the articles of the metaphysical exposition. Here I am adding only that the concept of change and, with it, the concept of motion (as change of locus) is possible only through and in the presentation of time. If this presentation were not an (inner) intuition a priori, no concept of any kind could make the possibility of change comprehensible, that is, the possibility of a conjunction of contradictorily opposed predicates in one and the same object (for example, the being in one locus and the non-being, in the same locus, of the same thing). Only in time both contradictorily opposed determinations can be met with in one thing, namely, successively. Our concept of time therefore explains the possibility of a great many synthetic cognitions a priori, as exhibited, for instance, in the general doctrine of motion.

§ 6
Conclusions from these concepts

a) Time does not exist by itself or inhere in things as an objective determination, as something that would remain, if abstraction were made from all subjective conditions of intuiting them. For in the first case it would be something that is actual without an actual object. In the second case, as a determination or an order inherent in the things themselves, time could not be antecedent to objects as their condition and be cognized and intuited a priori through synthetic propositions.

b) Time is nothing but the form of the inner sense, that is, of intuiting ourselves and our inner state. For time cannot be a determination of outer appearances; it belongs neither to shape nor location, etc., but determines the relation of presentations in our inner state. And because this inner intuition does not yield any shape, we conceive of temporal succession, by analogy, as a line progressing to infinity, in which the manifold makes up a series of one dimension only.

c) Time is the formal condition a priori of all appearances of any kind. Space as the pure form of all outer intuition is restricted, as a condition a priori, to outer appearances. Because all presentations, no matter whether they have outer things for objects or not, belong, as determinations of the mind, to the inner state, this inner state, however, is subject to the formal condition of inner intuition which is time, time is a condition a priori of all appearance. This it is immediately as the condition of inner appearances (our soul) and thereby mediately also of outer appearances. All objects of the senses therefore stand necessarily in relations of time.

If abstraction is made from the sensibility of our intuition (from the manner of presentation peculiar to us) and if one speaks of things generatim, time is no longer objective. But time is necessarily objective in respect of all appearances, thus all things that may occur to us in experience. The proposition: All things as appearances (objects of sensible intuition) are in time, is a fundamental proposition that is objectively correct and has universality a priori.

Accordingly, our assertions teach the *empirical reality* of time, that is, its objective reality in respect of all objects that may ever be given to our senses. But we deny time any claim to absolute reality, that is, irrespective of the form of our sensible intuition. This constitutes its *transcendental ideality,* which does not permit us to ascribe time to objects in themselves, whether as substance or as inherence, once abstraction is made from the subjective conditions of our sensible intuition.

§ 7
Explanation

Against this theory, which concedes empirical reality to time but denies it absolute reality, I have heard a unanimous objection by men of insight: Changes are actual (as proved at least by the turn-over of our presentations). Now changes are possible only in time, consequently time is something actual. I grant the whole argument. Time is indeed something actual, namely, the actual form of inner intuition. These critics, however, did not consider that the object of the inner sense no less than external objects—without disputing their actuality as presentations—belong to appearance only, which always has two sides: the one where the object is viewed in itself (irrespective of the way of intuiting it, thus leaving its properties problematic) and the other where we look at the form of intuiting this object, a form to be sought not in the object in itself but in the subject to which it appears, although this form nevertheless pertains, actually and necessarily, to the object as appearance.

This reality of space and time does not weaken experiential cognition, for we are equally certain of it, whether these forms be inherent in the things in themselves or, of necessity, in our intuition of these things only. On the contrary, those who maintain the absolute reality of space and time come into conflict with the principles of experience itself. If they consider space and time as subsisting (as do most mathematical explorers of nature), they must assume two eternal and infinite self-contained non-entities [*Undinge*] which are there (without there being anything actual) only to comprise all that is actual. If others (some metaphysical theorists of nature) take space and time for relations gained by abstraction from experience, they must deny the validity, or at least the apodictic certainty, of mathematical doctrines a priori in respect of actual things (in space for instance). For such certainty cannot be obtained a posteriori. The former gain this much that they open the field of appearances for mathematical assertions, but they become tied down by those very conditions, when the understanding wants to go beyond this field. The latter gain an advantage in this respect since space and time do not interfere when they want to judge of objects not as appearances but in relation to the understanding only. However, lacking a true and objectively valid intuition a priori, they cannot account for the possibility of mathematical cognition a priori, nor can they bring experiential propositions into necessary agreement with those assertions. Both difficulties are removed in our theory.

Transcendental Aesthetic contains only these two elements: space and time, for even the concept of motion presupposes something empirical. In space, considered in itself, there is nothing that moves. Change also does not figure among the a-priori data of Transcendental

Aesthetic, for what changes is not time itself but something that is in time. It therefore presupposes perception.

§ 8
General Observations on the Transcendental Aesthetic

I. That our whole sensibility should be nothing but a disordered presentation of things, containing what pertains to them in themselves, though only in a coacervation of characteristics and partial presentations not consciously separated by us, is a falsification of the concept of sensibility and of appearance making the entire theory of it useless and empty. The presentation of a body in intuition contains nothing pertaining to an object in itself but mere appearance of something and the manner in which we are affected by it. Even if we could see through appearance to the bottom, it remains a world apart from cognition of the object in itself.

The Leibniz-Wolffian philosophy therefore has given all investigations into the nature and origin of our cognitions a totally wrong direction by considering the difference between the sensible and the intellectual as merely logical. This difference obviously does not concern distinctness or indistinctness but origin and content of our cognitions. Through sensibility we do not cognize the properties of things in themselves indistinctly but not at all.

If we call the rainbow a mere appearance, the rain, however, the matter in itself, this is quite right, as long as we understand the latter concept in its physical sense only, as that which in general experience under all different positions to the senses is determined in intuition in this and no other way. If, however, we take this empirical content generatim and ask, without bothering about its sameness for every human viewer, whether it presents an object in itself (which is not the raindrops, for they are, as appearances, already empirical objects), then the question concerning the relation of presentation to object is transcendental. Not only are these drops mere appearances, but even their round shape, nay even the space in which they fall are nothing in themselves but mere modifications or basic conformations of our sensible intuition. The transcendental object, however, remains unknown to us.

II. It may serve to confirm our theory of the ideality of both the outer and the inner sense, thus also of all objects of the senses as mere appearance, that everything in our cognition that belongs to intuition contains nothing but mere relations, of loci in an intuition (extension), change of loci (motion), and laws according to which that change is determined (moving forces). What is present in that locus, or what it does in the things themselves besides effecting a change of locus, is thereby not given. A matter is not cognized in itself by mere relations. One therefore may well judge that since the outer sense gives nothing but mere relational presentations, it can equally contain only the relation of an object to the subject and not the inner properties pertaining to that object in itself.

The same applies to the inner sense. Not only do presentations of the outer senses make up the material proper with which we fill our mind, but time, in which we posit them, which even precedes their consciousness in experience and, as a formal condition, underlies the manner in which we posit them in the mind, contains relations of being-one-after-another, of being simultaneous, and of what is simultaneous with succession (the perdurable [*das Beharrliche*]). That presentation which can precede any act of thinking something is intuition, and if it contains nothing but relations, the form of intuition. Since the form of intuition does not present anything except insofar as something is posited in the mind, this form of intuition cannot be anything but the manner in which the mind is affected by its own activity, that is by this positing of its [the activity's] presentation: it is an inner sense in respect of its form.

All that is presented through a sense is so far always appearance, and an inner sense would therefore either have to be completely ruled out, or the subject, which is its object, would be susceptible of being presented as appearance only (not as it would judge of itself, if its intuition were pure spontaneity, that is, an intellectual intuition). The difficulty herein is how a subject can intuit itself inwardly. But this difficulty is common to every theory.

The consciousness of oneself (apperception) is the simple presentation of the I, and if thereby alone all the manifold in the subject would be given spontaneously, the inner intuition would be intellectual. In man this consciousness requires inner perception of the previously given manifold, and the way it is given in the mind without spontaneity must be called, for the sake of this difference, sensibility. If the faculty of becoming conscious of oneself shall seek out (apprehend) what lies in the mind, it must affect the mind and can in this way alone produce an intuition of itself, the form of which, however, is a priori grounded in the mind and determines the manner in which the manifold has come together in it in the presentation of time. The mind then intuits itself not as it would present itself in immediate spontaneity but according to the manner in which it is affected from within, consequently not as it is, but as it appears to itself.

III. When I say that intuition in space and time presents both outer objects and the self-intuition of the mind as they affect the senses, that is, in their appearance [Erscheinung], this does not mean that these objects are mere illusion [Schein]. It would be my own fault if I said: bodies merely seem to be external to me, or my soul only seems to be given in my self-consciousness. If, however, one considers space and time as qualities to be found, as to their possibility, in matters in themselves, and if one then thinks of the resulting absurdities: two infinite things neither substance nor anything actually inhering in substances, yet existents, nay the necessary condition of all existing things, and even remaining if all existing things are removed from them, one cannot blame the good Berkeley for downgrading all bodies to mere illusion.

IV. The conditions of space and time have always been carefully excluded from the object of natural theology. But as conditions of all existence without difference they would also have to be conditions of God's existence. If then we don't want to make them objective forms of all things, we have no other alternative but to make them subjective forms of our outer, as well as inner mode of intuition.

It is possible that every finite thinking being herein must necessarily agree with man. Such universal validity would not stop the manner of intuiting in space and time from being a derivative rather than an original or intellectual intuition.

Conclusion of the Transcendental Aesthetic

Here we have one of the pieces for a solution of the general task of Transcendental Philosophy: How are synthetic propositions a priori possible?—space and time. When in a judgment a priori we want to go beyond a given concept, it is in space and time that we find what may be discovered a priori (in intuition corresponding to the concept) and synthetically be joined with the concept. Such synthetic judgments a priori therefore never extend beyond objects of the senses and can be valid only for objects of possible experience.

Of the proving grounds of speculative reason
to conclude the existence of a highest being

Every human reason begins with common experience, thereby putting some existent at the base. This ground, however, sinks, unless it rests on the immovable rock of the absolutely necessary. This itself, however, remains suspended without support, if beside and under it there is still empty space and it is not all-filling. It remains without support unless it is infinite as to reality and leaves no further room for any why.

If something, whatever it may be, exists, it must be conceded that something exists *necessarily*. For the accidental exists only if something else exists as its cause, and from this the same conclusion is valid up to a cause that is not accidental and hence is necessarily there without any condition. This is the argument on which reason founds its advance to the original being.

Now, reason looks for the concept of a being that fits a privileged existence such as is meant by unconditioned necessity. It does so not in order to draw an a-priori conclusion from the concept to the existence of this being, for if it dared to do that, it only need explore mere concepts without basing itself on a given existence. It rather wants to find among all concepts of possible things the one that excludes anything conflicting with absolute necessity. For according to the above conclusion reason already considers it established that something must exist with absolute necessity. If now it can shut out all that is incompatible with this necessity save one, this is the downright-necessary being, whether we comprehend its necessity, that is, can derive it from its concept alone or not.

Now that which in its concept contains the *therefore* for every *wherefore,* which in no way is defective and in every respect a sufficient condition, seems to be the being suited for absolute necessity, because in self-possession of all conditions of all that is possible it needs no condition itself. Among all concepts of possible things, the concept of a being of the highest reality would therefore be best suited for the concept of an unconditioned-necessary being, and even if it does not entirely satisfy it, we have no choice but clinging to it, because we are not permitted to cast the existence of a necessary being to the winds, if admitting it, though, cannot find anything in the whole field of possibility that could lay a better supported claim to such a pre-eminence in existence.

This is the natural course of human reason: First it convinces itself of the existence of *some* necessary being. In this it cognizes an unconditioned existence. Now it seeks the concept of what is independent of any condition and finds it in that which itself is the sufficient condition of everything else, that is, in what contains all reality. The unconfined All, however, is absolute unity and carries with it the concept of a unitary, namely, the highest being. And so reason concludes that the highest being, as the primordial ground of all things, exists [*dasei*] in a downright necessary way.

One cannot deny this concept a certain thoroughness if *resolutions* [*Entschließungen*] are under discussion, namely wherein to posit the existence of some necessary being, once its existence has been conceded and one agrees that one must take its side. If, however, nothing impels us to make up our mind and we would prefer to leave the matter undecided until the full weight of proving grounds were to force our acclaim, that is, if the issue is criticism [*Beurteilung*] of what we know and what we flatter ourselves to know, then the above conclusion needs the substitute of favoritism for its lack of a rightful claim.

Nevertheless, the above argument retains a certain importance and authority that cannot immediately be taken away from it. For suppose there are obligations which, although quite right in the idea of reason, would be without any reality in their application to ourselves, that is, would be without springs of action unless a highest being were presupposed that could give those practical laws efficacy and reinforcement: then we would also have an obligation to follow concepts which, though objectively inadequate, are preponderant and not surpassed, under standards of reason, by any better and more convincing cognition. The duty to choose would here change the equilibrium of speculative inconclusiveness by a practical addition, nay, reason would find no justification before itself, if under urgent motivating causes—although deficient insight—it had not followed these grounds of its judgment.

Only Three Kinds of Proving God's Existence out of Speculative Reason Are Possible

All roads one has chosen to that end either

1. start from determinate experience and thereby from the special quality of our world of the senses, ascending from it, according to laws of causality, to the highest cause outside the world, or
2. base themselves on indeterminate experience only, that is, on empirical existence, or
3. conclude out of mere concepts, entirely a priori, that a highest cause exists.

The first proof is the *physico-theological,* the second the *cosmological,* the third the *ontological* proof. There are, and can be, no more.

I shall show that reason achieves as little on the empirical road as on the transcendental one, that it spreads its wings in vain to transcend the world of the senses by sheer power of speculation. The order in which these proofs must be scrutinized will be the reverse of that taken by a gradually expanding reason. For we shall see that only the transcendental concept guides reason in these efforts, notwithstanding they are first occasioned by experience. I shall begin, therefore, with an examination of the transcendental proof and thereafter look into what the addition of empirical material might do to increase its proving force.

Section IV
Of the impossibility of an ontological proof of God's existence

The unconditioned necessity of *judgments* is not the unconditioned necessity of *matters.* For the absolute necessity of a judgment is only a conditioned necessity of the matter or of the predicate in the judgment. That a triangle has three angles is downright necessary, but the proposition does not say that three angles are downright necessary (without the condition of the given triangle).

Nevertheless, this logical necessity has exerted so powerful an illusion that when one formed an a-priori concept of a thing which—so one thought—also comprised existence in its extension, it was believed to be a secure conclusion: since existence belongs necessarily to the object of this concept—on condition that I posit this thing as given (existing)—its existence is also posited necessarily (according to the rule of identity), because its existence is thought together with a freely assumed concept and on condition that I posit the object of the concept.

If in an identical judgment I suspend the predicate and keep the subject, a contradiction results, and I therefore say: the predicate appertains necessarily to the subject. If, however, I suspend the subject together with the predicate, no contradiction arises, for nothing is left that could be contradicted. Positing a triangle and yet suspending its three angles is contradictory, but suspending the triangle together with its three angles is no contradiction. The same holds true of the concept of an absolutely necessary being. If you suspend its existence, you suspend the thing with all its predicates. Where should a contradiction come from? *God is omnipotent* is a judgment thought with its necessity. Omnipotence cannot be suspended, if you posit a deity, that is, an infinite being, whose concept is identical with the concept of omnipotence. If, however, you say: There is no God, neither omnipotence nor any other predicate is given, for they are all suspended together with the subject and there is not the slightest contradiction in this.

Just one escape is left, if you were to say: There are subjects that can not be suspended at all, which therefore must remain. That would be saying as much as: there are absolutely necessary subjects—the very presupposition whose correctness I have doubted and the possibility of which you wanted to show me. For I cannot in the least form the concept of a thing which, when suspended with all its predicates, would leave a contradiction, and without contradiction, I have, through mere pure concepts a priori, no criterion of impossibility.

Being [*Sein* [to be]], obviously, is no real predicate, that is, a concept of something that may be added to the concept of a thing. It is merely the positing of a thing, or of certain determinations, in themselves. In logical use it is merely the copula of a judgment. The proposition *God is omnipotent* contains two concepts that have their objects: God and omnipotence. The word "is" is not yet another predicate over and above these but only that which posits the predicate in reference to the subject. If I take the subject (God) together with all its predicates (among them omnipotence) and say: *God is,* or: there is a God, I do not posit a new predicate with the concept of God but only the subject in itself with all its predicates, and that is, the *object* in reference to my *concept.* Both must contain the same, and by thinking the object of the concept as plain given (through the expression: it is) nothing further can accrue to the concept (which merely expresses the possibility). The actual thus contains no more than the possible. A hundred actual thalers do not in the least contain more than a hundred possible thalers. For since these mean the concept, the actual thalers, however, the object and its position in itself, my concept would not express the entire object and therefore not be commensurate with it if the object contained more than the concept. But in the state of my assets there is more with a hundred actual thalers than there is with their mere concept (that is, their possibility). For in the case of actuality the object is not merely analytically contained in my concept (a determination of my state) but accrues synthetically to it, without however augmenting, through this being outside my concept, those hundred thalers of my thought in the least.

A thing may therefore be thought through as many predicates as I wish (even in a thoroughgoing determination), nothing accrues to it at all by adding that this thing is. For otherwise there would exist not the same but more than I had thought in the concept and I could not say that the very object of my concept exists. Even if in a thing I think all reality minus one, the missing reality does not accrue to it by saying that such a deficient thing exists, but it exists with the very same deficiency with which I have thought it. If now I think a being is the highest reality (without any deficiency), the question still remains whether it exists or not. For although nothing is missing in my concept of the possible real content of a thing generatim, something is missing in relation to my whole state of thought, namely that the cognition of that object is also possible a posteriori. If we want to think existence through the mere category alone, and not through connection with the content of experience, it is not surprising that we cannot specify any characteristic by which to distinguish it from mere possibility.

Whatever therefore the content of our concept of an object, we must go outside it to ascribe existence to it. In the case of objects of the senses this is done through nexus with some one of my perceptions according to empirical laws; but there is no means whatsoever of cognizing the existence of objects of pure thought, because their existence would have to be cognized entirely a priori. Our consciousness of all existence, however, belongs entirely to the unity of experience, and an existence outside this field, though it cannot be declared outright impossible, is a presupposition that cannot be justified in any way.

In certain respects the concept of a highest being is a very useful idea. An idea, however, because it is a mere idea, is completely incapable of expanding, by its own means, our cognition of what exists. It cannot even teach us anything further in respect of *possibility*. The connection of all real properties in a thing is a synthesis the possibility of which cannot be judged a priori at all, because to us the realities are not given specifically; and even if they were, judgment has no place therein, because the distinctive feature of the possibility of synthetic cognitions must always be sought in experience alone, to which, however, the object of an idea cannot belong. The illustrious Leibniz thus has by far not accomplished what he flattered himself to have gained, namely, insight a priori into the possibility of such a sublime ideal being.

All labor therefore is lost on the famous ontological (Cartesian) proof (out of concepts) of the existence of a highest being, and through mere ideas a man might well become richer in insights as much as a merchant in capital if, to improve his lot, he were to add to his cash balance a few zeros.

Section V

Of the impossibility of a cosmological proof of God's existence

Picking from a self-contrived idea the existence of its corresponding object was something quite unnatural and an innovation of schoolwit. There was reason's prior need, indeed, to assume, for the sake of all existence, something a priori and unconditionally necessary where it could stop in its ascent, and to seek a concept which, if possible, might satisfy that requirement. But this natural course was concealed and instead of ending at this concept, one tried to begin with it in order to derive necessity of existence from it, which resulted in the derailed ontological proof.

The cosmological proof retains the connection of absolute necessity with the highest reality but takes the natural course of concluding the unlimited reality from the presupposed unconditioned necessity of some being. Thus it brings everything onto the track of a, I don't know whether rational or rationalizing, but at least natural mode of concluding. It starts with experience (it is not carried out entirely a priori), and since the object of all possible experience is called world, it is called the cosmological proof. Leibniz called it the proof *a contigentia mundi*. It concludes: If something exists, an absolutely necessary being must also exist. Now, at least I myself exist, therefore an absolutely necessary being also exists. The proof continues: The necessary being can be determined only in one way, that is, only by one of all possible opposed predicates, consequently it must be *thoroughgoingly* determined by its concept. There is only one concept of a thing possible that contains its thoroughgoing determination a priori, namely that of the *ens realissimum*. This concept therefore is the only one through which a necessary being can be thought, that is, a highest being exists of necessity.

If it is a correct proposition: every plain necessary being is at the same time the *ens realissimum* (the *nervus probandi* of the cosmological proof), it must at least be possible to convert it, like all affirmative universal judgments, *per accidens:* some *entia realissima* are downright necessary beings. Now, one *ens realissimum* is in no way distinguished from another, and what is valid of some beings contained under this concept is valid also of all. In this case I therefore can also convert *simpliciter:* every *ens realissimum* is a necessary being. Since this proposition is a priori determined solely out of its concepts, the mere concept of the *ens realissimum* must carry with it also its absolute necessity—the very assertion of the ontological argument, which the cosmological proof did not want to acknowledge but nevertheless covertly used in its conclusions. It commits an *ignoratio elenchi* in that it promises to lead us on to a new path but, after a short detour, takes us back to the old track.

In the cosmological proof a whole nest of dialectical arrogations is hidden, which transcendental critique can easily detect and destroy:

1. The transcendental principle of a conclusion from the accidental to a cause, which has meaning only in the world of the senses but outside it does not make any sense at all.

2. The unjustified conclusion from the impossibility of an infinite series of ascending causes in the world of the senses to a first cause beyond experience.
3. Reason's false self-satisfaction in respect of completion of this series by finally removing any kind of condition, without which no concept of necessity can take place. Since at this stage there is nothing further to comprehend, this is taken for completion of our concept.
4. Confusion of the logical possibility of a concept of all united reality (without internal contradiction) with the transcendental possibility, which requires a principle of the feasibility of such a synthesis and, again, appertains only to the field of possible experiences; and so forth.

The unconditioned necessity so indispensably needed by us as the last carrier of all things is the veritable abyss for human reason. Even eternity, depicted by Haller in such awesome sublimity, does not nearly stagger the mind as much, for it only measures the duration of things without carrying them. One cannot dispel the thought, but one also can not bear it, that a being conceived by us as the highest among all possible beings should, as it were, say to himself: I am from eternity to eternity, apart from me there is nothing, except what is something solely through my will. *But whence am I?* Here everything below us sinks, and the highest no less than the smallest perfection floats without support before speculative reason, which at no cost to itself and without any hindrance can make both vanish.

*Disclosure and explanation of the dialectical illusion
in all transcendental proofs of the existence
of a necessary being*

Both the preceding proofs were transcendental, that is, they were attempted independently of empirical conditions. For although the cosmological proof bases itself on an unspecified experience (of whatever kind), it is conducted out of pure principles of reason in relation to an existence given through empirical consciousness generatim and even abandons this guidance to find support in pure concepts alone.

If one presupposes that something exists, it is very peculiar that one cannot avoid the conclusion that also something exists necessarily. On this quite natural (though for that reason still not secure) conclusion rests the cosmological argument. Whatever there may exist, however, nothing prevents me from thinking its non-existence. I must indeed assume something necessary for all that exists, but I cannot think a single thing is in itself necessary. That means: I can never *complete* the regress to conditions of existence without assuming a necessary being, but I can never *begin* with it.

If (1) for existing things generatim I must think something that is necessary, if, however, (2) I am not allowed to think any thing as necessary in itself, it inevitably follows that necessity and contingency must not concern the things themselves, because otherwise a contradiction would occur. Neither of these propositions thus is objective. They are subjective principles of reason which, as heuristic and *regulative,* take care of nothing but reason's formal interest.

It thus follows that the absolutely necessary must be assumed as *outside the world,* because it shall serve only as a principle of the greatest possible unity of appearances, as their supreme ground, which you can never reach *in the world,* because the second rule commands always to consider any empirical cause of unity as derivative.

According to these considerations, the ideal of the highest being is nothing but a regulative principle of reason. We thereby regard all conjunction in the world *as if* it were springing from an all-sufficient necessary cause, in order to found on it the rule of a systematic and lawful unity in explaining that conjunction; the ideal is not the assertion of an in itself necessary existence. At the same time, however, it is unavoidable to conceive of this principle by means of a transcendental subreption as constitutive and to think this unity hypostatically. Just as space is taken for a downright necessary self-subsisting something and an object given a priori in itself because it makes possible all shapes as merely different limitations of itself, so it happens quite naturally that the ideal of the highest being is hypostasized, since the systematic unity of nature cannot be set up as a principle of reason's empirical use unless we base it on the idea of an *ens realissimum* as the supreme cause. We thereby conceive of this idea as an actual object, and of this object again, because it is the supreme condition, as necessary, thus transforming a regulative principle into a constitutive one. The supposititious character of this step becomes obvious when the supreme being, whose unconditioned necessity was needed in respect of the world, is contemplated as a thing by itself: then this necessity is not capable of any concept, and I must therefore have met with it in my reason as a formal condition of thought only, not as a material and hypostatic condition of existence.

Section VI

Of the impossibility of a physico-theological proof

If neither the concept of things generatim nor the experience of any existence leads to the desired result, there still remains one means: We may try whether a specific experience, thus the quality and arrangement of things of the present world might not provide a ground of proof that could help us to gain a secure conviction of the existence of a highest being. We would call such a proof the physico-theological proof.

The present world, whether one traces it out in the infinity of space or in unlimited spatial division, opens to us so immense a stage of manifoldness, order, purposiveness, and beauty, that even according to the acquaintance our weak understanding has gained of it, all language regarding so many unfathomable marvels loses its impact, all numbers lose their power, and even our thoughts all their delimiting force. Our judgment of the whole must fall into speechless but all the more telling wonder. Everywhere we see a chain of causes and effects, of means and ends, of regularity in arising and disappearing; and as nothing has entered of itself into the state in which it is, it points further and further to something else as its cause, which makes the very same inquiry necessary, so that in this way the entire universe would have to sink into the abyss of nothing, unless one assumed something original and independent that outside this infinite array of the accidental were holding and securing it as the cause of its origin and at the same time of its continuance.

This highest cause, how large shall one think it? We are not acquainted with the entire content of the world. But since with regard to causality we need an outermost and uppermost being, what prevents us from placing it, in its degree of perfection, *above everything else that is possible?* This we can easily accomplish, though only through the delicate outline of an abstract concept, if we conceive of all possible perfection as united in this being as in a unitary substance. That concept tends to satisfy reason's requirement of economy in principles, it is in itself free from contradictions and, through the guidance of such an idea toward order and purposiveness, beneficial to expanding reason's use even in the midst of experience without being decisively contrary to any experience.

This proof should always be mentioned with respect. It is the oldest and clearest proof, the one most commensurate with common human reason, and any attempt to detract from it would be futile. No doubts of subtle abstract speculation can weigh down reason so much that it should not be lifted, by a look at the marvels of nature and the majesty of the universe, from brooding irresolution like out of a dream, to raise itself from height to height to the all highest, from any conditioned to its condition and to the supreme and unconditioned originator.

Although we have nothing to set against the reasonableness and usefulness of this procedure but rather encourage it, its claim to apodictic certainty and approval without any favoritism or extraneous support cannot be sanctioned. The physico-theological proof can never demonstrate the existence of a highest being by itself but must always leave it to the ontological proof to supplement this defect. The latter still contains the only possible ground of proof (if indeed a speculative proof takes place at all).

The chief moments of the physico-theological proof are the following:
1. Everywhere in the world there are distinct signs of an arrangement carried out with great wisdom according to a definite design.
2. The nature of different things could not of itself harmonize with determinate final purposes through such a variety of concerting means, unless an organizing principle according to underlying ideas had been instrumental in their selection and design.
3. There exists therefore a sublime and wise cause (or several causes) which must be the cause of the world, not merely as blind all-powerful nature, through fecundity, but as intelligence, through freedom.
4. From the observed unity of the mutual reference of parts of the world as members of an art-structure, the unity of this cause can be concluded with certainty, elsewhere, however, according to principles of analogy, with probability.

Without contesting here a conclusion of natural reason by analogy in likening nature's organisms to man-made artifacts—which kind of reasoning might not stand the sharpest scrutiny of transcendental critique—one must yet concede that if we are to name a cause, we cannot proceed here more securely than by this analogy. Reason could not justify before itself a passing from the causality it knows to obscure and unsupportable grounds of explanation.

Accordingly, the conclusion proceeds from the order and purposiveness we can observe in the world and which is an entirely accidental arrangement, to the existence of its proportional cause. Thus it would, strictly speaking, only prove the form to be the product of a highest wisdom, but not matter, that is, substance in the world. The proof could at best set forth a world *architect* who is always very restricted by the material at hand, but not a world *creator* whose idea dominates everything. If we wanted to prove the accidental character of matter itself, we would have to resort to a transcendental argument, the very procedure that was to be avoided here.

The step to absolute totality is entirely impossible on the empirical road. It has, however, been taken in the physico-theological proof. By what means does one try to bridge that gap?

After having come to admire the greatness of the wisdom, power, etc., of the originator of the world, one suddenly leaves this empirical argument and reverts to the accidental character of the world that was initially concluded from its order and purposiveness. From the accidental alone, one now proceeds through mere transcendental concepts to the existence of the plain necessary, and from the concept of absolute necessity of the first cause to its thoroughgoingly determined and determining concept, namely that of an all-comprising reality. The physico-theological proof, in its quandary, switched to the cosmological proof, and since the latter is only a veiled ontological proof, it actually carried out its intention merely through pure reason, although it had initially denied all relationship with it and staked everything on plausible proofs from experience.

Physico-theologians therefore have no cause for professing such aloofness in face of the transcendental kind of proof and looking down on it, with the conceit of clairvoyant naturalists, as on cobwebs of sinister-brooding minds. For with a little self-examination they would find that after proceeding a fair distance on the ground of nature and experience, and seeing their object as distant as before, they suddenly leave this ground and make a transition to the realm of mere possibilities, where on the wings of ideas they hope to get near what had eluded all empirical investigation. Now, after having, in their opinion, gained a firm foothold through such a mighty leap, they spread the now determinate concept—not knowing how they arrived at it—over the entire field of creation and explain, poorly enough and far below its dignity, the ideal, the exclusive product of pure reason, by experience, not admitting that they arrived at this presupposition on a path other than experience.

Since besides the physico-theological proof, the cosmological proof, and the ontological proof of the existence of a highest being no other road is open to speculative reason, the ontological proof, out of pure concepts of reason alone, is the only proof possible, if indeed a proof is possible at all of a proposition towering so high above all empirical use of the understanding.

From *Critique of Pure Reason,* by Immanuel Kant. Concise text in a new faithful terminologically improved translation exhibiting the structure of Kant's argument in thesis and proof. With introduction and glossary by Wolfgang Schwarz. Aalen, 1982. Used by permission of Scientia Verlag und Antiquariat.

G. W. F. HEGEL

Today individualism and the resentment of all authority are very widespread. The selection from Hegel (1770–1831) is a classic analysis of the dynamics of illegitimate authority. It can stimulate one to seek to understand the nature of legitimate authority. The relation between a master and slave represents one stage in the growth of human consciousness from its most primitive state toward the realization of its affinity with the Absolute.

Hegel is best known for his development of a dialectical method in which reality is understood as the historical manifestation and realization of the Absolute. He interpreted past thinkers and historical movements from the hermeneutical perspective of their contribution to the historical realization of the Absolute.

Unlike many of the writers of the Enlightenment, Hegel was highly sympathetic toward religion, and in particular Christianity. His immediate philosophic predecessors—for example, Kant—reduced Christianity to moral teachings. Hegel, however, treated the doctrine of the person of Christ as the God-man and the doctrine of the Trinity with a certain respect. They expressed ultimate truth in a less adequate way than did philosophy, but nonetheless in a valid, historically necessary, and legitimate fashion. Hegel's culturally acceptable version of Christianity was readily accepted by many theologians, and thus aroused Kierkegaard, who became Hegel's most persistent and profound Christian critic.

Lordship and Bondage
(*Phenomenology of Spirit,* B.IV.A)

178. Self-consciousness exists in and for itself when, and by the fact that, it so exists for another; that is, it exists only in being

acknowledged. The Notion of this its unity in its duplication embraces many and varied meanings. Its moments, then, must on the one hand be held strictly apart, and on the other hand must in this differentiation at the same time also be taken and known as not distinct, or in their opposite significance. The twofold significance of the distinct moments has in the nature of self-consciousness to be infinite, or directly the opposite of the determinateness in which it is posited. The detailed exposition of the Notion of this spiritual unity in its duplication will present us with the process of Recognition.

179. Self-consciousness is faced by another self-consciousness; it has come *out of itself.* This has a twofold significance: first, it has lost itself, for it finds itself as an *other* being; secondly, in doing so it has superseded the other, for it does not see the other as an essential being, but in the other sees its own self.

180. It must supersede this otherness of itself. This is the supersession of the first ambiguity, and is therefore itself a second ambiguity. First, it must proceed to supersede the *other* independent being in order thereby to become certain of *itself* as the essential being; secondly, in so doing it proceeds to supersede its *own* self, for this other is itself.

181. This ambiguous supersession of its ambiguous otherness is equally an ambiguous return *into itself.* For first, through the supersession, it receives back its own self, because, by superseding *its* otherness, it again becomes equal to itself; but secondly, the other self-consciousness equally gives it back again to itself, for it saw itself in the other, but supersedes this being of itself in the other and thus lets the other again go free.

182. Now, this movement of self-consciousness in relation to another self-consciousness has in this way been represented as the action of *one* self-consciousness, but this action of the one has itself the double significance of being both its own action and the action of the other as well. For the other is equally independent and self-contained, and there is nothing in it of which it is not itself the origin. The first does not have the object before it merely as it exists primarily for desire, but as something that has an independent existence of its own, which, therefore, it cannot utilize for its own purposes, if that object does not of its own accord do what the first does to it. Thus the movement is simply the double movement of the two self-consciousnesses. Each sees the *other* do the same as it does; each does itself what it demands of

the other, and therefore also does what it does only in so far as the other does the same. Action by one side only would be useless because what is to happen can only be brought about by both.

183. Thus the action has a double significance not only because it is directed against itself as well as against the other, but also because it is indivisibly the action of one as well as of the other.

184. In this movement we see repeated the process which presented itself as the play of Forces, but repeated now in consciousness. What in that process was *for us,* is true here of the extremes themselves. The middle term is self-consciousness which splits into the extremes; and each extreme is this exchanging of its own determinateness and an absolute transition into the opposite. Although, as consciousness, it does indeed come *out of itself,* yet, though out of itself, it is at the same time kept back within itself, is *for itself,* and the self outside it, is for *it.* It is aware that it at once is, and is not, another consciousness, and equally that this other is *for itself* only when it supersedes itself as being for itself, and is for itself only in the being-for-self of the other. Each is for the other the middle term, through which each mediates itself with itself and unites with itself; and each is for itself, and for the other, an immediate being on its own account, which at the same time is such only through this mediation. They *recognize* themselves as *mutually recognizing* one another.

185. We have now to see how the process of this pure Notion of recognition, of the duplicating of self-consciousness in its oneness, appears to self-consciousness. At first, it will exhibit the side of the inequality of the two, or the splitting-up of the middle term into the extremes which, as extremes, are opposed to one another, one being only *recognized,* the other only *recognizing.*

186. Self-consciousness is, to begin with, simple being-for-self, self-equal through the exclusion from itself of everything else. For it, its essence and absolute object is 'I'; and in this immediacy, or in this [mere] being, of its being-for-self, it is an *individual.* What is 'other' for it is an unessential, negatively characterized object. But the 'other' is also a self-consciousness; one individual is confronted by another individual. Appearing thus immediately on the scene, they are for one another like ordinary objects, *independent* shapes, individuals submerged in the being [or immediacy] of *Life* — for the object in its immediacy is here determined as Life. They are, *for each other,* shapes of consciousness

which have not yet accomplished the movement of absolute abstraction, of rooting-out all immediate being, and of being merely the purely negative being of self-identical consciousness; in other words, they have not as yet exposed themselves to each other in the form of pure being-for-self, or as self-consciousnesses. Each is indeed certain of its own self, but not of the other, and therefore its own self-certainty still has no truth. For it would have truth only if its own being-for-self had confronted it as an independent object, or, what is the same thing, if the object had presented itself as this pure self-certainty. But according to the Notion of recognition this is possible only when each is for the other what the other is for it, only when each in its own self through its own action, and again through the action of the other, achieves this pure abstraction of being-for-self.

187. The presentation of itself, however, as the pure abstraction of self-consciousness consists in showing itself as the pure negation of its objective mode, or in showing that it is not attached to any specific *existence*, not to the individuality common to existence as such, that it is not attached to life. This presentation is a twofold action: action on the part of the other, and action on its own part. In so far as it is the action of the *other*, each seeks the death of the other. But in doing so, the second kind of action, action on its own part, is also involved; for the former involves the staking of its own life. Thus the relation of the two self-conscious individuals is such that they prove themselves and each other through a life-and-death struggle. They must engage in this struggle, for they must raise their certainty of being *for themselves* to truth, both in the case of the other and in their own case. And it is only through staking one's life that freedom is won; only thus is it proved that for self-consciousness, its essential being is not [just] being, not the *immediate* form in which it appears, not its submergence in the expanse of life, but rather that there is nothing present in it which could not be regarded as a vanishing moment, that it is only pure *being-for-self*. The individual who has not risked his life may well be recognized as a *person*, but he has not attained to the truth of this recognition as an independent self-consciousness. Similarly, just as each stakes his own life, so each must seek the other's death, for it values the other no more than itself; its essential being is present to it in the form of an 'other', it is outside of itself and must rid itself of its self-externality. The other is an *immediate* consciousness entangled in a variety of

213

relationships, and it must regard its otherness as a pure being-for-self or as an absolute negation.

188. This trial by death, however, does away with the truth which was supposed to issue from it, and so, too, with the certainty of self generally. For just as life is the *natural* setting of consciousness, independence without absolute negativity, so death is the *natural* negation of consciousness, negation without independence, which thus remains without the required significance of recognition. Death certainly shows that each staked his life and held it of no account, both in himself and in the other; but that is not for those who survived this struggle. They put an end to their consciousness in its alien setting of natural existence, that is to say, they put an end to themselves, and are done away with as *extremes* wanting to be *for themselves,* or to have an existence of their own. But with this there vanishes from their interplay the essential moment of splitting into extremes with opposite characteristics; and the middle term collapses into a lifeless unity which is split into lifeless, merely immediate, unopposed extremes; and the two do not reciprocally give and receive one another back from each other consciously, but leave each other free only indifferently, like things. Their act is an abstract negation, not the negation coming from consciousness, which supersedes in such a way as to preserve and maintain what is superseded, and consequently survives its own supersession.

189. In this experience, self-consciousness learns that life is as essential to it as pure self-consciousness. In immediate self-consciousness the simple 'I' is absolute mediation, and has as its essential moment lasting independence. The dissolution of that simple unity is the result of the first experience; through this there is posited a pure self-consciousness, and a consciousness which is not purely for itself but for another, i.e. is a merely *immediate* consciousness, or consciousness in the form of *thinghood.* Both moments are essential. Since to begin with they are unequal and opposed, and their reflection into a unity has not yet been achieved, they exist as two opposed shapes of consciousness; one is the independent consciousness whose essential nature is to be for itself, the other is the dependent consciousness whose essential nature is simply to live or to be for another. The former is lord, the other is bondsman.

190. The lord is the consciousness that exists *for itself,* but no longer merely the Notion of such a consciousness. Rather, it is a consciousness

existing *for itself* which is mediated with itself through another consciousness, i.e. through a consciousness whose nature it is to be bound
up with an existence that is independent, or thinghood in general. The
lord puts himself into relation with both of these moments, to a *thing*
as such, the object of desire, and to the consciousness for which
thinghood is the essential characteristic. And since he is (a) *qua* the
Notion of self-consciousness an immediate relation of *being-for-self,*
but (b) is now at the same time mediation, or a being-for-self which
is for itself only through another, he is related (a) immediately to both,
and (b) mediately to each through the other. The lord relates himself
mediately to the bondsman through a being [a thing] that is independent, for it is just this which holds the bondsman in bondage; it is his
chain from which he could not break free in the struggle, thus proving
himself to be dependent, to possess his independence in thinghood.
But the lord is the power over this thing, for he proved in the struggle
that it is something merely negative; since he is the power over this thing
and this again is the power over the other [the bondsman], it follows
that he holds the other in subjection. Equally, the lord relates himself
mediately to the thing through the bondsman; the bondsman, *qua* self-
consciousness in general, also relates himself negatively to the thing,
and takes away its independence; but at the same time the thing is
independent *vis-à-vis* the bondsman, whose negating of it, therefore,
cannot go the length of being altogether done with it to the point of
annihilation; in other words, he only *works* on it. For the lord on the
other hand, the *immediate* relation becomes through this mediation
the sheer negation of the thing, or the enjoyment of it. What desire
failed to achieve, he succeeds in doing, viz. to have done with the thing
altogether, and to achieve satisfaction in the enjoyment of it. Desire
failed to do this because of the thing's independence; but the lord, who
has interposed the bondsman between it and himself, takes to himself
only the dependent aspect of the thing and has the pure enjoyment of
it. The aspect of its independence he leaves to the bondsman, who
works on it.

191. In both of these moments the lord achieves his recognition
through another consciousness; for in them, that other consciousness
is expressly something unessential, both by its working on the thing,
and by its dependence on a specific existence. In neither case can it
be lord over the being of the thing and achieve absolute negation of

it. Here, therefore, is present this moment of recognition, viz. that the other consciousness sets aside its own being-for-self, and in so doing itself does what the first does to it. Similarly, the other moment too is present, that this action of the second is the first's own action; for what the bondsman does is really the action of the lord. The latter's essential nature is to exist only for himself; he is the sheer negative power for whom the thing is nothing. Thus he is the pure, essential action in this relationship, while the action of the bondsman is impure and unessential. But for recognition proper the moment is lacking, that what the lord does to the other he also does to himself, and what the bondsman does to himself he should also do to the other. The outcome is a recognition that is one-sided and unequal.

192. In this recognition the unessential consciousness is for the lord the object, which constitutes the *truth* of his certainty of himself. But it is clear that this object does not correspond to its Notion, but rather that the object in which the lord has achieved his lordship has in reality turned out to be something quite different from an independent consciousness. What now really confronts him is not an independent consciousness, but a dependent one. He is, therefore, not certain of *being-for-self* as the truth of himself. On the contrary, his truth is in reality the unessential consciousness and its unessential action.

193. The *truth* of the independent consciousness is accordingly the servile consciousness of the bondsman. This, it is true, appears at first *outside* of itself and not as the truth of self-consciousness. But just as lordship showed that its essential nature is the reverse of what it wants to be, so too servitude in its consummation will really turn into the opposite of what it immediately is; as a consciousness forced back into itself, it will withdraw into itself and be transformed into a truly independent consciousness.

194. We have seen what servitude is only in relation to lordship. But it is a self-consciousness, and we have now to consider what as such it is in and for itself. To begin with, servitude has the lord for its essential reality; hence the *truth* for it is the independent consciousness that is *for itself*. However, servitude is not yet aware that this truth is implicit in it. But it does in fact contain within itself this truth of pure negativity and being-for-self, for it has experienced this its own essential nature. For this consciousness has been fearful, not of this or that particular thing or just at odd moments, but its whole being has been seized with dread. In that experience it has been quite unmanned, has trembled

in every fibre of its being, and everything solid and stable has been shaken to its foundations. But this pure universal movement, the absolute melting-away of everything stable, is the simple, essential nature of self-consciousness, absolute negativity, *pure being-for-self,* which consequently is *implicit* in this consciousness. This moment of pure being-for-self is also *explicit* for the bondsman, for in the lord it exists for him as his *object.* Furthermore, his consciousness is not this dissolution of everything stable merely in principle; in his service he *actually* brings this about. Through his service he rids himself of his attachment to natural existence in every single detail; and gets rid of it by working on it.

195. However, the feeling of absolute power both in general, and in the particular form of service, is only implicitly this dissolution, and although the fear of the lord is indeed the beginning of wisdom, consciousness is not therein aware that it is a being-for-self. Through work, however, the bondsman becomes conscious of what he truly is. In the moment which corresponds to desire in the lord's consciousness, it did seem that the aspect of unessential relation to the thing fell to the lot of the bondsman, since in that relation the thing retained its independence. Desire has reserved to itself the pure negating of the object and thereby its unalloyed feeling of self. But that is the reason why this satisfaction is itself only a fleeting one, for it lacks the side of objectivity and permanence. Work, on the other hand, is desire held in check, fleetingness staved off; in other words, work forms and shapes the thing. The negative relation to the object becomes its *form* and something *permanent,* because it is precisely for the worker that the object has independence. This *negative* middle term or the formative *activity* is at the same time the individuality or pure being-for-self of consciousness which now, in the work outside of it, acquires an element of permanence. It is in this way, therefore, that consciousness, *qua* worker, comes to see in the independent being [of the object] its *own* independence.

196. But the formative activity has not only this positive significance that in it the pure being-for-self of the servile consciousness acquires an existence; it also has, in contrast with its first moment, the negative significance of *fear.* For, in fashioning the thing, the bondsman's own negativity, his being-for-self, becomes an object for him only through his setting at nought the existing *shape* confronting him. But this objective *negative* moment is none other than the alien being before

which it has trembled. Now, however, he destroys this alien negative moment, posits *himself* as a negative in the permanent order of things, and thereby becomes *for himself,* someone existing on his own account. In the lord, the being-for-self is an 'other' for the bondsman, or is only *for* him [i.e. is not his own]; in fear, the being-for-self is present in the bondsman himself; in fashioning the thing, he becomes aware that being-for-self belongs to *him,* that he himself exists essentially and actually in his own right. The shape does not become something other than himself through being made external to him; for it is precisely this shape that is his pure being-for-self, which in this externality is seen by him to be the truth. Through this rediscovery of himself by himself, the bondsman realizes that it is precisely in his work wherein he seemed to have only an alienated existence that he acquires a mind of his own. For this reflection, the two moments of fear and service as such, as also that of formative activity, are necessary, both being at the same time in a universal mode. Without the discipline of service and obedience, fear remains at the formal stage, and does not extend to the known real world of existence. Without the formative activity, fear remains inward and mute, and consciousness does not become explicitly *for itself.* If consciousness fashions the thing without that initial absolute fear, it is only an empty self-centred attitude; for its form or negativity is not negativity *per se,* and therefore its formative activity cannot give it a consciousness of itself as essential being. If it has not experienced absolute fear but only some lesser dread, the negative being has remained for it something external, its substance has not been infected by it through and through. Since the entire contents of its natural consciousness have not been jeopardized, determinate being still *in principle* attaches to it; having a 'mind of one's own' is self-will, a freedom which is still enmeshed in servitude. Just as little as the pure form can become essential being for it, just as little is that form, regarded as extended to the particular, a universal formative activity, an absolute Notion; rather it is a skill which is master over some things, but not over the universal power and the whole of objective being.

◆ ◆ ◆

SØREN KIERKEGAARD

During the nineteenth century little attention was paid to Søren Kierkegaard (1813–1855). It was not until the twentieth century that he was "discovered" by theologians such as Karl Barth who were facing the same sorts of problems that Kierkegaard had seen many years before. Chief among these problems was one about history. Since the Enlightenment, discussions about Christianity had tended to assume that Christian faith was simply a matter of believing Christian doctrines as matters of historical fact. Kierkegaard, however, went to great lengths to point out that faith is primarily a matter of "inwardness" or "subjectivity." This is to say, it is a personal appropriation that can never be achieved when one maintains "objective" distance from the object of faith. Kierkegaard believed that this distance occurred not only when considering historical evidences and facts (a problem he inherited from Lessing), but also in philosophical systems such as Hegel's. Recognizing that even to put the matter so straightforwardly itself belied his deeper meaning, Kierkegaard therefore wrote most of his philosophical works under pseudonyms such as Johannes Climacus, the named author of *Concluding Unscientific Postscript*. The following selection is taken from the conclusion of that book. It should be noted, however, that Kierkegaard did write, under his own name, a number of works that assumed faith and were intended to aid growth in faith.

Objective and Subjective Christianity
(*Concluding Unscientific Postscript,* Conclusion)

OBJECTIVELY, WHAT IT IS TO BECOME
OR TO BE A CHRISTIAN IS DEFINED
IN THE FOLLOWING WAY:

1. A Christian is one who accepts the doctrine of Christianity. But if it is the doctrine which is to decide in the last resort whether one is a Christian, then instantly attention is directed outward, in order to learn to know in the minutest detail what the doctrine of Christianity is, because this indeed is to decide, not what Christianity is, but whether I am a Christian. That same instant begins the erudite, the anxious, the timorous effort at approximation. Approximation can be protracted as long as you please, and in the end the decision whereby one becomes a Christian is relegated to oblivion.

This incongruity has been remedied by the assumption that everyone in Christendom is a Christian, we are all of us what one in a way calls Christians. With this assumption things go better with the objective theories. We are all Christians. The Bible-theory has now to investigate quite objectively what Christianity is (and yet we are in fact Christians, and the objective information is assumed to make us Christians, the objective information which we who are Christians shall now for the first time learn to know—for if we are not Christians, the road here taken will never lead us to become such). The Church theory assumes that we are Christians, but now we have to be assured in a purely objective way what Christianity is, in order that we may defend ourselves against the Turk and the Russian and the Roman yoke, and gallantly fight out the battle of Christianity so that we may make our age, as it were, a bridge to the peerless future which already is glimpsed. This is sheer aesthetics. Christianity is an existence-communication, the task is to become a Christian and continue to be such, and the most dangerous of all illusions is to be so sure of being such that one has to defend the whole of Christendom against the Turk—instead of being alert to defend our own faith against the illusion about the Turk.

2. One says, No, not every acceptance of the Christian doctrine make one a Christian; what it principally depends upon is appropriation,

that one appropriates and holds fast this doctrine quite differently from anything else, that one is ready to live in it and to die in it, to venture one's life for it, etc.

This seems as if it were something. However, the category "quite differently" is a mediocre category, and the whole formula, which makes an attempt to define more subjectively what it is to be a Christian, is neither one thing nor the other, in a way it avoids the difficulty involved in the distraction and deceit of approximation, but it lacks categorical definition. The pathos of approximation which is talked of here is that of immanence; one can just as well say that an enthusiastic lover is so related to his love: he holds fast to it and appropriates it quite differently from anything else, he is ready to live in it and die in it, he will venture everything for it. To this extent there is no difference between a lover and a Christian with respect to inwardness, and one must again recur to the *what,* which is the doctrine — and with that we again come under No. 1.

The pathos of appropriation needs to be so defined that it cannot be confused with any other pathos. The more subjective interpretation is right in insisting that it is appropriation which decides the matter, but it is wrong in its definition of appropriation, which does not distinguish it from every other immediate pathos.

Neither is this distinction made when one defines appropriation as faith, but at once imparts to faith headway and direction towards reaching an understanding, so that faith becomes a provisional function whereby one holds what essentially is to be an object for understanding, a provisional function wherewith poor people and stupid men have to be content, whereas *Privatdocents* and clever heads go further. The mark of being a Christian (i.e. faith) is appropriated, but in such a way that it is not specifically different from other intellectual appropriation where a preliminary assumption serves as a provisional function looking forward to understanding. Faith is not in this case the specific mark of the relationship to Christianity, and again it will be the *what* of faith which decides whether one is a Christian or not. But therewith the thing is again brought back under No. 1.

That is to say, the appropriation by which a Christian is a Christian must be so specific that it cannot be confused with anything else.

3. One defines the thing of becoming and being a Christian, not objectively by the *what* of the doctrine, nor subjectively by appropriation,

not by what has gone on in the individual, but by what the individual has undergone: that he was baptized. Though one adjoins to baptism the assumption of a confession of faith, nothing decisive will be gained, but the definition will waver between accentuating the *what* (the path of approximation) and talking indefinitely about acceptance and acceptance and appropriation, etc., without any specific determination.

If being baptized is to be the definition, attention will instantly turn outward towards the reflection, whether I have really been baptized. Then begins the approximation with respect to a historical fact.

If, on the other hand, one were to say that he did indeed receive the Spirit in baptism and by the witness it bears together with his spirit, he knows that he was baptized—then the inference is inverted, he argues from the witness of the Spirit within him to the fact that he was baptized, not from the fact of being baptized to the possession of the Spirit. But if the inference is to be drawn in this way, baptism is quite rightly not regarded as the mark of the Christian, but inwardness is, and so here in turn there is needed a specific definition of inwardness and appropriation whereby the witness of the Spirit in the individual is distinguished from all other (universally defined) activity of spirit in man.

It is noteworthy moreover that the orthodoxy which especially has made baptism the decisive mark is continually complaining that among the baptized there are so few Christians, that almost all, except for an immortal little band, are spiritless baptized pagans—which seems to indicate that baptism cannot be the decisive factor with respect to becoming a Christian, not even according to the latter view of those who in the first form insist upon it as decisive with respect to becoming a Christian.

SUBJECTIVELY, WHAT IT IS TO BECOME A CHRISTIAN
IS DEFINED THUS:

The decision lies in the subject. The appropriation is the paradoxical inwardness which is specifically different from all other inwardness. The thing of being a Christian is not determined by the *what* of Christianity but by the *how* of the Christian. This *how* can only correspond with one thing, the absolute paradox. There is therefore no vague talk to the effect that being a Christian is to accept, and to accept, and to accept quite differently, to appropriate, to believe, to appropriate by faith quite differently (all of them purely rhetorical and fictitious definitions); but *to believe* is specifically different from all other appropriation and inwardness. Faith is the objective uncertainty due to the repulsion of the absurd held fast by the passion of inwardness, which in this instance is intensified to the utmost degree. This formula fits only the believer, no one else, not a lover, not an enthusiast, not a thinker, but simply and solely the believer who is related to the absolute paradox.

Faith therefore cannot be any sort of provisional function. He who from the vantage point of a higher knowledge would know his faith as a factor resolved in a higher idea has *eo ipso* ceased to believe. Faith *must* not *rest content* with unintelligibility; for precisely the relation to or the repulsion from the unintelligible, the absurd, is the expression for the passion of faith.

This definition of what it is to be a Christian prevents the erudite or anxious deliberation of approximation from enticing the individual into byways so that he becomes erudite instead of becoming a Christian, and in most cases a smatterer instead of becoming a Christian; for the decision lies in the subject. But inwardness has again found its specific mark whereby it is differentiated from all other inwardness and is not disposed of by the chatty category "quite differently" which fits the case of every passion at the moment of passion.

The psychologist generally regards it as a sure sign that a man is beginning to give up a passion when he wishes to treat the object of it objectively. Passion and reflection are generally exclusive of one another. Becoming objective in this way is always retrogression, for passion is man's perdition, but it is his exaltation as well. In case dialectic and reflection are not used to intensify passion, it is a retrogression to become objective; and even he who is lost through passion has not lost so much as he who lost passion, for the former had the possibility.

Thus it is that people in our age have wanted to become objective with relation to Christianity; the passion by which every man is a Christian has become too small a thing for them, and by becoming objective we all of us have the prospect of becoming . . . a *Privatdocent*.

But this situation in turn has made the strife in Christendom so comic, because in so many ways the strife consists merely in exchanging weapons, and because the strife about Christianity is waged in Christendom by Christians or between Christians who, all of them by being objective and going further, are about to give up being Christians. At the time when the Danish Government transferred the English three per cent loan from Wilson to Rothschild there was an outcry raised in the papers, there was held a general assembly of people who did not possess the bonds but had borrowed one in order to take part in the meeting as bondholders. It was resolved that a protest should be made against the action of the government by refusing to accept the new bonds. And the meeting was made up of people who owned no bonds and therefore would hardly incur the embarrassment of being compelled by the government to accept the new bonds. The thing of being a Christian is on the point of losing the interest of passion, yet the strife is waged *pro* and *contra,* one argues from himself as a postulate: "If this is not Christianity, then I am no Christian, which nevertheless I surely am"; and the situation has been so inverted that one is interested in Christianity in order to know what Christianity is, not interested in knowing what Christianity is in order to be a Christian. The name of Christ is used as those people used the borrowed bonds— in order to take part in the general assembly where the fate of the Christians is decided by Christians who for their own sake do not care a fig about being Christians. For whose sake then do they do all this?

Precisely because people in our age and in the Christendom of our time do not appear to be sufficiently aware of the dialectic of inward appropriation, or of the fact that the "how" of the individual is an expression just as precise and more decisive for what he has, than is the "what" to which he appeals—precisely for this reason there crop up the strangest and (if one is in the humor and has time for it) the most laughable confusions, more comic than even the confusions of paganism, because in them there was not so much at stake, and because the contradictions were not so strident.

But tit for tat, if friendship is to be maintained and if one is to continue to be an optimist. He who, experimenting in the domain of passion, excludes himself from all the bright and smiling prospects of becoming *Privatdocent* and from what that brings in, ought at least to have a little humoristic compensation because he takes so much to heart what others, aiming at something higher, regard as a bagatelle— the little humoristic compensation that his passion sharpens his sense for the comical. He who, though he is a friend of humanity, exposes himself to be abhorred as an egoist, seeing he does not concern himself with Christianity for the sake of other people, ought on the score that he is a friend of laughter to have a little subsidy from the State. It really does not do at all to have the reproach of being an egoist and have no advantage from it—in this way indeed one is not an egoist.

An orthodox champion fights in defense of Christianity with the most frightful passion, he protests with the sweat of his brow and with the most concerned demeanor that he accepts Christianity pure and simple, he will live and die in it—and he forgets that such acceptance is an all too general expression for the relation to Christianity. He does everything in Jesus' name and uses Christ's name on every occasion as a sure sign that he is a Christian and is called to fight in defense of Christendom in our age—and he has no inkling of the little ironical secret that a man merely by describing the "how" of his inwardness can show indirectly that he is a Christian without mentioning God's name.* A man becomes converted New Year's Eve precisely at six o'clock. With that he is fully prepared. Fantastically decked out with the fact of conversion, he now must run out and proclaim Christianity . . . in a Christian land. Well, of course, even though we are all baptized, every man may well need to become a Christian in another sense. But here is the distinction: there is no lack of information in a Christian land, something else is lacking, and this is a something which the one man cannot directly communicate to the other. And in such fantastic categories would a converted man work for Christianity; and yet he proves (just in proportion as he is the more busy in spreading and spreading) that he himself is not a Christian. For to be a Christian is something so deeply reflected that it does not admit of the aesthetical dialectic which allows one man to be for others

---

*In relation to love (by which I would illustrate again the same thing) it does not hold good in the same sense that a man merely by defining his "how" indicates what or whom it is he loves. All lovers have the "how" of love in common, the particular person must supply the name of his beloved. But with respect to believing (*sensu strictissimo*) it holds good that this "how" is appropriate only to one as its object. If anybody would say, "Yes, but then one can also learn the 'how' of faith by rote and patter"; to this one must reply that it cannot be done, for he who declares it directly contradicts himself, because the content of the assertion must constantly be reduplicated in the form of expression, and the isolation contained in the definition must reduplicate itself in the form.

something he is not for himself. On the other hand, a scoffer attacks Christianity and at the same time expounds it so reliably that it is a pleasure to read him, and one who is in perplexity about finding it distinctly set forth may almost have recourse to him.

All ironical observations depend upon paying attention to the "how," whereas the gentleman with whom the ironist has the honor to converse is attentive only to the "what." A man protests loudly and solemnly, "This is my opinion." However, he does not confine himself to delivering this formula verbatim, he explains himself further, he ventures to vary the expressions. Yes, for it is not so easy to vary as one thinks it is. More than one student would have got *laudabilis* for style if he had not varied his expressions, and a great multitude of men possess the talent which Socrates so much admired in Polos: they never say the same thing—about the same. The ironist then is on the watch, he of course is not looking out for what is printed in large letters or for that which by the speaker's diction betrays itself as a formula (our gentleman's "what"), but he is looking out for a little subordinate clause which escapes the gentleman's haughty attention, a little beckoning predicate, etc., and now he beholds with astonishment (glad of the variation—*in variatione voluptas*) that the gentleman *has not* that opinion—not that he is a hypocrite, God forbid! that is too serious a matter for an ironist—but that the good man has concentrated his force in bawling it out instead of possessing it within him. To that extent the gentleman may be right in asserting that he has that opinion which with all his vital force he persuades himself he has, he may do everything for it in the quality of talebearer, he may risk his life for it, in very much troubled times he may carry the thing so far as to lose his life for this opinion*—with that, how the deuce can I doubt that the man had this opinion; and yet there may have been living contemporaneously with him an ironist who even in the hour when the unfortunate gentleman is executed cannot resist laughing, because he knows by the circumstantial evidence he has gathered that the man had never been clear about the thing himself. Laughable it is, nor is it disheartening that such a thing can occur; for he who with quiet introspection is honest

---

*In turbulent times when the government must defend its existence by the penalty of death, it would not be unthinkable that a man might be executed for an opinion which indeed in a juridical and civil sense he had, but hardly in an intellectual sense.

before God and concerned for himself, the Deity saves from being in error, though he be never so simple, him the Deity leads by the suffering of inwardness to the truth. But meddlesomeness and noise is the sign of error, the sign of an abnormal condition, like wind in the stomach, and this thing of stumbling by chance upon getting executed in a tumultuous turn of affairs is not the sort of suffering which essentially characterizes inwardness.

It is said to have chanced in England that a man was attacked on the highway by a robber who had made himself unrecognizable by wearing a big wig. He falls upon the traveller, seizes him by the throat and shouts, "Your purse!" He gets the purse and keeps it, but the wig he throws away. A poor man comes along the same road, puts it on and arrives at the next town where the traveller had already denounced the crime, he is arrested, is recognized by the traveller, who takes his oath that he is the man. By chance, the robber is present in the court-room, sees the misunderstanding, turns to the judge and says, "It seems to me that the traveller has regard rather to the wig than to the man," and he asks permission to make a trial. He puts on the wig, seizes the traveller by the throat, crying, "Your purse!" — and the traveller recognizes the robber and offers to swear to it — the only trouble is that already he has taken an oath. So it is, in one way or another, with every man who has a "what" and is not attentive to the "how": he swears, he takes his oath, he runs errands, he ventures life and blood, he is executed — all on account of the wig.

If my memory is not very bad, I have already recounted this story once in this work; yet I desire to end the whole book with it. I believe that no one can with truth accuse me of having varied it so that it has not remained the same.

From *Concluding Unscientific Postscript*, by Søren Kierkegaard. Translated by David F. Swenson and Walter Lowrie. Copyright 1941 © renewed 1969 by Princeton University Press. Pages 537–544 reprinted by permission of Princeton University Press.

WILHELM DILTHEY

The German philosopher Wilhelm Dilthey (1833–1911) was the son of a Protestant clergyman and was originally trained in theology. His contributions to nineteenth-century philosophy were vast and far-reaching. But chief among those contributions were his efforts to give a sound methodological basis to the human sciences (*Geisteswissenschaften*), which have come to include theology. Arguing that the goal of the human sciences is to understand life from categories derived from life itself, Dilthey turned to history for that understanding. Historical expressions of the inner life as we find them in texts, though, have to be interpreted, he argued. Thus we must seek out their historical context and social climate. By doing so we are then able to reconstruct the inner experience of people otherwise quite different from ourselves. Thus the human sciences are objective, Dilthey claims, but differ from the natural sciences by being historical. The effect of this line of reasoning caused a revolution in how theology understands itself. It also provides the basis of a method for interpreting biblical texts that began in Schleiermacher and continues in many circles today. The following selection is taken from drafts that Dilthey wrote during the later years of his life which were published posthumously.

The Understanding of Other Persons and Their Life-Expressions

Understanding and interpretation is the method used throughout the human sciences. It unites all their functions and contains all their truths. At each instance understanding opens up a world.

Understanding of other people and their life-expressions is developed on the basis of experience (*Erlebnis*) and self-understanding and the constant interaction between them. Here, too, it is not a matter of logical construction or psychological dissection but of an epistemological analysis. We must now establish what understanding can contribute to historical knowledge.

(1) LIFE-EXPRESSIONS

What is given always consists of life-expressions. Occurring in the world of the senses they are manifestations of mental content which they enable us to know. By "life-expressions" I mean not only expressions which intend something or seek to signify something but also those which make a mental content intelligible for us without having that purpose.

The mode and accomplishment of the understanding differs according to the various classes of life-expressions.

Concepts, judgments and larger thought-structures form the first of these classes. As constituent parts of knowledge, separated from the experience in which they occurred, what they have in common is conformity to logic. They retain their identity, therefore, independently of their position in the context of thought. Judgment asserts the validity of a thought independently of the varied situations in which it occurs, the difference of time and people involved. This is the meaning of the law of identity. Thus the judgment is the same for the man who makes it and the one who understands it; it passes, as if transported, from the speaker to the one who understands it. This determines how we understand any logically perfect system of thought. Understanding, focusing entirely on the content which remains identical in every context, is, here, more complete than in relation to any other life-expression. At the same time such an expression does not reveal to the one who understands it anything about its relation to the obscure and rich life of the mind. There is no hint of the particular life from which it arose; it follows from its nature that it does not require us to go back to its psychological context.

Actions form another class of life-expressions. An action does not spring from the intention to communicate; however, the purpose to which it is related is contained in it. There is a regular relation between an action and some mental content which allows us to make probable inferences. But it is necessary to distinguish the state of mind which produced the action by which it is expressed from the circumstances of life by which it is conditioned. Action, through the power of a decisive motive, steps from the plenitude of life into one-sidedness. However much it may have been considered it expresses only a part of our nature. It annihilates potentialities which lie in that nature. So action, too, separates itself from the background of the context of life and, unless accompanied by an explanation of how circumstances, purposes, means and context of life are linked together in it, allows no comprehensive account of the inner life from which it arose.

How different it is with the expressions of a "lived experience"! A particular relation exists between it, the life from which it sprang, and the understanding to which it gives rise. For expressions can contain more of the psychological context than any introspection can discover. They lift it from depths which consciousness does not illuminate. But it is characteristic of emotive expressions that their relation to the mental content expressed in them can only provide a limited basis for under-standing. They are not to be judged as true or false but as truthful or untruthful. For dissimulation, lie and deception can break the relation between the expression and the mental content which is expressed.

The important distinction which thus emerges is the basis for the highest significance which life-expressions can achieve in the human studies. What springs from the life of the day is subject to the power of its interests. The interpretation of the ephemeral is also determined by the moment. It is terrible that in the struggle of practical interests every expression can be deceptive and its interpretation changed with the change in our situation. But in great works, because some mental content separates itself from its creator, the poet, artist or writer, we enter a sphere where deception ends. No truly great work of art can, according to the conditions which hold good and are to be developed later, wish to give the illusion of a mental content foreign to its author; indeed, it does not want to say anything about its author. Truthful in itself it stands — fixed, visible and permanent; this makes its methodical and certain understanding possible. Thus there arises in the confines between science and action an area in which life discloses itself at a depth inaccessible to observation, reflection and theory.

(2) THE ELEMENTARY FORMS OF UNDERSTANDING

Understanding arises, first of all, in the interests of practical life where people are dependent on dealing with each other. They must communicate with each other. The one must know what the other wants. So first the elementary forms of understanding arise. They are like the letters of the alphabet which, joined together, make higher forms of understanding possible. By such an elementary form I mean the interpretation of a single life-expression. Logically it can be expressed as an argument from analogy, based on the congruence between the analogy and what it expresses. In each of the classes listed individual life-expressions can be interpreted in this way. A series of letters combined into words which form a sentence is the expression of an assertion. A facial expression signifies pleasure or pain. The elementary acts of which continuous activities are composed, such as picking up an object, letting a hammer drop, cutting wood with a saw, indicate the presence of certain purposes. In this elementary understanding we do not go back to the whole context of life which forms the permanent subject of life-expressions. Neither are we conscious of any inference from which this understanding could have arisen.

The fundamental relationship on which the process of elementary understanding rests is that of the expression to what is expressed. Elementary understanding is not an inference from an effect to a cause. Nor must we, more cautiously, conceive it as a procedure which goes back from the given reality to some part of the context of life which made the effect possible. Certainly the latter relation is contained in the circumstances themselves and thus the transition from one to the other is, as it were, always at the door, but it need not enter.

What is thus related is linked in a unique way. The relation between life-expressions and the world of mind which governs all understanding, obtains here in its most elementary form; according to this, understanding tends to spell out mental content which becomes its goal; yet the expressions given to the senses are not submerged in this content. How, for instance, both the gesture and the terror are not two separate things but a unity, is based on the fundamental relation of expression to mental content. To this must be added the generic character of all elementary forms of understanding which is to be discussed next.

231

(3) OBJECTIVE MIND AND ELEMENTARY UNDERSTANDING

I have shown how significant the objective mind is for the possibility of knowledge in the human studies. By this I mean the manifold forms in which what individuals hold in common have objectified themselves in the world of the senses. In this objective mind the past is a permanently enduring present for us. Its realm extends from the style of life and the forms of social intercourse to the system of purposes which society has created for itself and to custom, law, state, religion, art, science and philosophy. For even the work of genius represents ideas, feelings and ideals commonly held in an age and environment. From this world of objective mind the self receives sustenance from earliest childhood. It is the medium in which the understanding of other persons and their life-expressions takes place. For everything in which the mind has objectified itself contains something held in common by the I and the Thou. Every square planted with trees, every room in which seats are arranged, is intelligible to us from our infancy because human planning, arranging and valuing—common to all of us—have assigned a place to every square and every object in the room. The child grows up within the order and customs of the family which it shares with other members and its mother's orders are accepted in this context. Before it learns to talk it is already wholly immersed in that common medium. It learns to understand the gestures and facial expressions, movements and exclamations, words and sentences, only because it encounters them always in the same form and in the same relation to what they mean and express. Thus the individual orientates himself in the world of objective mind.

This has an important consequence for the process of understanding. Individuals do not usually apprehend life-expressions in isolation but against a background of knowledge about common features and a relation to some mental content.

This placing of individual life-expressions into a common context is facilitated by the articulated order in the objective mind. It embraces panicular homogeneous systems like law or religion, which have a firm, regular structure. Thus, in civil law, the imperatives enunciated in legal clauses designed to secure the highest possible degree of perfection in the conduct of human affairs, are related to judicial procedures, law courts and the machinery for carrying out what they decide. Within such a context many kinds of typical differences exist. Thus, the individual life-expressions which confront the understanding subject can be considered as belonging to a common sphere, to a type. The resulting relationship between the life-expression and the world of mind not only places the expression into its context but also supplements its mental content. A sentence is intelligible because a language, the meaning of words and of inflections, as well as the significance of syntactical arrangements, is common to a community. The fixed order of behaviour within a culture makes it possible for greetings or bows to signify, by their nuances, a certain mental attitude to other people and to be understood as doing so. In different countries the crafts developed particular procedures and particular instruments for special purposes; when, therefore, the craftsman uses a hammer or saw, his purpose is intelligible to us. In this sphere the relation between life-expressions and mental content is always fixed by a common order. This explains why this relation is present in the apprehension of an individual expression and why—without conscious inference based on the relation between expression and what is expressed—both parts of the process are welded into a unity in the understanding.

In elementary understanding the connection between expression and what is expressed in a particular case is, logically speaking, inferred from the way the two are commonly connected; by means of this common connection we can say of the expression that it expresses some mental content. So we have an argument from analogy; a finite number of similar cases makes it probable that a subject has a particular attribute.

The doctrine of the difference between elementary and higher forms of understanding here put forward justifies the traditional distinction between pragmatic and historical interpretation by basing the difference on the relation—inherent in understanding—between its elementary and higher forms.

(4) THE HIGHER FORMS OF UNDERSTANDING

The transition from elementary to higher forms of understanding is already prepared for in the former. The greater the inner distance between a particular given life-expression and the person who tries to understand it, the more often uncertainties arise. An attempt is made to overcome them. A first transition to higher forms of understanding is made when understanding takes the normal context of a life-expression and the mental content expressed in it for its point of departure. When a person encounters, as a result of his understanding, an inner difficulty or a contradiction of what he already knows, he is forced to re-examine the matter. He recalls cases in which the normal relation between life-expression and inner content did not hold. Such a deviation occurs when we withdraw our inner states, ideas or intentions from observation, by an inscrutable attitude or by silence. Here the mere absence of a visible expression is misinterpreted by the observer. But, beyond this, we must frequently reckon on an intention to deceive. Facial expressions, gestures and words contradict the mental content. So, for different reasons, we must consider other expressions or go back to the whole context of life in order to still our doubts.

The interactions of practical life also require judgments about the character and capacities of individuals. We constantly take account of interpretations of individual gestures, facial expressions, actions or combinations of these; they take place in arguments from analogy but our understanding takes us further; trade and commerce, social life, profession and family point to the need to gain insight into the people surrounding us so that we can make sure how far we can count on them. Here the relation between expression and what is expressed becomes that between the multiplicity of expressions of another person and the inner context behind them. This leads us to take account of changing circumstances. Here we have an induction from individual life-expressions to the whole context of a life. Its presupposition is knowledge of mental life and its relation to environment and circumstances. As the series of available life-expressions is limited and the underlying context uncertain, only probable conclusions are possible. If we can infer how a person we have understood would act in new circumstances, the deduction from an inductively arrived insight into a mental context can only achieve expectations and possibilities. The transition from an, only probable, mental context to its reaction in new circumstances can be anticipated but not forecast with certainty. As we shall soon see, the presupposition can be infinitely elaborated but cannot be made certain.

But not all higher forms of understanding rest on the relations between product and producer. It is clear that such an assumption is not even true in the elementary forms of understanding; but a very important part of the higher ones is also based on the relation between expression and what is expressed. In many cases the understanding of a mental creation is merely directed to the context in which the individual, successively apprehended, parts form a whole. If understanding is to produce knowledge of the world of mind as efficiently as possible, it is most important that its independent forms should be appreciated. If a play is performed, it is not only the naive spectator who is wholly absorbed in the plot without thinking of the author; even the cognoscenti can be wholly captivated by the action. Their understanding is directed towards the plot, the characters and the fateful interplay of different factors. Only so will they enjoy the full reality of the cross-section of life presented and understand and relive the action as the poet intended. All this understanding of mental creations is dominated by the relation between expressions and the world of mind expressed in them. Only when the spectator notices that what he has just accepted as a piece of reality is the poet's artistically planned creation does understanding pass from being governed by the relation between expression and what is expressed to being dominated by that between creation and creator.

The common characteristic of the forms of higher understanding mentioned is that by means of an induction from the expressions given they make the whole context comprehensible. The basic relation determining the progress from outer manifestations to inner content is either, in the first instance, that of expression to what is expressed or, frequently, that of product to producer. The procedure rests on elementary understanding which, as it were, makes the elements for reconstruction available. But higher understanding is distinguishable from elementary by a further feature which completely reveals its character.

The subject-matter of understanding is always something individual. In its higher forms it draws its conclusions about the pattern within a work, a person, or a situation, from what is given in the book or person and combined by induction. It was shown previously in our analysis of lived experience (*Erlebnis*) and of our understanding of self that the individual constitutes an intrinsic value in the world of the mind; indeed it is the only intrinsic value we can ascertain without doubt. Thus we are concerned with the individual not merely as an example of man in general but as a totality in himself. Quite independently of the practical interest which constantly forces us to reckon with other people, this concern, be it noble or wicked, vulgar or foolish, occupies a considerable place in our lives. The secret of personality lures us on to new attempts at deeper understanding for its own sake. In such understanding, the realm of individuals, embracing men and their creations, opens up. The unique contribution of understanding in the human studies lies in this; the objective mind and the power of the individual together determine the mind-constructed world. History rests on the understanding of these two.

But we understand individuals by virtue of their kinship, by the features they have in common. This process presupposes the connection between what is common to man and the differentiation of these common features into a variety of individual mental existences; through it we constantly accomplish the practical task of mentally living through, as it were, the unfolding of individuality. The material for accomplishing this task is formed by the facts combined by induction. Each fact has an individual character and is grasped as such; it, therefore, contains something which makes possible the comprehension of the individual features of the whole. But the presupposition on which this procedure is based assumes more and more developed forms as we become absorbed in the particular and the comparison of it with other things; thus the business of understanding takes us into ever greater depths of the mind-constructed world. Just as the objective mind contains a structural order of types, so does mankind, and this leads from the regularity and structure of general human nature to the types through which understanding grasps individuals. If we assume that these are not distinguished qualitatively, but, as it were, through emphasis on particular elements—however one may express this psychologically—then this represents the inner principle of the rise of individuality. And, if it were possible, in the act of understanding, both to grasp the changes brought about by circumstances in the life and state of the mind, as the outer principle of the rise of individuality, and the varied emphasis on the structural elements as the inner principle, then the understanding of human beings and of poetic and literary works would be a way of approaching the greatest mystery of life. And this, in fact, is the case. To appreciate this we must focus on what cannot be represented by logical formulae (i.e. schematic and symbolic representations which alone are at issue here).

(5) EMPATHY, RE-CREATING AND RE-LIVING

The approach of higher understanding to its object is determined by its task of discovering a vital connection in what is given. This is only possible if the context which exists in one's own experience and has been encountered in innumerable cases is always — and with all the potentialities contained in it — present and ready. This state of mind involved in the task of understanding we call empathy, be it with a man or a work. Thus every line of a poem is retransformed into life through the inner context of lived experience from which the poem arose. Potentialities of the soul are evoked by the comprehension — by means of elementary understanding — of physically presented words. The soul follows the accustomed paths in which it enjoyed and suffered, desired and acted in similar situations. Innumerable roads are open, leading to the past and dreams of the future; innumerable lines of thought emerge from reading. Even by indicating the external situation the poem makes it easier for the poet's words to evoke the appropriate mood. Relevant here is what I have mentioned before, namely that expressions may contain more than the poet or artist is conscious of and, therefore, may recall more. If, therefore, understanding requires the presence of the vital coherence of our mental life this can be described as a projection of the self into some given expression.

On the basis of this empathy or transposition there arises the highest form of understanding in which the totality of mental life is active — re-creating or re-living. Understanding as such moves in the reverse order to the sequence of events. But full empathy depends on understanding moving with the order of events so that it keeps step with the course of life. It is in this way that empathy or transposition expands. Re-experiencing follows the line of events. We progress with the history of a period, with an event abroad or with the mental processes of a person close to us. Re-experiencing is perfected when the event has been filtered through the consciousness of a poet, artist or historian and lies before us in a fixed and permanent work.

In a lyrical poem we can follow the pattern of lived experiences in the sequence of lines, not the real one which inspired the poet, but the one, which, on the basis of this inspiration, he places in the mouth of an ideal person. The sequence of scenes in a play allows us to re-live the fragments from the life of the person on the stage. The narrative of the novelist or historian, which follows the historical course of events, makes us re-experience it. It is the triumph of re-experiencing that it supplements the fragments of a course of events in such a way that we believe ourselves to be confronted by continuity.

But what does this re-experiencing consist of? We are only interested in what the process accomplishes; there is no question of giving a psychological explanation. So we shall not discuss the relation of this concept to those of sympathy and empathy, though their relevance is clear from the fact that sympathy strengthens the energy of re-living. We must focus on the significance of re-living for grasping the world of mind. It rests on two factors; envisaging an environment or situation vividly always stimulates re-experiencing; imagination can strengthen or diminish the emphasis on attitudes, powers, feelings, aspirations and ideas contained in our own lives and this enables us to re-produce the mental life of another person. The curtain goes up and Richard appears. A flexible mind, following his words, facial expressions and movements, can now experience something which lies outside any possibility in its real life. The fantastic forest of *As You Like It* transposes us into a mood which allows us to re-produce all eccentricities.

This re-living plays a significant part in the acquisition of mental facts, which we owe to the historian and the poet. Life progressively limits a man's inherent potentialities. The shaping of each man's nature determines his further development. In short, he always discovers, whether he considers what determines his situation or the acquired characteristics of his personality, that the range of new perspectives on life and inner turns of personal existence is limited. But understanding opens for him a wide realm of possibilities which do not exist within the limitations of his real life. The possibility of experiencing religious states in one's own life is narrowly limited for me as for most of my contemporaries. But, when I read through the letters and writings of Luther, the reports of his contemporaries, the records of religious disputes and councils, and those of his dealings with officials, I experience a religious process, in which life and death are at issue, of such eruptive power and energy as is beyond the possibility of direct experience for a man of our time. But I can re-live it. I transpose myself into the circumstances; everything in them makes for an extraordinary development of religious feelings. I observe in the monasteries a technique of dealing with the invisible world which directs the monk's soul constantly towards transcendent matters; theological controversies become matters of inner life. I observe how what is thus formed in the monasteries *is spread* through innumerable channels — sermons, confessions, teaching and writings — to the laity; and then *I notice* how councils and religious movements *have spread* the doctrine of the invisible church and universal priesthood everywhere and how it comes to be related to the liberation of personality in the secular sphere. Finally, I see that what has been achieved by such struggles in lonely cells can survive, in spite of the church's opposition. Christianity as a force for shaping family, professional and political life converges with the spirit of the Age in the cities and wherever sophisticated work is done as by Hans Sachs or Dürer. As Luther leads this movement we can understand his development through the links between common human features, the religious sphere, this historical setting and his personality. Thus this process reveals a religious world in him and his companions of the first period of the Reformation which widens our horizon of the possibilities of human existence. Only in this way do they become accessible to us. Thus the inner-directed man can experience many other existences in his imagination. Limited by circumstances he can yet glimpse alien beauty in the world and areas of life beyond his reach. Put generally: man, tied and limited by the reality of life is liberated not only by art — as has often been explained — but also by historical understanding. This effect of history, which its modern detractors have not noticed, is widened and deepened in the further stages of historical consciousness.

(6) EXPLICATION OR INTERPRETATION

Re-creating and re-living what is alien and past shows clearly how understanding rests on special, personal talent. But, as this is a significant and permanent condition of historical science, personal talent becomes a technique which develops with the development of historical consciousness. It is dependent on permanently fixed life-expressions being available so that understanding can always return to them. The methodological understanding of permanently fixed life-expressions we call explication. As the life of the mind only finds its complete, exhaustive and therefore, objectively comprehensible expression in language, explication culminates in the interpretation of the written records of human existence. This art is the basis of philology. The science of this art is hermeneutics.

The explication of surviving remnants [from the human past] is inherently and necessarily linked to their critical examination. This arises from difficulties of explication and leads to the purification of texts, and the rejection of documents, works and traditions. Explication and critical examination have, in the course of history, developed new methodological tools, just as science has constantly refined its experiments. Their transmission from one generation of philologists and historians to another rests predominantly on personal contact with the great virtuosi and the tradition of their achievements. Nothing in the sphere of scholarship appears so personally conditioned and tied to personal contact as this philological art. Its reduction to rules by hermeneutics was characteristic of a stage in history when attempts were made to introduce rules into every sphere; this hermeneutic systematization corresponded to theories of artistic creation which considered it as production governed by rules. In the great period when historical consciousness dawned in Germany, Friedrich Schlegel, Schleiermacher and Boeckh replaced this hermeneutic systematization by a doctrine of ideals which based the new deeper understanding on a conception of mental creation; Fichte had laid its foundations and Schlegel had intended to develop it in his sketch of a science of criticism. On this new conception of creation rests Schleiermacher's bold assertion that one has to understand an author better than he understood himself. In this paradox there is an element of truth which can be psychologically explained.

Today hermeneutics enters a context in which the human studies acquire a new important task. It has always defended the certainty of understanding against historical scepticism and wilful subjectivity; first when it contested allegorical interpretation, again when it justified the great Protestant doctrine of the intrinsic comprehensibility of the Bible against the scepticism of the Council of Trent, and then when, in the face of all doubts, it provided theoretical foundations for the confident progress of philology and history by Schlegel, Schleiermacher and Boeckh. Now we must relate hermeneutics to the epistemological task of showing the possibility of historical knowledge and finding the means for acquiring it. The basic significance of understanding has been explained; we must now, starting from the logical forms of understanding, ascertain to what degree it can achieve validity.

We found the starting-point for ascertaining how far assertions in the human studies correspond to reality in the character of lived experience which is a becoming aware of reality.

When lived experience is raised to conscious attention in elementary acts of thought, these merely reveal relations which are contained in the experience. Discursive thought represents what is contained in lived experience. Understanding rests primarily on the relationship, contained in any experience which can be characterized as an act of understanding, of expression to what is expressed. This relation can be experienced in its uniqueness. As we can only transcend the narrow sphere of our experience by interpreting other life-expressions, understanding achieves central significance for the construction of the human studies. But it was also clear that it could not be considered simply as an act of thought; transposition, re-creation, re-living—these facts pointed towards the totality of mental life which was active in it. In this respect it is connected with lived experience which, after all, is merely a becoming aware of the whole mental reality in a particular situation. So all understanding contains something irrational because life is irrational; it cannot be represented by a logical formula. The final, but quite subjective, certainty derived from this re-living cannot be replaced by an examination of the cognitive value of the inferences by which understanding can be represented. These are the limits set to the logical treatment of understanding by its own nature.

Though laws and forms of thought are clearly valid in every part of science and scholarship and even the methods of research are extensively interrelated, understanding introduces procedures which have no analogy in the methods of science. For they rest on the relation between expressions and the inner states expressed in them.

We must distinguish understanding from those preliminary grammatical and historical procedures which merely serve to place the student of a written document (*fixiert Vorliegenden*) from the past or a distant place and linguistically foreign, in the position of a reader from the author's own time and environment.

In the elementary forms of understanding we infer from a number of cases in which a series of similar life-expressions reflects similar mental content that the same relation will hold in other similar cases. From the recurrence of the same meaning of a word, a gesture, an overt action, we infer their meaning in a fresh case. One notices immediately, however, how little this form of inference achieves. In fact, as we saw, expressions are also reflections of something general; we make inferences by assigning them to a type of gesture or action or range of usage. The reference from the particular to the particular contains a reference to the general which is always represented. The relation becomes even clearer when, instead of inferring the relation between a series of particular, similar, expressions and the mental life expressed, we argue from analogy about some composite, individual, facts. Thus from the regular connection between particular features in a composite character we infer that this combination will reveal an, as yet unobserved, trait in a new situation. By this kind of inference we assign a mystical writing which has been newly discovered, or has to be chronologically re-classified, to a particular circle of mystics at a particular time. Such an argument always tends to infer the structure of such products from individual cases and thus to justify the new case more profoundly. So, in fact, the argument from analogy when applied to a new case becomes an induction. These two forms of inference can only be relatively distinguished in understanding. As a result, our expectations of a successful inference in a new case are invariably limited—how much no general rule can determine but only an evaluation of the varying circumstances. A logic of the human studies would have to discover rules for such evaluation.

So understanding itself, because it is based on all this, has to be considered as induction. This induction is not of the type in which a general law is inferred from an incomplete series of cases; it is rather one which co-ordinates these cases into a structure or orderly system by treating them as parts of a whole. The sciences and the human studies share this type of induction. Kepler discovered the elliptical path of the planet Mars by such an induction. Just as he inferred a simple mathematical regularity from observations and calculations by means of a geometrical intuition, so understanding must try to link words into meaning and the meaning of the parts into the structure of the whole given in the sequence of words. Every word is both determined and undetermined. It contains a range of meanings. The means of syntactically relating these words are, also, within limits, ambiguous; meaning arises when the indeterminate is determined by a construction. In the same way the value of the whole, which is made up of sentences, is ambiguous within limits and must be determined from the whole. This determining of determinate-indeterminate particulars is characteristic . . . .

KARL MARX

In 1841 Ludwig Feuerbach, a disciple of Hegel, published a book entitled *The Essence of Christianity,* in which he claimed that the idea of God is a human projection resulting from the alienation of the human self and its historical, social activity. In his brief but groundbreaking "Theses on Feuerbach" Karl Marx (1818–1883) criticized Feuerbach for failing to complete his suggestions: for failing to see that even the very idea of a human self is itself a projection that is the result of historical, material human activity. The significance of this realization for Marx led to his own distinctive political and economic analyses, which in time had their own influence on Christian theology. However, he has also made an important contribution to hermeneutics by inviting would-be interpreters of history and texts to see, in a way that even Hegel could not, the crucial bearing of our material history and activity on our thought, including our theological thought.

Theses on Feuerbach

(1)

The chief defect of all previous materialism (including Feuerbach's) is that the object, actuality, sensuousness is conceived only in the form of the *object or perception* [*Anschauung*], but not as *sensuous human activity, practice* [*Praxis*], not subjectively. Hence in opposition to materialism the *active* side was developed by idealism — but only abstractly since idealism naturally does not know actual, sensuous activity as such. Feuerbach wants sensuous objects actually different from thought objects: but he does not comprehend human activity itself as objective. Hence in *The Essence of Christianity* he regards only the theoretical attitude as the truly human attitude, while practice is understood and fixed only in its dirtily Jewish form of appearance. Consequently he does not comprehend the significance of "revolutionary," of "practical-critical" activity.

(2)

The question whether human thinking can reach objective truth — is not a question of theory but a *practical* question. In practice man must prove the truth, that is, actuality and power, this-sidedness of his thinking. The dispute about the actuality or non-actuality of thinking — thinking isolated from practice — is a purely *scholastic* question.

(3)

The materialistic doctrine concerning the change of circumstances and education forgets that circumstances are changed by men and that the educator must himself be educated. Hence this doctrine must divide society into two parts — one of which towers above [as in Robert Owen, Engels added].

The coincidence of the change of circumstances and of human activity or self change can be comprehended and rationally understood only as *revolutionary practice.*

(4)

Feuerbach starts out from the fact of religious self-alienation, the duplication of the world into a religious and secular world. His work consists in resolving the religious world into its secular basis. But the fact that the secular basis becomes separate from itself and establishes an independent realm in the clouds can only be explained by the cleavage and self-contradictoriness of the secular basis. Thus the latter must itself be both understood in its contradiction and revolutionized in practice. For instance, after the earthly family is found to be the secret of the holy family, the former must then be theoretically and practically nullified.

(5)

Feuerbach, not satisfied with *abstract thinking,* wants *perception;* but he does not comprehend sensuousness as *practical,* human-sensuous activity.

(6)

Feuerbach resolves the religious essence into the *human* essence. But the essence of man is no abstraction inhering in each single individual. In its actuality it is the ensemble of social relationships.

Feuerbach, who does not go into the criticism of this actual essence, is hence compelled

1. to abstract from the historical process and to establish religious feeling as something self-contained, and to presuppose an abstract — *isolated* — human individual;
2. to view the essence of man merely as "species," as the inner, dumb generality which unites the many individuals *naturally.*

(7)

Feuerbach does not see, consequently, that "religious feeling" is itself a social product and that the abstract individual he analyzes belongs to a particular form of society.

(8)

All social life is essentially *practical.* All mysteries which lead theory to mysticism find their rational solution in human practice and the comprehension of this practice.

(9)

The highest point attained by perceptual materialism, that is, materialism that does not comprehend sensuousness as practical activity, is the view of separate individuals and civil society.

(10)

The standpoint of the old materialism is civil society; the standpoint of the new is human society or socialized humanity.

(11)

The philosophers have only *interpreted* the world in various ways; the point is, to *change* it.

✦ ✦ ✦

From *Writings of the Young Marx on Philosophy and Society*. Edited and translated by L. D. Easton and K. H. Guddat. Garden City, New York: Anchor Books, 1967. Reprinted by permission of the editors.

MARTIN HEIDEGGER

One definition of philosophy might be "a search for ultimate reality and an attempt to say what it is." This is a search in which theology clearly also has an interest. However, at various points in the history of philosophy this search has been called into question. Kant, for example, argued that we cannot get behind appearances. While later philosophy (e.g., Hegel) turned to look at the history of these appearances as a way of saying what really is, a serious question arises whether even this approach is legitimate. Martin Heidegger (1884–1976) in his large and dense *Being and Time* (1927) at first attempted to give an analysis of phenomena in order to discover how they disclosed Being itself. Yet shortly after finishing that work he began to question the enterprise as "too metaphysical"; that is, he began to realize that ultimate reality, Being, cannot be frozen in words no matter how we arrive at them. Only it can disclose itself. Any attempt to say what Being is misfires, for such attempts do not—and cannot—express Being; they can only disclose its manifestations in particular beings. In much of his later work Heidegger turned to an analysis of language as the "house of Being" in an attempt not to say what Being is but to let Being disclose itself. He developed an intense interest in poetry at this time. Heidegger's work has been extremely influential on numerous twentieth-century theologians, for example, Rudolf Bultmann, and remains an important source in hermeneutical theory.

The Way Back
into the Ground of Metaphysics

Descartes, writing to Picot, who translated the *Principia Philosophiae* into French, observed: "Thus the whole of philosophy is like a tree:

the roots are metaphysics, the trunk is physics, and the branches that issue from the trunk are all the other sciences . . ." (*Opp. ed. Ad. et Ta.* IX, 14)

Sticking to this image, we ask: In what soil do the roots of the tree of philosophy have their hold? Out of what ground do the roots—and through them the whole tree—receive their nourishing juices and strength? What element, concealed in the ground, enters and lives in the roots that support and nourish the tree? What is the basis and element of metaphysics? What is metaphysics, viewed from its ground? What is metaphysics itself, at bottom?

Metaphysics thinks about beings as beings. Wherever the question is asked what beings are, beings as such are in sight. Metaphysical representation owes this sight to the light of Being. The light itself, i.e., that which such thinking experiences as light, does not come within the range of metaphysical thinking; for metaphysics always represents beings only as beings. Within this perspective, metaphysical thinking does, of course, inquire about the being which is the source and originator of this light. But the light itself is considered sufficiently illuminated as soon as we recognize that we look through it whenever we look at beings.

In whatever manner beings are interpreted—whether as spirit, after the fashion of spiritualism; or as matter and force, after the fashion of materialism; or as becoming and life, or idea, will, substance, subject, or *energeia;* or as the eternal recurrence of the same events—every time, beings as beings appear in the light of Being. Wherever metaphysics represents beings, Being has entered into the light. Being has arrived in a state of unconcealedness ('Aλήθεια). But whether and how Being itself involves such unconcealedness, whether and how it manifests itself in, and as, metaphysics, remains obscure. Being in its revelatory essence, i.e. in its truth, is not recalled. Nevertheless, when metaphysics gives answers to its question concerning beings as such, metaphysics speaks out of the unnoticed revealedness of Being. The truth of Being may thus be called the ground in which metaphysics, as the root of the tree of philosophy, is kept and from which it is nourished.

Because metaphysics inquires about beings as beings, it remains concerned with beings and does not devote itself to Being as Being. As the root of the tree, it sends all nourishment and all strength into the trunk and its branches. The root branches out in the soil to enable the tree to grow out of the ground and thus to leave it. The tree of philosophy grows out of the soil in which metaphysics is rooted. The ground is the element in which the root of the tree lives, but the growth of the tree is never able to absorb this soil in such a way that it disappears in the tree as part of the tree. Instead, the roots, down to the subtlest tendrils, lose themselves in the soil. The ground is ground for the roots, and in the ground the roots forget themselves for the sake of the tree. The roots still belong to the tree even when they abandon themselves, after a fashion, to the element of the soil. They squander themselves and their element on the tree. As roots, they do not devote themselves to the soil — at least not as if it were their life to grow only into this element and to spread out in it. Presumably, the element would not be the same element either if the roots did not live in it.

Metaphysics, insofar as it always represents only beings as beings, does not recall Being itself. Philosophy does not concentrate on its ground. It always leaves its ground — leaves it by means of metaphysics. And yet it never escapes its ground.

Insofar as a thinker sets out to experience the ground of metaphysics, insofar as he attempts to recall the truth of Being itself instead of merely representing beings as beings, his thinking has in a sense left metaphysics. From the point of view of metaphysics, such thinking goes back into the ground of metaphysics. But what still appears as ground from this point of view is presumably something else, once it experienced in its own terms — something as yet unsaid, according to which the essence of metaphysics, too, is something else and not metaphysics.

Such thinking, which recalls the truth of Being, is no longer satisfied with mere metaphysics, to be sure; but it does not oppose and think against metaphysics either. To return to our image, it does not tear up the root of philosophy. It tills the ground and plows the soil for this root. Metaphysics remains the basis of philosophy. The basis of thinking, however, it does not reach. When we think of the truth of Being, metaphysics is overcome. We can no longer accept the claim of metaphysics that it takes care of the fundamental involvement in "Being" and that it decisively determines all relations to beings as such. But this "overcoming of metaphysics" does not abolish metaphysics. As long as man remains the *animal rationale* he is also the *animal metaphysicum*. As long as man understands himself as the rational animal, metaphysics belongs, as Kant said, to the nature of man. But if our thinking should succeed in its efforts to go back into the ground of metaphysics, it might well help to bring about a change in human nature, accompanied by a transformation of metaphysics.

If, as we unfold the question concerning the truth of Being, we speak of overcoming metaphysics, this means: recalling Being itself. Such recalling goes beyond the tradition of forgetting the ground of the root of philosophy. The thinking attempted in *Being and Time* (1927) sets out on the way to prepare an overcoming of metaphysics, so understood. That, however, which prompts such thinking can only be that which is to be recalled. That Being itself and how Being itself concerns our thinking does not depend upon our thinking alone. That Being itself, and the manner in which Being itself, strikes a man's thinking, that rouses his thinking and stirs it to rise from Being itself to respond and correspond to Being as such.

Why, however, should such an overcoming of metaphysics be necessary? Is the point merely to underpin that discipline of philosophy which was the root hitherto, or to supplant it with a yet more basic discipline? Is it a question of changing the philosophic system of instruction? No. Or are we trying to go back into the ground of metaphysics in order to uncover a hitherto overlooked presupposition of philosophy, and thereby to show that philosophy does not yet stand on an unshakable foundation and therefore cannot yet be the absolute science? No.

It is something else that is at stake with the arrival of the truth of Being or its failure to arrive: it is neither the state of philosophy nor philosophy itself alone, but rather the proximity or remoteness of that from which philosophy, insofar as it means the representation of beings as such, receives its nature and its necessity. What is to be decided is nothing less than this: can Being itself, out of its own unique truth, bring about its involvement in human nature; or shall metaphysics, which turns its back to its ground, prevent further that the involvement of Being in man may generate a radiance out of the very essence of this involvement itself—a radiance which might lead man to belong to Being?

In its answers to the question concerning beings as such, metaphysics operates with a prior conception of Being. It speaks of Being necessarily and hence continually. But metaphysics does not induce Being itself to speak, for metaphysics does not recall Being in its truth, nor does it recall truth as unconcealedness, nor does it recall the nature of unconcealedness. To metaphysics the nature of truth always appears only in the derivative form of the truth of knowledge and the truth of propositions which formulate our knowledge. Unconcealedness, however, might be prior to all truth in the sense of *veritas*. Ἀλήθεια might be the word that offers a hitherto unnoticed hint concerning the nature of *esse* which has not yet been recalled. If this should be so, then the representational thinking of metaphysics could certainly never reach this nature of truth, however zealously it might devote itself to historical studies of pre-Socratic philosophy; for what is at stake here is not some renaissance of pre-Socratic thinking: any such attempt would be vain and absurd. What is wanted is rather some regard for the arrival of the hitherto unexpressed nature of unconcealedness, for it is in this form that Being has announced itself. Meanwhile the truth of Being has remained concealed from metaphysics during its long history from Anaximander to Nietzsche. Why does metaphysics not recall it? Is the failure to recall it merely a function of some kinds of metaphysical thinking? Or is it an essential feature of the fate of metaphysics that its own ground eludes it because in the rise of un-concealedness its very core, namely concealedness, stays away in favor of the unconcealed which appears in the form of beings?

Metaphysics, however, speaks continually and in the most various ways of Being. Metaphysics gives, and seems to confirm, the appearance that it asks and answers the question concerning Being. In fact, meta-physics never answers the question concerning the truth of Being, for it never asks this question. Metaphysics does not ask this question because it thinks of Being only by representing beings as beings. It means all beings as a whole, although it speaks of Being. It refers to Being and means beings as beings. From its beginning to its completion, the propositions of metaphysics have been strangely involved in a persis-tent confusion of beings and Being. This confusion, to be sure, must be considered an event and not a mere mistake. It cannot by any means be charged to a mere negligence of thought or a carelessness of expres-sion. Owing to this persistent confusion, the claim that metaphysics poses the question of Being lands us in utter error.

Due to the manner in which it thinks of beings, metaphysics almost seems to be, without knowing it, the barrier which keeps man from the original involvement of Being in human nature.

What if the absence of this involvement and the oblivion of this absence determined the entire modern age? What if the absence of Being abandoned man more and more exclusively to beings, leaving him forsaken and far from any involvement of Being in his nature, while this forsakenness itself remained veiled? What if this were the case—and had been the case for a long time now? What if there were signs that this oblivion will become still more decisive in the future?

Would there still be occasion for a thoughtful person to give himself arrogant airs in view of this fateful withdrawal with which Being presents us? Would there still be occasion, if this should be our situation, to deceive ourselves with pleasant phantasms and to indulge, of all things, in an artificially induced elation? If the oblivion of Being which has been described here should be real, would there not be occasion enough for a thinker who recalls Being to experience a genuine horror? What more can his thinking do than to endure in dread this fateful withdrawal while first of all facing up to the oblivion of Being? But how could thought achieve this as long as its fatefully granted dread seems to it no more than a mood of depression? What does such dread, which is fated by Being, have to do with psychology or psychoanalysis?

Suppose that the overcoming of metaphysics involved the endeavor to commence with a regard for the oblivion of Being—the attempt to learn to develop such a regard, in order to experience this oblivion and to absorb this experience into the involvement of Being in man, and to preserve it there: then, in the distress of the oblivion of Being, the question "What is metaphysics?" might well become the most necessary necessity for thought.

Thus everything depends on this: that our thinking should become more thoughtful in its season. This is achieved when our thinking, instead of implementing a higher degree of exertion, is directed toward a different point of origin. The thinking which is posited by beings as such, and therefore representational and illuminating in that way, must be supplanted by a different kind of thinking which is brought to pass by Being itself and, therefore, responsive to Being.

All attempts are futile which seek to make representational thinking which remains metaphysical, and only metaphysical, effective and useful for immediate action in everyday public life. The more thoughtful our thinking becomes and the more adequate it is to the involvement of Being in it, the purer our thinking will stand *eo ipso* in the one action appropriate to it: recalling what is meant for it and thus, in a sense, what is already meant.

But who still recalls what is meant? One makes inventions. To lead our thinking on the way on which it may find the involvement of the truth of Being in human nature, to open up a path for our thinking on which it may recall Being itself in its truth—to do that the thinking attempted in *Being and Time* is "on its way." On this way—that is, in the service of the question concerning the truth of Being—it becomes necessary to stop and think about human nature; for the experience of the oblivion of Being, which is not specifically mentioned because it still had to be demonstrated, involves the crucial conjecture that in view of the unconcealedness of Being the involvement of Being in human nature is an essential feature of Being. But how could this conjecture, which is experienced here, become an explicit question before every attempt had been made to liberate the determination of human nature from the concept of subjectivity and from the concept of the *animal rationale?* To characterize with a single term both the involvement of Being in human nature and the essential relation of man to the openness ("there") of Being as such, the name of "being there [*Dasein*]" was chosen for that sphere of being in which man stands as man. This term was employed, even though in metaphysics it is used interchangeably with *existentia,* actuality, reality, and objectivity, and although this metaphysical usage is further supported by the common [German] expression "*menschliches Dasein*." Any attempt, therefore, to re-think *Being and Time* is thwarted as long as one is satisfied with the observation that, in this study, the term "being there" is used in place of "consciousness." As if this were simply a matter of using different words! As if it were not the one and only thing at stake here: namely, to get men to think about the involvement of Being in human nature and thus, from our point of view, to present first of all an experience of human nature which may prove sufficient to direct our inquiry. The term "being there" neither takes the place of the term "consciousness" nor does the "object" designated as "being there" take the place of what we think of when we speak of "consciousness." "Being there" names that which should first of all be experienced, and subsequently thought of, as a place—namely, the location of the truth of Being.

What the term "being there" means throughout the treatise on *Being and Time* is indicated immediately . . . by its introductory key sentence:

"*The 'essence' of being there lies in its existence.*" [*Das "Wesen" des Daseins liegt in seiner Existenz.*]

To be sure, in the language of metaphysics the word "existence" is a synonym of "being there": both refer to the reality of anything at all that is real, from God to a grain of sand. As long, therefore, as the quoted sentence is understood only superficially, the difficulty is merely transferred from one word to another, from "being there" to "existence." In *B.&T.* the term "existence" is used exclusively for the being of man. Once "existence" is understood rightly, the "essence" of being there can be recalled: in its openness, Being itself manifests and conceals itself, yields itself and withdraws; at the same time, this truth of Being does not exhaust itself in being there, nor can it by any means simply be identified with it after the fashion of the metaphysical proposition: all objectivity is as such also subjectivity.

What does "existence" mean in *B.&T.?* The word designates a mode of Being; specifically, the Being of those beings who stand open for the openness of Being in which they stand, by standing it. This "standing it," this enduring, is experienced under the name of "care." The ecstatic essence of being there is approached by way of care, and, conversely, care is experienced adequately only in its ecstatic essence. "Standing it," experienced in this manner, is the essence of the *ekstasis* which must be grasped by thought. The ecstatic essence of existence is therefore still understood inadequately as long as one thinks of it as merely "standing out," while interpreting the "out" as meaning "away from" the inside of an immanence of consciousness and spirit. For in this manner, existence would still be understood in terms of "subjectivity" and "substance"; while, in fact, the "out" ought to be understood in terms of the openness of Being itself. The *stasis* of the ecstatic consists—strange as it may sound—in standing in the "out" and "there" of unconcealedness in which Being itself is present. What is meant by "existence" in the context of an inquiry that is prompted by, and directed toward, the truth of Being, can be most beautifully designated by the word "instancy [*Inständigkeit*]." We must think at the same time, however, of standing in the openness of Being, of enduring and outstanding this standing-in (care), and of out-braving the utmost (Being toward death); for it is only together that they constitute the full essence of existence.

The being that exists is man. Man alone exists. Rocks are, but they do not exist. Trees are, but they do not exist. Horses are, but they do not exist. Angels are, but they do not exist. God is, but he does not exist. The proposition "man alone exists" does not mean by any means that man alone is a real being while all other beings are unreal and mere appearances or human ideas. The proposition "man exists" means: man is that being whose Being is distinguished by the open-standing standing-in in the unconcealedness of Being, from Being, in Being. The existential nature of man is the reason why man can represent beings as such, and why he can be conscious of them. All consciousness presupposes ecstatically understood existence as the *essentia* of man— *essentia* meaning that as which man is present insofar as he is man. But consciousness does not itself create the openness of beings, nor is it consciousness that makes it possible for man to stand open for beings. Whither and whence and in what free dimension could the intentionality of consciousness move, if instancy were not the essence of man in the first instance? What else could be the meaning—if anybody has ever seriously thought about this—of the word *sein* in the [German] words *Bewusstsein* ["consciousness"; literally: "being conscious"] and *Selbstbewusstsein* ["self-consciousness"] if it did not designate the existential nature of that which is in the mode of existence? To be a self is admittedly one feature of the nature of that being which exists; but existence does not consist in being a self, nor can it be defined in such terms. We are faced with the fact that metaphysical thinking understands man's selfhood in terms of substance or —and at bottom this amounts to the same—in terms of the subject. It is for this reason that the first way which leads away from metaphysics to the ecstatic existential nature of man must lead through the metaphysical conception of human selfhood (*B.&T.*, §§63 and 64).

The question concerning existence, however, is always subservient to that question which is nothing less than the only question of thought. This question, yet to be unfolded, concerns the truth of Being as the concealed ground of all metaphysics. For this reason the treatise which sought to point the way back into the ground of metaphysics did not bear the title "Existence and Time," nor "Consciousness and Time," but *Being and Time*. Nor can this title be understood as if it were parallel to the customary juxtapositions of Being and Becoming, Being and Seeming, Being and Thinking, or Being and Ought. For in all these cases Being is limited, as if Becoming, Seeming, Thinking, and Ought did not belong to Being, although it is obvious that they are not nothing and thus belong to Being. In *Being and Time,* Being is not something other than Time: "Time" is called the first name of the truth of Being, and this truth is the presence of Being and thus Being itself. But why "Time" and "Being"?

By recalling the beginnings of history when Being unveiled itself in the thinking of the Greeks, it can be shown that the Greeks from the very beginning experienced the Being of beings as the presence of the present. When we translate εἶναι as 'being,' our translation is linguistically correct. Yet we merely substitute one set of sounds for another. As soon as we examine ourselves it becomes obvious that we neither think εἶναι, as it were, in Greek nor have in mind a correspondingly clear and univocal concept when we speak of "being." What, then, are we saying when instead of εἶναι we say "being," and instead of "being," εἶναι and *esse?* We are saying nothing. The Greek, Latin, and German word all remain equally obtuse. As long as we adhere to the customary usage we merely betray ourselves as the pacemakers of the greatest thoughtlessness which has ever gained currency in human thought and which has remained dominant until this moment. This εἶναι, however, means: to be present [*anwesen;* this verb form, in place of the idiomatic *"anwesend sein,"* is Heidegger's neology]. The true being of this being present [*das Wesen dieses Anwesens*] is deeply concealed in the earliest names of Being. But for us εἶναι and οὐσία as παρ—and ἀπουσία means this first of all: in being present there moves, unrecognized and concealed, present time and duration—in one word, Time. Being as such is thus unconcealed owing to Time. Thus Time points to unconcealedness, i. e., the truth of Being. But the Time of which we should think here is not experienced through the changeful career of beings. Time is evidently of an altogether different nature which neither has been recalled by way of the time concept of metaphysics nor ever can be recalled in this way. Thus Time becomes the first name, which is yet to be heeded, of the truth of Being, which is yet to be experienced.

A concealed hint of Time speaks not only out of the earliest metaphysical names of Being but also out of its last name, which is "the eternal recurrence of the same events." Through the entire epoch of metaphysics, Time is decisively present in the history of Being, without being recognized or thought about. To this Time, space is neither co-ordinated nor merely subordinated.

Suppose one attempts to make a transition from the representation of beings as such to recalling the truth of Being: such an attempt, which starts from this representation, must still represent, in a certain sense, the truth of Being, too; and any such representation must of necessity be heterogeneous and ultimately, insofar as it is a representation, inadequate for that which is to be thought. This relation, which comes out of metaphysics and tries to enter into the involvement of the truth of Being in human nature, is called understanding. But here understanding is viewed, at the same time, from the point of view of the unconcealedness of Being. Understanding is a project thrust forth and ecstatic, which means that it stands in the sphere of the open. The sphere which opens up as we project, in order that something (Being in this case) may prove itself as something (in this case, Being as itself in its unconcealedness), is called the sense. (Cf. B.&T., p. 151) "The sense of Being" and "the truth of Being" mean the same.

Let us suppose that Time belongs to the truth of Being in a way that is still concealed: then every project that holds open the truth of Being, representing a way of understanding Being, must look out into Time as the horizon of any possible understanding of Being. (Cf. B.&T., §§31–34 and 68.)

The preface to *Being and Time,* on the first page of the treatise, ends with these sentences: "To furnish a concrete elaboration of the question concerning the sense of 'Being' is the intention of the following treatise. The interpretation of Time as the horizon of every possible attempt to understand Being is its provisional goal."

All philosophy has fallen into the oblivion of Being which has, at the same time, become and remained the fateful demand on thought in *B.&T.;* and philosophy could hardly have given a clearer demonstration of the power of this oblivion of Being than it has furnished us by the somnambulistic assurance with which it has passed by the real and only question of *B.&T.* What is at stake here is, therefore, not a series of misunderstandings of a book but our abandonment by Being.

Metaphysics states what beings are as beings. It offers a λόγος (statement) about the ὄντα (beings). The later title "ontology" characterizes its nature, provided, of course, that we understand it in accordance with its true significance and not through its narrow scholastic meaning.

Metaphysics moves in the sphere of the ὄν ᾗ ὄν: it deals with beings as beings. In this manner, metaphysics always represents beings as such in their totality; it deals with the beingness of beings (the οὐσία of the ὄν). But metaphysics represents the beingness of beings [*die Siendheit des Seienden*] in a twofold manner: in the first place, the totality of beings as such with an eye to their most universal traits (ὄν καθόλου, κοινόν;) but at the same time also the totality of beings as such in the sense of the highest and therefore divine being (ὄν καθόλου, ἀκρότατον, θεῖον). In the metaphysics of Aristotle, the unconcealedness of beings as such has specifically developed in this twofold manner. (Cf. Met. Γ, Ε, Κ.)

Because metaphysics represents beings as beings, it is, two-in-one, the truth of beings in their universality and in the highest being. According to its nature, it is at the same time ontology in the narrower sense and theology. This ontotheological nature of philosophy proper (πρώτη φιλοσοφία) is, no doubt, due to the way in which the ὄν opens up in it, namely as ὄν. Thus the theological character of ontology is not merely due to the fact that Greek metaphysics was later taken up and transformed by the ecclesiastic theology of Christianity. Rather it is due to the manner in which beings as beings have from the very beginning disconcealed themselves. It was this unconcealedness of beings that provided the possibility for Christian theology to take possession of Greek philosophy—whether for better or for worse may be decided by the theologians, on the basis of their experience of what is Christian; only they should keep in mind what is written in the First Epistle of Paul the Apostle to the Corinthians: "οὐχὶ ἐμώρανεν ὁ θεός τὴν σοφίαν τοῦ κόσμου; Has not God let the wisdom of this world become foolishness?" (I Cor. 1:20) The σοφία τοῦ κόσμου [wisdom of this world], however, is that which, according to 1:22, the Ἕλληνες ζητοῦσιν, the Greeks seek. Aristotle even calls the πρώτη φιλοσοφία (philosophy proper) quite specifically ζητουμένη—what is sought. Will Christian theology make up its mind one day to take seriously the word of the apostle and thus also the conception of philosophy as foolishness?

As the truth of beings as such, metaphysics has a twofold character. The reason for this twofoldness, however, let alone its origin, remains unknown to metaphysics; and this is no accident, nor due to mere neglect. Metaphysics has this twofold character because it is what it is: the representation of beings as beings. Metaphysics has no choice.

Being metaphysics, it is by its very nature excluded from the experience of Being; for it always represents beings (ὄν) only with an eye to what of Being has already manifested itself as beings (ᾗ ὄν). But metaphysics never pays attention to what has concealed itself in this very ὄν insofar as it became unconcealed.

Thus the time came when it became necessary to make a fresh attempt to grasp by thought what precisely is said when we speak of ὄν or use the word "being" [seiend]. Accordingly, the question concerning the ὄν was reintroduced into human thinking. (Cf. B.&T., Preface.) But this reintroduction is no mere repetition of the Platonic-Aristotelian question; instead it asks about that which conceals itself in the ὄν.

Metaphysics is founded upon that which conceals itself here as long as metaphysics studies the ὄν ᾗ ὄν. The attempt to inquire back into what conceals itself here seeks, from the point of view of metaphysics, the fundament of ontology. Therefore this attempt is called, in Being and Time . . . "fundamental ontology" [Fundamentalontologie]. Yet this title, like any title, is soon seen to be inappropriate. From the point of view of metaphysics, to be sure, it says something that is correct; but precisely for that reason it is misleading, for what matters is success in the transition from metaphysics to recalling the truth of Being. As long as this thinking calls itself "fundamental ontology" it blocks and obscures its own way with this title. For what the title "fundamental ontology" suggests is, of course, that the attempt to recall the truth of Being—and not, like all ontology, the truth of beings—is itself (seeing that it is called "fundamental ontology") still a kind of ontology. In fact, the attempt to recall the truth of Being sets out on the way back into the ground of metaphysics, and with its first step it immediately leaves the realm of all ontology. On the other hand, every philosophy which revolves around an indirect or direct conception of "transcendence" remains of necessity essentially an ontology, whether it achieves a new foundation of ontology or whether it assures us that it repudiates ontology as a conceptual freezing of experience.

Coming from the ancient custom of representing beings as such, the very thinking that attempted to recall the truth of Being became entangled in these customary conceptions. Under these circumstances it would seem that both for a preliminary orientation and in order to prepare the transition from representational thinking to a new kind of thinking recalls [*das andenkende Denken*], that nothing could be more necessary than the question: What is metaphysics?

The unfolding of this question in the following lecture culminates in another question. This is called the basic question of metaphysics: Why is there any being at all and not rather Nothing? Meanwhile [since this lecture was first published in 1929], to be sure, people have talked back and forth a great deal about dread and the Nothing, both of which are spoken of in this lecture. But one has never yet deigned to ask oneself why a lecture which moves from thinking of the truth of Being to the Nothing, and then tries from there to think into the nature of metaphysics, should claim that this question is the basic question of metaphysics. How can an attentive reader help feeling on the tip of his tongue an objection which is far more weighty than all protests against dread and the Nothing? The final question provokes the objection that an inquiry which attempts to recall Being by way of the Nothing returns in the end to a question concerning beings. On top of that, the question even proceeds in the customary manner of metaphysics by beginning with a causal "Why?" To this extent, then, the attempt to recall Being is repudiated in favor of representational knowledge of beings on the basis of beings. And to make matters still worse, the final question is obviously the question which the metaphysician Leibniz posed in his *Principes de la nature et de la grace: "Pourquoi il y a plutôt quelque chose que rien?"* (Opp. ed. Gerh. tom. VI, 602.n. 7).

Does the lecture, then fall short of its intention? After all, this would be quite possible in view of the difficulty of effecting a transition from metaphysics to another kind of thinking. Does the lecture end up by asking Leibniz' metaphysical question about the supreme cause of all things that have being? Why, then, is Leibniz' name not mentioned, as decency would seem to require?

Or is the question asked in an altogether different sense? If it does not concern itself with beings and inquire about their first cause among all beings, then the question must begin from that which is not a being. And this is precisely what the question names, and it capitalizes the word: the Nothing. This is the sole topic of the lecture. The demand seems obvious that the end of the lecture should be thought through, for once, in its own perspective which determines the whole lecture. What has been called the basic question of metaphysics would then have to be understood and asked in terms of fundamental ontology as the question that comes out of the ground of metaphysics and as the question about this ground.

But if we grant this lecture that in the end it thinks in the direction of its own distinctive concern, how are we to understand this question?

The question is: Why is there any being at all and not rather Nothing? Suppose that we do not remain within metaphysics to ask metaphysically in the customary manner; suppose we recall the truth of Being out of the nature and the truth of metaphysics; then this might be asked as well: How did it come about that beings take precedence everywhere and lay claim to every "is" while that which is not a being is understood as Nothing, though it is Being itself, and remains forgotten? How did it come about that with Being It really is nothing and that the Nothing really is not? Is it perhaps from this that the as yet unshaken presumption has entered into all metaphysics that "Being" may simply be taken for granted and that Nothing is therefore made more easily than beings? That is indeed the situation regarding Being and Nothing. If it were different, then Leibniz could not have said in the same place by way of an explanation: "*Car le rien est plus simple et plus facile que quelque chose* [For the nothing is simpler and easier than any thing]."

What is more enigmatic: that beings are, or that Being is? Or does even this reflection fail to bring us close to that enigma which has occurred with the Being of beings?

Whatever the answer may be, the time should have ripened meanwhile for thinking through the lecture "What is Metaphysics?" which has been subjected to so many attacks, from its end, for once—from *its* end and not from an imaginary end.

❖ ❖ ❖

HANS-GEORG GADAMER

Heidegger's call for "an end to metaphysics," his call to become involved with Being as it discloses itself rather than objectifying it in timeless, universal formulations has had great influence in hermeneutical studies. One of the most important examples is Hans-Georg Gadamer (1900–) and his *Truth and Method*. In this work, Gadamer, a student of Heidegger, challenges the hermeneutical tradition that began with Schleiermacher and continued through Dilthey which attempted to make hermeneutics and, indeed, all of the humanities including history into objective, universal sciences. Rather, Gadamer claims, interpretation is not and cannot be a matter of stating timelessly what a text means. Instead it is a matter of standing within a historical tradition of interpretation in which the text is engaged through a "historically effected consciousness" (*wirkungsgeschichtliches Bewusstsein*). Gadamer poses the "hermeneutical problem" as one more akin to legal judgment than to establishing what we normally call historical fact, although, he adds, even historical facts finally need to be seen as matters of interpretation. The "hermeneutical problem" is one that is especially seen in the interpretation of theological texts.

The Exemplary Significance of Legal Hermeneutics
(Truth and Method, II.II.2c)

If this is the case, the gap between hermeneutics of the human sciences and legal hermeneutics cannot be as wide as is generally assumed. The dominant view is, of course, that only with the rise of historical consciousness was understanding raised to a method of objective science and that hermeneutics came into its own when it was elaborated into a general theory of the understanding and interpretation of texts. Legal hermeneutics does not belong in this context, for its purpose is not to understand given texts, but to be a practical measure filling a kind of gap in the system of legal dogmatics. It is thought, then, that it has nothing to do with the task of hermeneutics in the human sciences, which is the understanding of traditionary material.

But in that case *theological hermeneutics* cannot claim any independent systematic significance. Schleiermacher consciously placed it wholly within *general hermeneutics* and merely regarded it as a special application of it. Since then, scientific theology's claim to be a discipline on a par with the modern historical sciences seems to depend on the fact that no laws and rules are to be applied in interpreting Scripture other than those used in understanding any other traditionary material. Thus there could no longer be any such thing as a specifically theological hermeneutics.

It is a paradoxical position if we, nevertheless, try to revive the old truth and the old unity of hermeneutical discipline within modern science. It seems that methodology of the human sciences moves into modernity when it detaches itself from all dogmatic ties. Legal hermeneutics was separated from theory of understanding as a whole because it has a dogmatic purpose, just as, by giving up its dogmatic commitment, theological hermeneutics was united with philological-historical method.

In this situation we can take special interest in the divergence between legal and historical hermeneutics and consider those cases in which legal and historical hermeneutics are concerned with the same object — i.e., cases in which legal texts are interpreted legally, in court, and also understood historically. So we will consider the approaches taken by the legal historian and the jurist to the same legal text. We can turn here to the excellent writings of E. Betti and pursue our own thinking from there. Our question is *whether or not there is a unequivocal distinction between dogmatic and historical interest.*

That there is a difference is clear. The jurist understands the meaning of the law from the present case and for the sake of this present case. By contrast, the legal historian has no case from which to start, but he seeks to determine the meaning of the law by constructing the whole range of its applications. It is only in all its applications that the law becomes concrete. Thus the legal historian cannot be content to take the original application of the law as determining its original meaning. As a historian he will, rather, have to take account of the historical change that the law has undergone. In understanding, he will have to mediate between the original application and the present application of the law.

In my view it would not be enough to say that the task of the historian was simply to "reconstruct the original meaning of the legal formula" and that of the jurist to "harmonize that meaning with the present living actuality." This kind of division would mean that the definition of the jurist is more comprehensive and includes the task of the legal historian. Someone who is seeking to understand the correct meaning of a law must first know the original one. Thus he must think in terms of legal history—but here historical understanding serves merely as a means to an end. On the other hand, the historian as such has no dogmatic task. As a historian he approaches the historical object in order to determine its historical value, whereas the jurist, in addition, applies what has been learned in this way to the legal present. This is what Betti says.

We may ask, however, whether he has viewed and described the task of the historian in a sufficiently comprehensive way. In our particular example, where does the historical element come in? In regard to a law still in force we naturally assume that its legal meaning is clear and that the legal practice of the present simply follows the original meaning. If this were always the case, the question about the meaning of a law would be both juridically and historically the same. For the jurist too the hermeneutical task would be just to establish the original meaning of the law and apply it as the right one. Hence as late as 1840, Savigny, in his *System des römischen Rechts,* regarded the task of legal hermeneutics as purely historical. Just as Schleiermacher saw no problem in the interpreter's having to identify himself with the original reader, so Savigny ignores the tension between the original and the present legal sense.

It has emerged clearly enough in the course of time that this is a legally untenable fiction. Ernst Forsthoff has shown in a valuable study that for purely legal reasons it was necessary for an awareness of historical change to develop, which involved distinguishing between the original meaning of a law and that applied in current legal practice. It is true that the jurist is always concerned with the law itself, but he determines its normative content in regard to the given case to which it is to be applied. In order to determine this content exactly, it is necessary to have historical knowledge of the original meaning, and only for this reason does the judge concern himself with the historical value that the law has through the act of legislation. But he cannot let himself be bound by what, say, an account of the parliamentary proceedings tells him about the intentions of those who first passed the law. Rather, he has to take account of the change in circumstances and hence define afresh the normative function of the law.

It is quite different with the legal historian. He is apparently concerned only with the original meaning of the law, the way in which it was meant, and the validity it had when it was first promulgated. But how can he know this? Can he know it without being aware of the change in circumstances that separates his own present time from that past time? Must he not then do exactly the same thing as the judge does—i.e., distinguish between the original meaning of the text of the law and the legal meaning which he as someone who lives in the present automatically assumes? The hermeneutical situation of both the historian and the jurist seems to me to be the same in that, when faced with any text, we have an immediate expectation of meaning. There can be no such thing as a direct access to the historical object that would objectively reveal its historical value. The historian has to undertake the same reflection as the jurist.

Thus the actual content of what is understood in each of the two ways is the same. The above description of the historian's approach, then, is inadequate. Historical knowledge can be gained only by seeing the past in its continuity with the present—which is exactly what the jurist does in his practical, normative work of "ensuring the unbroken continuance of law and preserving the tradition of the legal idea."

We must consider, though, whether the case we have been discussing is really characteristic of the general problem of historical understanding. The model from which we started was the understanding of a law still in force. Here the historian and the dogmatist were concerned with the same object. But is this not a special case? A legal historian who turns to the legal cultures of the past, and certainly any other historian who is seeking to understand a past that no longer has any direct continuity with the present, would not recognize himself in the case we have been considering—namely a law still in force. He would say that legal hermeneutics has a special dogmatic task that is quite foreign to the context of historical hermeneutics.

In fact the situation seems to me just the opposite. Legal hermeneutics serves to remind us what the real procedure of the human sciences is. Here we have the model for the relationship between past and present that we are seeking. The judge who adapts the transmitted law to the needs of the present is undoubtedly seeking to perform a practical task, but his interpretation of the law is by no means merely for that reason an arbitrary revision. Here again, to understand and to interpret means to discover and recognize a valid meaning. The judge seeks to be in accord with the "legal idea" in mediating it with the present. This is, of course, a legal mediation. It is the legal significance of the law—and not the historical significance of the law's promulgation or of particular cases of its application—that he is trying to understand. Thus his orientation is not that of a historian, but he has an orientation to his own history, which is his present. Thus he can always approach as a historian those questions that he has implicitly concluded as a judge.

On the other hand, the historian, who has no juridical task before him but is trying to discover the legal meaning of this law—like anything else that has been handed down in history—cannot disregard the fact that he is concerned with a legal creation that needs to be understood in a legal way. He must be able to think not only historically but also legally. It is true that it is a special case when a historian is examining a legal text that is still valid today. But this special case shows us what determines our relationship to any traditionary text. Trying to understand the law in terms of its historical origin, the historian cannot disregard its continuing effect: it presents him with the questions that he has to ask of historical tradition. Is this not true of every text—i.e., that it must be understood in terms of what it says? Does this not mean that it always needs to be restated? And does not this restatement always take place through its being related to the present? Inasmuch as the actual object of historical understanding is not events but their "significance," it is clearly an incorrect description of this understanding to speak of an object existing in itself and of the subject's approach to it. The truth is that historical understanding always implies that the tradition reaching us speaks into the present and must be understood in this mediation—indeed, *as* this mediation. *In reality then, legal hermeneutics is no special case but is, on the contrary, capable of restoring the hermeneutical problem to its full breadth and so re-establishing the former unity of hermeneutics, in which jurist and theologian meet the philologist.*

We saw above that one of the conditions of understanding in the human sciences is belonging to tradition. Let us now try to verify this by seeing how this structural element of understanding obtains in the case of legal and theological hermeneutics. This condition is clearly not so much a limiting condition as one that makes understanding possible. The way the interpreter belongs to his text is like the way the point from which we are to view a picture belongs to its perspective. It is not a matter of looking for this viewpoint and adopting it as one's standpoint. The interpreter similarly finds his point of view already given, and does not choose it arbitrarily. Thus it is an essential condition of the possibility of legal hermeneutics that the law is binding on all members of the community in the same way. Where this is not the case—for example in an absolutist state, where the will of the absolute ruler is above the law—hermeneutics cannot exist, "since an absolute ruler can explain his words in a sense that abrogates the general rules of interpretation." For in this instance the law is not interpreted in such a way that the particular case is decided justly according to the right sense of the law. On the contrary, the will of a monarch who is not bound by the law can effect whatever seems just to him without regard for the law—that is, without the effort of interpretation. The need to understand and interpret arises only when something is enacted in such a way that it is, as enacted, irrevocable and binding.

The work of interpretation is *to concretize* the law in each specific case—i.e., it is a work of *application*. The creative supplementing of the law that is involved is a task reserved to the judge, but he is subject to the law in the same way as is every other member of the community. It is part of the idea of a rule of law that the judge's judgment does not proceed from an arbitrary and unpredictable decision, but from the just weighing up of the whole. Anyone who has immersed himself in the particular situation is capable of undertaking this just weighing-up. This is why in a state governed by law, there is legal certainty—i.e., it is in principle possible to know what the exact situation is. Every lawyer and every counsel is able, in principle, to give correct advice—i.e., he can accurately predict the judge's decision on the basis of the existing laws. Applying the law is not simply a matter of knowing the law. If one has to give a legal judgment on a particular case, of course it is necessary to know the law and all the elements that have determined it. But the only belonging under the law necessary here is that the legal order is recognized as valid for everyone and that no one is exempt from it. Hence it is always possible to grasp the existing legal order as such — i.e., to assimilate dogmatically any past supplement to the law. Consequently there is an essential connection between legal hermeneutics and legal dogmatics, and in it hermeneutics has the more important place. For the idea of a perfect legal dogmatics, which would make every judgment a mere act of subsumption, is untenable.

Let us now consider the case of *theological hermeneutics,* as developed by Protestant theology, as it applies to our question. Here there is a genuine parallel to legal hermeneutics, for here too dogmatics cannot claim any primacy. The proclamation is genuinely concretized in preaching, as is the legal order in judgment. But there is still a big difference between them. Unlike a legal verdict, preaching is not a creative supplement to the text it is interpreting. Hence the gospel acquires no new content in being preached that could be compared with the power of the judge's verdict to supplement the law. It is not the case that the gospel of salvation becomes more clearly determined only through the preacher's thoughts. As a preacher, he does not speak before the community with the same dogmatic authority that a judge does. Certainly preaching too is concerned with interpreting a valid truth, but this truth is proclamation; and whether it is successful or not is not decided by the ideas of the preacher, but by the power of the word itself, which can call men to repentance even though the sermon is a bad one. The proclamation cannot be detached from its fulfillment. The dogmatic establishment of pure doctrine is a secondary matter. Scripture is the word of God, and that means it has an absolute priority over the doctrine of those who interpret it.

Interpretation should never overlook this. Even as the scholarly interpretation of the theologian, it must never forget that Scripture is the divine proclamation of salvation. Understanding it, therefore, cannot simply be a scientific or scholarly exploration of its meaning. Bultmann once wrote, "The interpretation of the biblical writings is subject to exactly the same conditions as any other literature." But the meaning of this statement is ambiguous, for the question is whether all literature is not subject to conditions of understanding other than those formal general ones that have to be fulfilled in regard to every text. Bultmann himself points out that all understanding presumes a living relationship between the interpreter and the text, his previous connection with the subject matter it deals with. He calls this hermeneutical requirement *fore-understanding,* because it is clearly not something to be attained through the process of understanding but is already presupposed. Thus Hofmann, whom Bultmann quotes with approval, writes that scriptural hermeneutics presupposes a relationship to the content of the Bible.

We may ask, however, what kind of "presupposition" this is. Is it something that is given with human life itself? Does there exist in every man a prior connection with the truth of divine revelation because man as such is concerned with the question of God? Or must we say that it is first from God—i.e., from faith—that human existence experiences itself as being affected by the question of God? But then the sense of the presupposition implied in the concept of fore-understanding becomes questionable. For then the presupposition would not be valid universally but only from the viewpoint of true faith.

In regard to the Old Testament this is a venerable hermeneutical problem. Which is the right interpretation of it, the Jewish one or the Christian one in light of the New Testament? Or are both legitimate interpretations—i.e., do they have something in common, and is this what is really being understood by the interpreter? The Jew who understands the text of the Old Testament in a different way than the Christian shares with him the presupposition that he too is concerned with the question of God. At the same time, he will hold that a Christian theologian misunderstands the Old Testament if he takes its truths as qualified by the New Testament. Hence the presupposition that one is moved by the question of God already involves a claim to knowledge concerning the true God and his revelation. Even unbelief is defined in terms of the faith that is demanded of one. The existential fore-understanding from which Bultmann starts can only be a Christian one.

We could perhaps try to escape this conclusion by saying that it is enough to *know* that religious texts are to be understood only as texts that answer the question of God. There need be no claim on the religious commitment of the interpreter himself. But what would a Marxist, who understands religious utterances only as the reflection of class interests, say? He will not accept the presupposition that human existence as such is moved by the question of God. This presupposition is obviously held only by someone who already recognizes the alternative of belief or unbelief in the true God. Thus the hermeneutical significance of fore-understanding in theology seems itself theological. After all, the history of hermeneutics shows how the examination of the texts is determined by a very precise fore-understanding. As a Protestant art of interpreting Scripture, modern hermeneutics is clearly related in a polemical way to the dogmatic tradition of the Catholic church. It has itself a dogmatic denominational significance. This does not mean that such theological hermeneutics is dogmatically predisposed, so that it reads out of the text what it has put into it. Rather, it really risks itself. But it assumes that the word of Scripture addresses us and that only the person who allows himself to be addressed — whether he believes or doubts — understands. Hence the primary thing is application.

We can, then, distinguish what is truly common to all forms of hermeneutics: the meaning to be understood is concretized and fully realized only in interpretation, but the interpretive activity considers itself wholly bound by the meaning of the text. Neither jurist nor theologian regards the work of application as making free with the text.

The task of concretizing something universal and applying it to oneself seems, however, to have a very different function in the historical sciences. If we ask what application means here and how it occurs in the kind of understanding undertaken in the human sciences, we can acknowledge that a certain class of traditionary material is applied in the same way the jurist does in regard to the law and the theologian the proclamation. Just as in the one case the judge seeks to dispense justice and in the other the preacher to proclaim salvation, and as, in both, the meaning of what is proclaimed finds its fullest realization in the proclamation of justice and the proclamation of the gospel, so in the case of a philosophical text or a work of literature we can see that these texts require a special activity of the reader and interpreter, and that we do not have the freedom to adopt a historical distance toward them. It will be seen that here understanding always involves applying the meaning understood.

But does application essentially and necessarily belong to understanding? From the point of view of modern science the answer will be that it does not, and it will be said that the kind of application that makes the interpreter the person to whom the text was originally addressed, as it were, is quite unscientific and is to be wholly excluded from the historical sciences. What makes modern scholarship scientific is precisely the fact that it objectifies tradition and methodically eliminates the influence of the interpreter and his time on understanding. It may often be difficult to attain this goal, and it will be difficult to preserve the distinction between historical and dogmatic interest in the case of texts that are addressed to no one in particular and claim to be valid for anyone who receives the tradition. A good example of this is the problem of scientific theology and its relation to the tradition of Scripture. It may seem in this case that the balance between historico-scientific and dogmatic interpretation is to be found in the private world of the person. It may be the same with the philosopher and also with our aesthetic consciousness when it finds itself addressed by a work of art. But according to this view, science claims to remain independent of all subjective applications by reason of its method.

This is the kind of argument that would have to be presented by proponents of the modern theory of science. Those cases in which the interpreter cannot immediately substitute for the original addressee will be considered exemplary—i.e., where a text has a quite specific addressee, such as the partner to an agreement, or the recipient of a bill or an order. Here, to understand the meaning of the text fully, we must, as it were, put ourselves in the place of the addressee, and insofar as this transposition serves to give the text its full concrete form, we can regard this also as an achievement of interpretation. But this transposing of ourselves into the position of the original reader (Schleiermacher) is something quite different from application. It actually skips the task of mediating between then and now, between the Thou and the I, which is what we mean by application and which legal hermeneutics also regards as its task.

Let us take the example of understanding an order. An order exists only where there is someone to obey it. Here, then, understanding belongs to a relationship between persons, one of whom has to give the order. To understand the order means to apply it to the specific situation to which it pertains. It is true that one makes the other repeat the order to make sure it has been understood, but that does not alter the fact that it is given its real meaning when it is carried out and concretized in accordance with its meaning. This is why there is such a thing as an explicit refusal to obey that is not simply disobedience but derives from the meaning of the order and its concretization. A person who refuses to obey an order has understood it, and because he applies it to the situation and knows what obedience would mean in that situation, he refuses. The criterion of understanding is clearly not in the order's actual words, nor in the mind of the person giving the order, but solely in the understanding of the situation and in the responsible behavior of the person who obeys. Even when an order is written down so one can be sure it will be correctly understood and executed, no one assumes that it makes everything explicit. The comic situation in which orders are carried out literally but not according to their meaning is well known. Thus there is no doubt that the recipient of an order must perform a definite creative act in understanding its meaning.

If we now imagine a *historian* who regards a traditionary text as such an order and seeks to understand it, he is, of course, in a situation quite different from that of the original addressee. He is not the person to whom the order is addressed and so cannot relate it to himself. But if he really wants to understand the order, then he must, idealiter, perform *the same act* as that performed by the intended recipient of the order. The latter too, who applies the order to himself, is well able to distinguish between understanding and obeying an order. It is possible for him not to obey even when—indeed, precisely when—he has understood it. It may be difficult for the historian to reconstruct the original situation in which the order arose. But he will understand it fully only when he has thus made the order concrete. This, then, is the clear hermeneutical demand: to understand a text in terms of the specific situation in which it was written.

According to the self-understanding of science, then, it can make no difference to the historian whether a text was addressed to a particular person or was intended "to belong to all ages." The general requirement of hermeneutics is, rather, that every text must be understood according to the aim appropriate to it. But this means that historical scholarship first seeks to understand every text in its own terms and does not accept the content of what it says as true, but leaves it undecided. Understanding is certainly concretization, but one that involves keeping a hermeneutical distance. Understanding is possible only if one keeps oneself out of play. This is the demand of science. According to this self-interpretation of the methodology of the human sciences, it is generally said that the interpreter imagines an addressee for every text, whether expressly addressed by the text or not. This addressee is in every case the original reader, and the interpreter knows that this is a different person from himself. This is obvious, when thus negatively expressed. A person trying to understand a text, whether literary critic or historian, does not, at any rate, apply what it says to himself. He is simply trying to understand what the author is saying, and if he is simply trying to understand, he is not interested in the objective truth of what is said as such, not even if the text itself claims to teach truth. On this the philologist and the historian are in agreement.

Hermeneutics and historical study, however, are clearly not the same thing. By examining the methodological differences between the two, we will discover that *what they really have in common* is not what they are generally thought to have. The historian has a different orientation to the texts of the past, in that he is trying to discover something about the past through them. He therefore uses other traditionary material to supplement and verify what the texts say. He considers it as more or less of a weakness when the philologist regards his text as a work of art. A work of art is a whole, self-sufficient world. But the interest of the historian knows no such self-sufficiency. Against Schleiermacher, Dilthey once said, "Philology would like to see self-contained existence everywhere." If a work of literature from the past makes an impression on a historian, this will have no hermeneutical significance for him. It is fundamentally impossible for him to regard himself as the addressee of the text and accept its claim on him. Rather, he examines the text to find something it is not, of itself, attempting to provide. This is true even of traditionary material which itself purports to be historical representation. Even the writer of history is subject to historical critique.

Thus the historian goes beyond hermeneutics, and the idea of interpretation acquires a new and more defined meaning. It no longer refers only to the explicit act of understanding a given text, as for the philologist. The concept of historical interpretation corresponds more to the idea of the *expression,* which is not understood by historical hermeneutics in its classical and traditional sense — i.e., as a rhetorical term that refers to the relation of language to thought. What the expression expresses is not merely what is supposed to be expressed in it—what is meant by it—but primarily what is also expressed by the words without its being intended—i.e., what the expression, as it were, "betrays." In this wider sense the word "expression" refers to far more than linguistic expression; rather, it includes everything that we have to get behind, and that at the same time enables us to get behind it. Interpretation here, then, does not refer to the sense intended, but to the sense that is hidden and has to be disclosed. In this sense every text not only presents an intelligible meaning but, in many respects, needs to be interpreted. The text is primarily a phenomenon of expression. It is understandable that the historian is interested in this aspect. For the documentary value of, say, a report depends in part on what the text, as a phenomenon of expression, displays. From this, one can discover what the writer intended without saying, what party he belonged to, with what views he approached things, or even what degree of lack of principle or dishonesty is to be expected of him. These subjective elements affecting the credibility of the witness must be taken into consideration. But, above all, the content of the traditionary material must itself be interpreted, even if its subjective reliability is established—i.e., the text is understood as a document whose true meaning can be discovered only behind its literal meaning, by comparing it with other data that allow us to estimate its historical value.

Thus *for the historian it is a basic principle that tradition is to be interpreted in a sense different than the texts, of themselves, call for.* He will always go back behind them and the meaning they express to inquire into the reality they express involuntarily. Texts must be treated in the same way as other available historical material—i.e., as the so-called relics of the past. Like everything else, they need explication—i.e., to be understood in terms of not only what they say but what they exemplify.

The concept of interpretation reaches its culmination here. Interpretation is necessary where the meaning of a text cannot be immediately understood. It is necessary wherever one is not prepared to trust what a phenomenon immediately presents to us. The psychologist interprets in this way by not accepting the expressions of life in their intended sense but delving back into what was taking place in the unconscious. Similarly, the historian interprets the data of tradition in order to discover the true meaning that is expressed and, at the same time, hidden in them.

Thus there is a natural tension between the historian and the philologist who seeks to understand a text for the sake of its beauty and its truth. The historian's interpretation is concerned with something that is not expressed in the text itself and need have nothing to do with the intended meaning of the text. There is a fundamental conflict here between the historical and the literary consciousness, although this tension scarcely exists now that historical consciousness has also altered the orientation of the critic. He has given up the claim that his texts have a normative validity for him. He no longer regards them as models of the best that has been thought and said, but looks at them in a way that they themselves did not intend to be looked at; he looks at them as a historian. This has made philology and criticism subsidiary disciplines of historical studies. This could be glimpsed already in classical philology when it began to call itself the science of antiquity (Wilamowitz). It is a department of historical research concerned primarily with language and literature. The philologist is a historian, in that he discovers a historical dimension in his literary sources. Understanding, then, is for him a matter of placing a given text in the context of the history of language, literary form, style, and so on, and thus ultimately mediating it with the whole context of historical life. Only occasionally does his own original nature come through. Thus, in judging the ancient historians, he tends to give these great writers more credence than the historian finds justified. This ideological credulity, which makes the philologist overestimate the value of his texts as evidence, is the last vestige of his old claim to be the friend of "eloquence" and the mediator of classical literature.

Let us now inquire whether this description of the procedure of the human sciences, in which the historian and the critic of today are one, is accurate and whether the claim of historical consciousness to be universal is justified. In regard to *philology* it seems questionable. The critic is ultimately mistaking his own nature, as a friend of eloquence, if he bows to the standard of historical studies. If his texts possess an exemplary character for him, this may be primarily in regard to form. The older humanism fervently believed that everything in classical literature was said in an exemplary way; but what is said in such a way is actually more than an exemplar of form. Eloquence (schöne Reden) is not called such simply because what is said is said beautifully, but also because something beautiful is said. It seeks to be more than mere rhetoric. It is particularly true of the national poetic traditions that we admire not only their poetic power, the imagination and art of their expression, but above all the great truth that speaks in them.

If in the work of the critic, then, there is still something of only acknowledging models, he is not in fact relating his texts merely to a reconstructed addressee but also to himself (though he is unwilling to accept this). But in accepting models there is always an understanding that does not leave their exemplarity undecided, but rather has already chosen and considers itself obligated to them. That is why relating oneself to an exemplar is always like following in someone's footsteps. And just as this is more than mere imitation, so this understanding is a continually new form of encounter and has itself the character of an event precisely because it does not simply leave things up in the air but involves application. The literary critic, as it were, weaves a little further on the great tapestry of tradition that supports us.

If we acknowledge this, then criticism and philology can attain their true dignity and proper knowledge of themselves only by being liberated from history. Yet this seems to me to be only half the truth. Rather, we should ask whether the picture of the historical approach, as set out here, is not itself distorted. Perhaps not only the approach of the critic and philologist but *also that of the historian* should be oriented not so much to the methodological ideal of the natural sciences as to the model offered us by legal and theological hermeneutics. It may be that the historical approach to texts differs specifically from the original bond of the critic to his texts. It may be that the historian tries to get behind the texts in order to force them to yield information that they do not intend, and are unable of themselves to give. With regard to the individual text, this would seem to be the case. The historian approaches his texts the way an investigating magistrate approaches his witnesses. But simply establishing facts, elicited from possibly prejudiced witnesses, does not make the historian. What makes the historian is understanding the significance of what he finds. Thus the testimony of history is like that given before a court. It is no accident that in German the same word is used for both, Zeugnis (testimony; witness). In both cases testimony aids in establishing the facts. But the facts are not the real objects of inquiry; they are simply material for the real tasks of the judge and of the historian — that is, respectively, to reach a just decision and to establish the historical significance of an event within the totality of his historical self-consciousness.

Thus the whole difference is possibly only a question of the criteria. One should not choose too nicely if one would reach the essentials. We have already shown that traditional hermeneutics artificially limited the dimensions of the phenomenon, and perhaps the same is true of the historical approach. Is it not the case here too that the really important things precede any application of historical methods? A historical hermeneutics that does not make the *nature of the historical question* the central thing, and does not inquire into a historian's motives in examining historical material, lacks its most important element.

If we accept this, then the relation between literary criticism and historical studies suddenly appears quite different. Although we spoke of the humanities as being under the alien control of historical studies, this is not the last word on the matter. Rather, it seems to me that the *problem of application,* of which we had to remind the critic, *also characterizes the more complicated situation of historical understanding.* All appearances seem to be against this, it is true, for historical understanding seems to fall entirely short of the traditionary text's claim to applicability. We have seen that history does not regard a text in terms of the text's intention but in terms of its own characteristic and different intention — i.e., as a historical source — using it to understand what the text did not at all intend to say but we nevertheless find expressed in it.

On closer examination, however, the question arises whether the historian's understanding is really different in structure from the critic's. It is true that he considers the texts from another point of view, but this difference of intention applies only to the individual text as such. For the historian, however, the individual text makes up, together with other sources and testimonies, the unity of the whole tradition. The whole unified tradition is his true hermeneutical object. It is this that he must understand in the same sense in which the literary critic understands his text in the unity of its meaning. Thus the historian too must perform a task of application. This is the important point: historical understanding proves to be a kind of literary criticism writ large.

But this does not mean that we share the hermeneutical approach of the historical school, the problems of which we outlined above. We spoke of the dominance of the philological schema in historical self-understanding and used Dilthey's foundation of the human sciences to show that the historical school's aim of seeing history as reality and not simply as unfolding complexes of ideas could not be achieved. We, for our part, are not maintaining, with Dilthey, that every event is as perfectly meaningful as a text. When I called history criticism writ large, this did not mean that historical studies are to be understood as part of intellectual history (Geistesgeschichte).

I am saying just the opposite. We have seen, I think more correctly, what is involved in reading a text. Of course the reader before whose eyes the great book of world history simply lies open does not exist. But neither does the reader exist who, when he has his text before him, simply reads what is there. Rather, all reading involves application, so that a person reading a text is himself part of the meaning he apprehends. He belongs to the text that he is reading. The line of meaning that the text manifests to him as he reads it always and necessarily breaks off in an open indeterminacy. He can, indeed he must, accept the fact that future generations will understand differently what he has read in the text. And what is true of every reader is also true of the historian. The historian is concerned with the whole of historical tradition, which he has to mediate with his own present existence if he wants to understand it and which in this way he keeps open for the future.

Thus *we too acknowledge that there is an inner unity between philology and literary criticism on the one hand and historical studies on the other,* but we do not see it in the universality of the historical method, nor in the objectifying replacement of the interpreter by the original reader, nor in historical critique of tradition as such but, on the contrary, in the fact that both perform an act of application that is different only in degree. If the philologist or critic understands the given text — i.e., understands himself in the text in the way we have said — the historian too understands the great text of world history he has himself discovered, in which every text handed down to us is but a fragment of meaning, one letter, as it were, and he understands himself in this great text. Both the critic and the historian thus emerge from the self-forgetfulness to which they had been banished by a thinking for which the only criterion was the methodology of modern science. Both find their true ground in *historically effected consciousness.*

279

This shows that the model of legal hermeneutics was, in fact, a useful one. When a judge regards himself as entitled to supplement the original meaning of the text of a law, he is doing exactly what takes place in all other understanding. *The old unity of the hermeneutical disciplines comes into its own again if we recognize that historically effected consciousness is at work in all hermeneutical activity, that of philologist as well as of the historian.*

The meaning of the application involved in all forms of understanding is now clear. Application does not mean first understanding a given universal in itself and then afterward applying it to a concrete case. It is the very understanding of the universal — the text — itself. Understanding proves to be a kind of effect and knows itself as such.

From *Truth and Method,* by Hans-Georg Gadamer. Second, revised edition. Translation revised by Joel Weinsheimer and Donald G. Marshall. Second, revised edition © 1989 by The Crossroad Publishing Company, Sheed & Ward Ltd. Reprinted by permission of the publishers.

✦ ✦

ANTONY FLEW

Logical positivism developed between the First and Second World Wars, largely in Vienna and Berlin, before spreading to the English-speaking world. Like classical positivism, in which the methods and results of the natural sciences are considered normative for all fields of inquiry, it added a new and powerful twist. Claiming to rely on the procedures of the physical sciences, it devised a criterion of meaning, the verification principle. According to this principle, unless a purported statement could in principle be verified or falsified by sense observation, it was meaningless. The positivists argued aggressively that the utterances of metaphysics, theology, ethics, and aesthetics were meaningless.

The selection from Antony Flew, which became widely accessible in 1955, was the first application of the falsification principle (a modification of the verification principle) to the claim that God is the designer of the universe and that God loves us. These issues were also raised by David Hume in his *Dialogues Concerning Natural Religion*. But the form in which Flew cast them became the way they were discussed in the philosophy of religion in English-speaking countries. Hermeneutical discussions seek better to understand what religious utterances and actions mean, but the dominant issue in English-speaking philosophy of religion for nearly three decades after Flew's article was whether they had any meaning at all.

The University Discussion

Let us begin with a parable. It is a parable developed from a tale told by John Wisdom in his haunting and revelatory article 'Gods'. Once upon a time two explorers came upon a clearing in the jungle. In the clearing were growing many flowers and many weeds. One explorer says, 'Some gardener must tend this plot'. The other disagrees, 'There is no gardener'. So they pitch their tents and set a watch. No gardener is ever seen. 'But perhaps he is an invisible gardener.' So they set up a barbed-wire fence. They electrify it. They patrol with bloodhounds. (For they remember how H. G. Wells's *The Invisible Man* could be both smelt and touched though he could not be seen.) But no shrieks ever suggest that some intruder has received a shock. No movements of the wire ever betray an invisible climber. The bloodhounds never give cry. Yet still the Believer is not convinced. 'But there is a gardener, invisible, intangible, insensible to electric shocks, a gardener who has no scent and makes no sound, a gardener who comes secretly to look after the garden which he loves.' At last the Sceptic despairs, 'But what remains of your original assertion? Just how does what you call an invisible, intangible, eternally elusive gardener differ from an imaginary gardener or even from no gardener at all?'

In this parable we can see how what starts as an assertion, that something exists or that there is some analogy between certain complexes of phenomena, may be reduced step by step to an altogether different status, to an expression perhaps of a 'picture preference'. The Sceptic says there is no gardener. The Believer says there is a gardener (but invisible, etc.). One man talks about sexual behaviour. Another man prefers to talk of Aphrodite (but knows that there is not really a superhuman person additional to, and somehow responsible for, all sexual phenomena). The process of qualification may be checked at any point before the original assertion is completely withdrawn and something of that first assertion will remain (Tautology). Mr. Wells's invisible man could not, admittedly, be seen, but in all other respects he was a man like the rest of us. But though the process of qualification may be, and of course usually is, checked in time, it is not always judiciously so halted. Someone may dissipate his assertion completely without noticing that he has done so. A fine brash hypothesis may thus be killed by inches, the death by a thousand qualifications.

And in this, it seems to me, lies the peculiar danger, the endemic evil, of theological utterance. Take such utterances as 'God has a plan', 'God created the world', 'God loves us as a father loves his children'. They look at first sight very much like assertions, vast cosmological assertions. Of course, this is no sure sign that they either are, or are intended to be, assertions. But let us confine ourselves to the cases where those who utter such sentences intend them to express assertions. (Merely remarking parenthetically that those who intend or interpret such utterances as crypto-commands, expressions of wishes, disguised ejaculations, concealed ethics, or as anything else but assertions, are unlikely to succeed in making them either properly orthodox or practically effective).

Now to assert that such and such is the case is necessarily equivalent to denying that such and such is not the case. Suppose then that we are in doubt as to what someone who gives vent to an utterance is asserting, or suppose that, more radically, we are sceptical as to whether he is really asserting anything at all, one way of trying to understand (or perhaps it will be to expose) his utterance is to attempt to find what he would regard as counting against, or as being incompatible with, its truth. For if the utterance is indeed an assertion, it will necessarily be equivalent to a denial of the negation of that assertion. And anything which would count against the assertion, or which would induce the speaker to withdraw it and to admit that it had been mistaken, must be part of (or the whole of) the meaning of the negation of that assertion. And to know the meaning of the negation of an assertion, is as near as makes no matter, to know the meaning of that assertion. And if there is nothing which a putative assertion denies then there is nothing which it asserts either: and so it is not really an assertion. When the Sceptic in the parable asked the Believer, 'Just how does what you call an invisible, intangible, eternally elusive gardener differ from an imaginary gardener or even from no gardener at all?' he was suggesting that the Believer's earlier statement had been so eroded by qualification that it was no longer an assertion at all.

Now it often seems to people who are not religious as if there was no conceivable event or series of events the occurrence of which would be admitted by sophisticated religious people to be a sufficient reason for conceding 'There wasn't a God after all' or 'God does not really love us then'. Someone tells us that God loves us as a father loves his children. We are reassured. But then we see a child dying of inoperable cancer of the throat. His earthly father is driven frantic in his efforts to help, but his Heavenly Father reveals no obvious sign of concern. Some qualification is made — God's love is 'not a merely human love' or it is 'an inscrutable love', perhaps — and we realize that such sufferings are quite compatible with the truth of the assertion that 'God loves us as a father (but, of course, . . .)'. We are reassured again. But then perhaps we ask: what is this assurance of God's (appropriately qualified) love worth, what is this apparent guarantee really a guarantee against? Just what would have to happen not merely (morally and wrongly) to tempt but also (logically and rightly) to entitle us to say 'God does not love us' or even 'God does not exist?' I therefore put to the succeeding symposiasts the simple central questions, 'What would have to occur or to have occurred to constitute for you a disproof of the love of, or of the existence of, God?'

From *New Essays in Philosophical Theology*. Edited by Antony Flew and Alasdair MacIntyre. Copyright © 1955 by Antony Flew and Alasdair MacIntyre, renewed 1983. Reprinted by permission of Macmillan Publishing Co. and SCM Press, Ltd.

LUDWIG WITTGENSTEIN

Although it was once widely believed that Wittgenstein (1889–1951) was a logical positivist, with the posthumous publication of his works, it became clear that he had been misunderstood. In fact, philosophers of religion have frequently used Wittgensteinian ideas to rebut the charge by logical positivists that religious utterances are meaningless.

In general, Wittgenstein sought to break the hold of a false picture or view of meaning: that the meaning of a word is what it stands for or what it refers to. In this false picture, words are treated as if they are *names* of things, either outside us in the sensible world or inside us as mental images or states of consciousness. But all words are not names, nor is their meaning to be found by finding something for them to refer to. Rather, to determine the meaning of a word we are, in many cases, to look at the ways it is used or how it functions in a particular "form of life," such as religion. Wittgenstein's own remarks on religious language are often oblique in order to keep the reader from misunderstanding the meaning or particular "grammar" of religious utterances.

Lectures on Religious Belief

I

An Austrian general said to someone: "I shall think of you after my death, if that should be possible." We can imagine one group who would find this ludicrous, another who wouldn't.

(During the war, Wittgenstein saw consecrated bread being carried in chromium steel. This struck him as ludicrous.)

Suppose that someone believed in the Last Judgement, and I don't, does this mean that I believe the opposite to him, just that there won't be such a thing? I would say: "not at all, or not always."

Suppose I say that the body will rot, and another says "No. Particles will rejoin in a thousand years, and there will be a Resurrection of you."

If some said: "Wittgenstein, do you believe in this?" I'd say: "No." "Do you contradict the man?" I'd say: "No."

If you say this, the contradiction already lies in this.

Would you say: "I believe the opposite", or "There is no reason to suppose such a thing"? I'd say neither.

Suppose someone were a believer and said: "I believe in a Last Judgement," and I said: "Well, I'm not so sure. Possibly." You would say that there is an enormous gulf between us. If he said "There is a German aeroplane overhead," and I said "Possibly I'm not so sure," you'd say we were fairly near.

It isn't a question of my being anywhere near him, but on an entirely different plane, which you could express by saying: "You mean something altogether different, Wittgenstein."

The difference might not show up at all in any explanation of the meaning.

Why is it that in this case I seem to be missing the entire point?

Suppose somebody made this guidance for this life: believing in the Last Judgment. Whenever he does anything, this is before his mind. In a way, how are we to know whether to say he believes this will happen or not?

Asking him is not enough. He will probably say he has proof. But he has what you might call an unshakeable belief. It will show, not by reasoning or by appeal to ordinary grounds for belief, but rather by regulating for in all his life.

This is a very much stronger fact—foregoing pleasures, always appealing to this picture. This in one sense must be called the firmest of all beliefs, because the man risks things on account of it which he would not do on things which are by far better established for him. Although he distinguishes between things well-established and not well-established.

Lewy: Surely, he would say it is extremely well-established.

First, he may use "well-established" or not use it at all. He will treat this belief as extremely well-established, and in another way as not well-established at all.

If we have a belief, in certain cases we appeal again and again to certain grounds, and at the same time we risk pretty little — if it came to risking our lives on the ground of this belief.

There are instances where you have a faith — where you say "I believe" — and on the other hand this belief does not rest on the fact on which our ordinary everyday beliefs normally do rest.

How should we compare beliefs with each other? What would it mean to compare them?

You might say: "We compare the states of mind."

How do we compare states of mind? This obviously won't do for all occasions. First, what you say won't be taken as the measure for the firmness of a belief? But, for instance, what risks you would take?

The strength of a belief is not comparable with the intensity of a pain.

An entirely different way of comparing beliefs is seeing what sorts of grounds he will give.

A belief isn't like a momentary state of mind. "At 5 o'clock he had a very bad toothache."

Suppose you had two people, and one of them, when he had to decide which course to take, thought of retribution, and the other did not. One person might, for instance, be inclined to take everything that happened to him as a reward or punishment, and another person doesn't think of this at all.

If he is ill, he may think: "What have I done to deserve this?" This is one way of thinking of retribution. Another way is, he thinks in a general way whenever he is ashamed of himself: "This will be punished."

Take two people, one of whom talks of his behaviour and of what happens to him in terms of retribution, the other one does not. These people think entirely differently. Yet, so far, you can't say they believe different things.

Suppose someone is ill and he says: "This is a punishment," and I say: "If I'm ill, I don't think of punishment at all." If you say: "Do you believe the opposite?" — you can call it believing the opposite, but it is entirely different from what we would normally call believing the opposite.

I think differently, in a different way. I say different things to myself. I have different pictures.

It is this way: if someone said: "Wittgenstein, you don't take illness as punishment, so what do you believe?"—I'd say: "I don't have any thoughts of punishment."

There are, for instance, these entirely different ways of thinking first of all—which needn't be expressed by one person saying one thing, another person another thing.

What we call believing in a Judgement Day or not believing in a Judgement Day—The expression of belief may play an absolutely minor role.

If you ask me whether or not I believe in a Judgement Day, in the sense in which religious people have belief in it, I wouldn't say: "No. I don't believe there will be such a thing." It would seem to me utterly crazy to say this.

And then I give an explanation: "I don't believe in . . .", but then the religious person never believes what I describe.

I can't say. I can't contradict that person.

In one sense, I understand all he says—the English words "God", "separate", etc. I understand. I could say: "I don't believe in this," and this would be true, meaning I haven't got these thoughts or anything that hangs together with them. But not that I could contradict the thing.

You might say: "Well, if you can't contradict him, that means you don't understand him. If you did understand him, then you might." That again is Greek to me. My normal technique of language leaves me. I don't know whether to say they understand one another or not.

These controversies look quite different from any normal controversies. Reasons look entirely different from normal reasons.

They are, in a way, quite inconclusive.

The point is that if there were evidence, this would in fact destroy the whole business.

Anything that I normally call evidence wouldn't in the slightest influence me.

Suppose, for instance, we knew people who foresaw the future; make forecasts for years and years ahead; and they described some sort of a Judgement Day. Queerly enough, even if there were such a thing, and even if it were more convincing than I have described but, belief in this happening wouldn't be at all a religious belief.

Suppose that I would have to forego all pleasures because of such a forecast. If I do so and so, someone will put me in fires in a thousand years, etc. I wouldn't budge. The best scientific evidence is just nothing.

A religious belief might in fact fly in the face of such a forecast, and say "No. There it will break down."

As it were, the belief as formulated on the evidence can only be the last result—in which a number of ways of thinking and acting crystallize and come together.

A man would fight for his life not to be dragged into the fire. No induction. Terror. That is, as it were, part of the substance of the belief.

That is partly why you don't get in religious controversies, the form of controversy where one person is *sure* of the thing, and the other says: 'Well, possibly.'

You might be surprised that there hasn't been opposed to those who believe in Resurrection those who say "Well, possibly."

Here believing obviously plays much more this role: suppose we said that a certain picture might play the role of constantly admonishing me, or I always think of it. Here, an enormous difference would be between those people for whom the picture is constantly in the foreground, and the others who just didn't use it at all.

Those who said: "Well, possibly it may happen and possibly not" would be on an entirely different plane.

This is partly why one would be reluctant to say: "These people rigorously hold the opinion (or view) that there is a Last Judgement". "Opinion" sounds queer.

It is for this reason that different words are used: 'dogma', 'faith'.

We don't talk about hypothesis, or about high probability. Nor about knowing.

In a religious discourse we use such expressions as: "I believe that so and so will happen," and use them differently to the way in which we use them in science.

Although, there is a great temptation to think we do. Because we do talk of evidence, and do talk of evidence by experience.

We could even talk of historic events.

It has been said that Christianity rests on an historic basis.

It has been said a thousand times by intelligent people that indubitability is not enough in this case. Even if there is as much evidence as for Napoleon. Because the indubitability wouldn't be enough to make me change my whole life.

It doesn't rest on an historic basis in the sense that the ordinary belief in historic facts could serve as a foundation.

Here we have a belief in historic facts different from a belief in ordinary historic facts. Even, they are not treated as historical, empirical, propositions.

Those people who had faith didn't apply the doubt which would ordinarily apply to *any* historical propositions. Especially propositions of a time long past, etc.

What is the criterion of reliability, dependability? Suppose you give a general description as to when you say a proposition has a reasonable weight of probability. When you call it reasonable, is this *only* to say that for it you have such and such evidence, and for others you haven't?

For instance, we don't trust the account given of an event by a drunk man.

Father O'Hara[1] is one of those people who make it a question of science.

Here we have people who treat this evidence in a different way. They base things on evidence which taken in one way would seem exceedingly flimsy. They base enormous things on this evidence. Am I to say they are unreasonable? I wouldn't call them unreasonable.

I would say, they are certainly not *reasonable,* that's obvious.

'Unreasonable' implies, with everyone, rebuke.

I want to say: they don't treat this as a matter of reasonability.

Anyone who reads the Epistles will find it said: not only that it is not reasonable, but that it is folly.

Not only is it not reasonable, but it doesn't pretend to be.

What seems to me ludicrous about O'Hara is his making it appear to be *reasonable.*

Why shouldn't one form of life culminate in an utterance of belief in a Last Judgement? But I couldn't either say "Yes" or "No" to the statement that there will be such a thing. Nor "Perhaps," nor "I'm not sure."

It is a statement which may not allow of any such answer.

If Mr. Lewy is religious and says he believes in a Judgement Day,

---

[1] Contribution to a Symposium on *Science and Religion* (Lond: Gerald Howe, 1931, pp. 107–116).

I won't even know whether to say I understand him or not. I've read the same things as he's read. In a most important sense, I know what he means.

If an atheist says: "There won't be a Judgment Day, and another person says there will," do they mean the same?—Not clear what criterion of meaning the same is. They might describe the same things. You might say, this already shows that they mean the same.

We come to an island and we find beliefs there, and certain beliefs we are inclined to call religious. What I'm driving at is, that religious beliefs will not . . . They have sentences, and there are also religious statements.

These statements would not just differ in respect to what they are about. Entirely different connections would make them into religious beliefs, and there can easily be imagined transitions were we wouldn't know for our life whether to call them religious beliefs or scientific beliefs.

You may say they reason wrongly.

In certain cases you would say they reason wrongly, meaning they contradict us. In other cases you would say they don't reason at all, or "It is an entirely different kind of reasoning." The first, you would say in the case in which they reason in a similar way to us, and make something corresponding to our blunders.

Whether a thing is a blunder or not—it is a blunder in a particular system. Just as something is a blunder in a particular game and not in another.

You could also say that where we are reasonable, they are not reasonable—meaning they don't use *reason* here.

If they do something very like one of our blunders, I would say, I don't know. It depends on further surroundings of it.

It is difficult to see, in cases in which it has all the appearances of trying to be reasonable.

I would definitely call O'Hara unreasonable. I would say, if this is religious beliefs, then it's all superstition.

But I would ridicule it, not by saying it is based on insufficient evidence. I would say: here is a man who is cheating himself. You can say: this man is ridiculous because he believes, and bases it on weak reasons.

II

The word 'God' is amongst the earliest learnt—pictures and catechisms, etc. But not the same consequences as with pictures of aunts. I wasn't shown [that which the picture pictured].

The word is used like a word representing a person. God sees, rewards, etc.

"Being shown all these things, did you understand what this word meant?" I'd say: "Yes and no. I did learn what it didn't mean. I made myself understand. I could answer questions, understand questions when they were put in different ways—and in that sense could be said to understand."

If the question arises as to the existence of a god or God, it plays an entirely different role to that of the existence of any person or object I ever heard of. One said, had to say, that one *believed* in the existence, and if one did not believe, this was regarded as something bad. Normally if I did not believe in the existence of something no one would think there was anything wrong in this.

Also, there is this extraordinary use of the word 'believe'. One talks of believing and at the same time one doesn't use 'believe' as one does ordinarily. You might say (in the normal use): "You only believe—oh well. . . ." Here it is used entirely differently; on the other hand it is not used as we generally use the word 'know'.

If I even vaguely remember what I was taught about God, I might say: "Whatever believing in God may be, it can't be believing in something we can test, or find means of testing." You might say: "This is nonsense, because people say they believe on *evidence* or say they believe on religious experiences." I would say: "The mere fact that someone says they believe on evidence doesn't tell me enough for me to be able to say now whether I can say of a sentence 'God exists' that your evidence is unsatisfactory or insufficient."

Suppose I know someone, Smith. I've heard that he has been killed in a battle in this war. One day you come to me and say: "Smith is in Cambridge." I inquire, and find you stood at Guildhall and saw at the other end a man and said: "That was Smith." I'd say: "Listen. This isn't sufficient evidence." If we had a fair amount of evidence he was killed I would try to make you say that you're being credulous. Suppose he was never heard of again. Needless to say, it is quite impossible to make inquiries: 'Who at 12:05 passed Market Place into Rose Crescent?" Suppose you say: "He was there". I would be extremely puzzled.

Suppose there is a feast on Mid-Summer Common. A lot of people stand in a ring. Suppose this is done every year and then everyone says he has seen one of his dead relatives on the other side of the ring. In this case, we could ask everyone in the ring. "Who did you hold by the hand?" Nevertheless, we'd all say that on that day we see our dead relatives. You could in this case say: "I had an extraordinary experience. I had the experience I can express by saying: 'I saw my dead cousin'." Would we say you are saying this on insufficient evidence? Under certain circumstances I would say this, under other circumstances I wouldn't. Where what is said sounds a bit absurd I would say: "Yes, in this case insufficient evidence." If altogether absurd, then I wouldn't.

Suppose I went to somewhere like Lourdes in France. Suppose I went with a very credulous person. There we see blood coming out of something. He says: "There you are, Wittgenstein, how can you doubt?" I'd say: "can it only be explained one way? Can't it be this or that?" I'd try to convince him that he'd seen nothing of any consequence. I wonder whether I would do that under all circumstances. I certainly know that I would under normal circumstances.

"Oughtn't one after all to consider this?" I'd say: "Come on. Come on." I would treat the phenomenon in this case just as I would treat an experiment in a laboratory which I thought badly executed.

"The balance moves when I will it to move." I point out it is not covered up, a draught can move it, etc.

I could imagine that someone showed an extremely passionate belief in such a phenomenon, and I couldn't approach his belief at all by saying: "This could just as well have been brought about by so and so" because he could think this blasphemy on my side. Or he might say: "It is possible that these priests cheat, but nevertheless in a different sense a miraculous phenomenon takes place there."

I have a statue which bleeds on such and such a day in the year. I have red ink, etc. "You are a cheat, but nevertheless the Deity uses you. Red ink in a sense, but not red ink in a sense."

Cf. Flowers at seance with label. People said: "Yes, flowers are materialized with label." What kind of circumstances must there be to make this kind of story not ridiculous?

I have a moderate education, as all of you have, and therefore know what is meant by insufficient evidence for a forecast. Suppose someone dreamt of the Last Judgement, and said he now knew what it would be like. Suppose someone said: "This is poor evidence." I would say: "If you want to compare it with the evidence for it's raining to-morrow it is no evidence at all." He may make it sound as if by stretching the point you may call it evidence. But it may be more than ridiculous as evidence. But now, would I be prepared to say: "You are basing your belief on extremely slender evidence, to put it mildly." Why should I regard this dream as evidence — measuring its validity as though I were measuring the validity of the evidence for meteorological events?

If you compare it with anything in Science which we call evidence, you can't credit that anyone could soberly argue: "Well, I had this dream . . . therefore . . . Last Judgement". You might say: "For a blunder, that's too big." If you suddenly wrote numbers down on the blackboard, and then said: "Now, I'm going to add," and then said: "2 and 21 is 13," etc. I'd say: "This is no blunder."

There are cases where I'd say he's mad, or he's making fun. Then there might be cases where I look for an entirely different interpretation altogether. In order to see what the explanation is I should have to see the sum, to see in what way it is done, what he makes follow from it, what are the different circumstances under which he does it, etc.

I mean, if a man said to me after a dream that he believed in the Last Judgement, I'd try to find what sort of impression it gave him. One attitude: "It will be in about 2,000 years. It will be bad for so and so and so, etc." Or it may be one of terror. In the case where there is hope, terror, etc., would I say there is insufficient evidence if he says: "I believe . . ."? I can't treat these words as I normally treat 'I believe so and so'. It would be entirely beside the point, and also if he said his friend so and so and his grandfather had had the dream and believed, it would be entirely beside the point.

I would not say "If a man said he dreamt it would happen tomorrow," would he take his coat?, etc.

Case where Lewy has visions of his dead friend. Cases where you don't try to locate him. And case where you try to locate him in a business-like way. Another case where I'd say: "We can pre-suppose we have a broad basis on which we agree."

In general, if you say: "He is dead" and I say: "He is not dead" no-one would say: "Do they mean the same thing by 'dead'?" In the case where a man has visions I wouldn't offhand say: "He means something different."

Cf. A person having persecution mania.

What is the criterion for meaning something different? Not only what he takes as evidence for it, but also how he reacts, that he is in terror, etc.

How am I to find out whether this proposition is to be regarded as an empirical proposition—'You'll see your dead friend again?' Would I say: "He is a bit superstitious?" Not a bit.

He might have been apologetic. (The man who stated it categorically was more intelligent than the man who was apologetic about it).

'Seeing a dead friend,' again means nothing much to me at all. I don't think in these terms. I don't say to myself: "I shall see so and so again" ever.

He always says it, but he doesn't make any search. He puts on a queer smile. "His story had that dreamlike quality." My answer would be in this case "Yes," and a particular explanation.

Take "God created man". Pictures of Michelangelo showing the creation of the world. In general, there is nothing which explains the meanings of words as well as a picture, and I take it that Michelangelo was as good as anyone can be and did his best, and here is the picture of the Deity creating Adam.

If we ever saw this, we certainly wouldn't think this the Deity. The picture has to be used in an entirely different way if we are to call the man in that queer blanket 'God', and so on. You could imagine that religion was taught by means of these pictures. "Of course, we can only express ourselves by means of picture." This is rather queer . . . I could show Moore the pictures of a tropical plant. There is a technique of comparison between picture and plant. If I showed him the picture of Michelangelo and said: "Of course, I can't show you the real thing, only the picture" . . . . The absurdity is, I've never taught him the technique of using this picture.

It is quite clear that the role of pictures of Biblical subjects and rôle of the picture of God creating Adam are totally different ones. You might ask this question: "Did Michelangelo think that Noah in the ark looked like this, and that God creating Adam looked like this?" He wouldn't have said that God or Adam looked as they look in this picture.

It might seem as though, if we asked such a question as: "Does Lewy

really mean what so and so means when he says so and so is alive ?"—
it might seem as though there were two sharply divided cases, one in
which he would say he didn't mean it literally. I want to say this it not
so. There will be cases where we will differ, and where it won't be a
question at all of more or less knowledge, so that we can come together.
Sometimes it will be a question of experience, so you can say: "Wait
another 10 years." And I would say: "I would disencourage this kind
of reasoning" and Moore would say: "I wouldn't disencourage it." That
is, one would *do* something. We would take sides, and that goes so
far that there would really be great differences between us, which might
come out in Mr. Lewy saying: "Wittgenstein is trying to undermine
reason", and this wouldn't be false. This is actually where such questions rise.

III

Today I saw a poster saying: "'Dead' Undergraduate speaks."
The inverted commas mean: "He isn't really dead." "He isn't what
people call dead. They call it 'dead' not quite correctly."
We don't speak of "door" in quotes.
It suddenly struck me: "If someone said 'He isn't really dead, although
by the ordinary criteria he is dead'— couldn't I say "He is not only dead
by the ordinary criteria; he is what we all call 'dead'."
If you now call him 'alive', you're using language in a queer way,
because you're almost deliberately preparing misunderstandings. Why
don't you use some other word, and let "dead" have the meaning it
already has?
Suppose someone said: "It didn't always have this meaning. He's not
dead according to the old meaning" or "He's not dead according to
the old idea".
What is it, to have different ideas of death? Suppose you say: "I have
the idea of myself being a chair after death" or "I have the idea of myself
being a chair in half-an-hour"—you all know under what circumstances
we say of something that it has become a chair.
Cf. (1) "This shadow will cease to exist."
(2) "This chair will cease to exist." You say that you know what this

chair ceasing to exist is like. But you have to think. You may find that
there isn't a use for this sentence. You think of the use.

I imagine myself on the death-bed. I imagine you all looking at the
air above me. You say "You have an idea".

Are you clear when you'd say you had ceased to exist?

You have six different ideas [of 'ceasing to exist'] at different times.

If you say: "I can imagine myself being a disembodied spirit. Wittgenstein, can you imagine yourself as a disembodied spirit?"—I'd say: "I'm
sorry. I [so far] connect nothing with these words."

I connect all sorts of complicated things with these words. I think
of what people have said of sufferings after death, etc.

"I have two different ideas, one of ceasing to exist after death, the
other of being a disembodied spirit."

What's it like to have two different ideas? What is the criterion for
one man having one idea, another man having another idea?

You gave me two phrases, "ceasing to exist", "being a disembodied
spirit". "When I say this, I think of myself having a certain set of
experiences." What is it like to think of this?

If you think of your brother in America, how do you know that what
you think is, that the thought inside you is, of your brother being in
America? Is this an experiential business?

Cf. How do you know that what you want is an apple? [Russell].

How do you know that you believe that your brother is in America?

A pear might be what satisfied you. But you wouldn't say: "What
I wanted was an apple."

Suppose we say that the thought is some sort of process in his mind,
or his saying something, etc.—then I could say: "All right, you call this
a thought of your brother in America, well, what is the connection
between this and your brother in America?"

Lewy: You might say that this is a question of convention.

Why is it that you don't doubt that it is a thought of your brother
in America?

One process [the thought] seems to be a shadow or a picture of
something else.

How do I know that a picture is a picture of Lewy?—Normally by
its likeness to Lewy, or, under certain circumstances, a picture of Lewy
may not be like him, but like Smith. If I give up the business of being

like [as a criterion], I get into an awful mess, because anything may be his portrait, given a certain method of projection.

If you said that the thought was in some way a picture of his brother in America—Yes, but by what method of projection is it a picture of this? How queer it is that there should be no doubt what it's a picture of.

If you're asked: "How do you know it is a thought of such and such?" the thought that immediately comes to your mind is one of a shadow, a picture. You don't think of a causal relation. The kind of relation you think of is best expressed by "picture", "shadow," etc.

The word "picture" is even quite all right—in many cases it is even in the most ordinary sense, a picture. You might translate my very words into a picture.

But the point is this, suppose you drew this, how do I know it is my brother in America? Who says it is him—unless it is here ordinary similarity?

What is the connection between these words, or anything substitutable for them, with my brother in America?

The first idea [you have] is that you are looking at your own thought, and are absolutely sure that it is a thought that so and so. You are looking at some mental phenomenon, and you say to yourself "obviously this is a thought of my brother being in America". It seems to be a super-picture. It seems, with thought, that there is no doubt whatever. With a picture, it still depends on the method of projection, whereas here it seems that you get rid of the projecting relation, and are absolutely certain that this is thought of that.

Smythies's muddle is based on the idea of a super-picture.

We once talked about how the idea of certain superlatives came about in Logic. The idea of a super-necessity, etc.

"How do I know that this is the thought of my brother in America?"— that *what* is the thought?

Suppose my thought consists of my *saying* "My brother is in America"—how do I know that I *say* my brother is in America?

How is the connection made?—We imagine at first a connection like strings.

Lewy: The connection is a convention. The word designates.

You must explain "designates" by examples. We have learnt a rule, a practice, etc.

Is thinking of something like painting or shooting at something?

It seems like a projection connection, which seems to make it indubitable, although there is not a projection relation at all.

If I said "My brother is in America"—I could imagine there being rays projecting from my words to my brother in America. But what if my brother isn't in America?—then the rays don't hit anything.

[If you say that the words refer to my brother by expressing the proposition that my brother is in America—the proposition being a middle link between the words and what they refer to] —What has the proposition, the mediate link, got to do with America?

The most important point is this—if you talk of painting, etc. your idea is that the connection exists *now,* so that it seem as though as long as I do this thinking, this connection exists.

Whereas, if we said it is a connection of convention, there would be no point in saying it exists while we think. There is a connection by convention—What do we mean?—This connection refers to events happening at various times. Most of all, it refers to a technique.

[Is thinking something going on at a particular time, or is it spread over the words?" "It comes in a flash." "Always?—it sometimes does come in a flash, although this may be all sorts of different things.]

If it does refer to a technique, then it can't be enough, in certain cases, to explain what you mean in a few words; because there is something which might be thought to be in conflict with the idea going on from 7 to 7.5, namely the practice of using it [the phrase.]

When we talked of: "So and so is an automaton", the strong hold of that view was [due to the idea] that you could say: "Well, I know what I mean" . . . , as though you were looking at something happening while you said the thing, entirely independent of what came before and after, the application [of the phrase]. It looked as though you could talk of understanding a word, without any reference to the technique of its usage. It looked as though Smythies said he could understand the sentence, and that we then had nothing to say.

What was it like to have different ideas of death?—What I meant was—Is having an idea of death something like having a picture, so that you can say "I have an idea of death from 5 to 5.1 etc."? "In whatever way anyone will use this word, I have now a certain idea"—if you call this "having an idea", then it is not what is commonly called "having an idea", because what is commonly called "having an idea", has a reference to the technique of the word, etc.

We are all here using the word "death", which is a public instrument, which has a whole technique [of usage]. Then someone says he has an idea of death. Something queer; because you might say "You are using the word 'death', which is an instrument functioning in a certain way."

If you treat this [your idea] as something private, with what right are you calling it an idea of death?—I say this, because we, also, have a right to say what is an idea of death.

He might say "I have my own private idea of death"—why call this an 'idea of death' unless it is something you connect with death. Although this [your 'idea'] might not interest us at all. [In this case,] it does not belong on the game played with 'death', which we all know and understand.

If what he calls his "idea of death" is to become relevant, it must become part of our game.

'My idea of death is the separation of the soul from the body'—if we know what to do with these words. He can also say: "I connect with the word 'death' a certain picture—a woman lying in her bed"—that may or may not be of some interest.

If he connects

with death, and this was his idea, this might be interesting psychologically.

"The separation of soul from body" [only had a public interest.] This may act like black curtains or it may not act like black curtains. I'd have to find out what the consequences [of your saying it] are. I am not, at least, at present at all clear. [You say this]—"So what?"—I know these words, I have certain pictures. All sorts of things go along with these words.

If he says this, I won't know yet what consequences he will draw. I don't know what he opposes this to.

Lewy: "You oppose it to being extinguished."

If you say to me—"Do you cease to exist?"—I should be bewildered, and would not know what exactly this is to mean. "If you don't cease to exist, you will suffer after death", there I begin to attach ideas, perhaps ethical ideas of responsibility. The point is, that although these are well-known words, and although I can go from one sentence to another sentence, or to pictures [I don't know what consequences you draw from this statement].

Suppose someone said: "What do you believe, Wittgenstein? Are you a sceptic? Do you know whether you will survive death?" I would really, this is a fact, say "I can't say. I don't know", because I haven't any clear idea what I'm saying when I'm saying "I don't cease to exist," etc.

Spiritualists make one kind of connection.

A Spiritualist says "Apparition" etc. Although he gives me a picture I don't like, I do get a clear idea. I know that much, that some people connect this phrase with a particular kind of verification. I know that some people don't—religious people e.g.—they don't refer to a verification, but have entirely different ideas.

A great writer said that, when he was a boy, his father set him a task, and he suddenly felt that nothing, not even death, could take away the responsibility [in doing this task]; this was his duty to do, and that even death couldn't stop it being his duty. He said that this was, in a way, a proof of the immortality of the soul—because if this lives on [the responsibility won't die.] The idea is given by what we call the proof. Well, if this is the idea, [all right].

If a Spiritualist wishes to give *me* an idea of what he means or doesn't mean by 'survival', he can say all sorts of things—

[If I ask what idea he has, I may be given what the Spiritualists say or I may be given what the man I quoted said, etc., etc.]

I would at least [in the case of the Spiritualist] have an idea of what this sentence is connected up with, and get more and more of an idea as I see what he does with it.

As it is, I hardly connect anything with it at all.

Suppose someone, before going to China, when he might never see me again, said to me: "We might see one another after death"—would I necessarily say that I don't understand him? I might say [want to say] simply, "Yes. I *understand* him entirely."

Lewy: "In this case, you might only mean that he expressed a certain attitude."

I would say "No, it isn't the same as saying 'I'm very fond of you'"— and it may not be the same as saying anything else. It says what it says. Why should you be able to substitute anything else?

Suppose I say: "The man used a picture."

"Perhaps now he sees he was wrong." What sort of remark is this?

"God's eye sees everything"—I want to say of this that it uses a picture. I don't want to belittle him. [the person who says it.]

Suppose I said to him "You've been using a picture", and he said "No, this is not all"— mightn't he have misunderstood me? What do I want to do [by saying this]? What would be the real sign of disagreement? What might be the real criterion of his disagreeing with me?

Lewy: "If he said: 'I've been making preparations [for death].'"

Yes, this might be a disagreement—if he himself were to use the word in a way in which I did not expect, or were to draw conclusions I did not expect him to draw. I wanted only to draw attention to a particular technique of usage. We should disagree, if he was using a technique I didn't expect.

We associate a particular use with a picture.

Smythies: 'This isn't all he does—associate a use with a picture.'

Wittgenstein: Rubbish. I meant: what conclusions are you going to draw? etc. Are eyebrows going to be talked of, in connection with the Eye of God?

"He could just as well have said so and so"—this [remark] is foreshadowed by the word "attitude". He couldn't just as well have said something else.

If I say he used a picture, I don't want to say anything he himself wouldn't say. I want to say that he draws these conclusions.

Isn't it as important as anything else, what picture he does use?

Of certain pictures we say that they might just as well be replaced by another—e.g. we could, under certain circumstances, have one projection of an ellipse drawn instead of another.

[He *may* say]: "I would have been prepared to use another picture, it would have had the same effect. . . ."

The whole *weight* may be in the picture.

We can say in chess that the exact shape of the chess-men plays no role. Suppose that the main pleasure was, to see people ride; then, playing it in writing wouldn't be playing the same game. Someone might say: "All he's done is change the shape of the head"—what more could he do?

When I say he's using a picture I'm merely making a *grammatical* remark: [What I say] can only be verified by the consequences he does or does not draw.

If Smythies disagrees, I don't take notice of this disagreement.

All I wished to characterize was the conventions he wished to draw. If I wished to say anything more I was merely being philosophically arrogant.

Normally, if you say "He is an automaton" you draw consequences, if you stab him, [he'll feel pain]. On the other hand, you may not wish to draw any such consequences, and this is all there is to it—except further muddles.

From *Lectures and Conversations on Aesthetics, Psychology, and Religious Belief,* by Ludwig Wittgenstein. Translated and edited by Cyril Barrett. Copyright © 1966 The University of California Press, Blackwell Publishers. Reprinted by permission of the University of California Press and Blackwell Publishers.

INDEX

DATE DUE